DR. COOKIE®'S GUIDE TO

Living Happily Ever

After with Your Cat

Also by Dr. Stefanie Schwartz

Canine and Feline Behavior Problems:
Instructions for Veterinary Clients

No More Myths: True Facts About Pet Care

First Aid for Dogs

First Aid for Cats

St. Martin's Griffin ✿ New York

DR. COOKIE®'S GUIDE TO

Living Happily Ever After with Your Cat

Written and Illustrated by
Stefanie Schwartz, DVM, MSc, DACVB

This book is lovingly dedicated

to my husband, Danny,

and to Hershel, Gracie, Teddi,

and, always, Sara, Merysa, and Jonathan

CONTENTS

Contents

PREFACE

After the butterfly is gone
It settles down:
A kitten.

—NETSUME SOSEKI, 1867–1916

The way I see it, there are two basic types of people in this world: animal people (including dog people and cat people) and people people. If you are like me, of course, it is entirely possible to be both a dog and a cat person. People people, who feel little or no emotional or spiritual bond to other animals, deserve each other's company and probably will not be reading this book anyway. *Dr. Cookie®'s Guide to Living Happily Ever After with Your Cat* is intended for cat people, cat and dog people, dog people who know and love cat people, and for any animal people or people people who have even the slightest curiosity about how to live happily ever after with a cat.

I must confess that I was raised a dog person. My introduction to the world of cats happened while I was a veterinary student, enriching my life and altering the course of my journey. Jonathan, the first cat to live with me, was even tempered, social, and uncommonly intelligent. He was, as his name implied, a princely cat. Unfortunately, he succumbed to a chronic and debilitating illness that took him from me prematurely. More than a decade after he left, he is still much missed. Jonathan redefined my existence. His nobility and sweetness opened my mind, my heart, and my soul to his kind: miraculous creatures who inspire, delight, and comfort those lucky enough to know them. Since I began living with and loving cats, nothing in my life has been the same. And I can't imagine living without cats ever again.

As a veterinarian in clinical practice, I have examined healthy and ailing cats. As a veterinary behavior consultant, I have encountered cats

with a wide variety of behavior problems. I have marveled at the abounding energy and enthusiasm of healthy kittens and at the dignity of fragile geriatric kitties. I have seen cats with short hair, long hair, or no hair. Some were slim and slinky, others stocky or stout, with striped, spotted, swirled, or solid coats of every shade. I've seen cats who remained passive and patient under duress, and others who became frenzied with little or no provocation. Green, blue, or golden eyes flashed in fear, shimmered in play, or radiated a serene welcome into their dominion. Every time I think I've seen or heard it all, I am challenged with a different dimension of the unique feline perspective.

The cats in my household currently outnumber the dogs by four to two. Sara Lee (as in "chocolate cake," my constant companion of over twenty-two years), Hershey (short for Hershel Walker, the only male and, oh, so proud of it, six years), Gracie Allen (a fluffy little thing but very sweet and smart, five years), and Tiadora (known as Teddi, the tiny runt who has enchanted us all, one year old) teach me on a daily basis how little any of us really know about cats. But what I know of them I know well and will share with you. Using anecdotes of my own cats and other cats I have met during almost twenty years of veterinary practice, I will explore some of the subtle and even intricate ways of the cat. Living happily ever after with a cat is a journey filled with amusement and awe. You, too, will be transformed and forever grateful for the experience.

Stefanie Schwartz, DVM, MSc, DACVB
Diplomate, American College of Veterinary Behaviorists
Dr. Cookie®
www.dr-cookie.com
Norwell, Massachusetts

DR. COOKIE'S GUIDE TO

Living Happily Ever
After with Your Cat

General Stuff About Living Happily Ever After with Your Cat

When I play with my cat, who knows if I am not a pastime to her more than she is to me?

—MICHEL EYQUEM DE MONTAIGNE, 1533–1592

HOW CATS SHOW AFFECTION

He gently reaches one paw up toward me and looks at me longingly as if to say, "Pick me up, please." Hershey wraps his chunky, manly man cat arms around my neck and hugs me. He purrs and rubs his cheeks against me, purrs and gives little Hershey kisses to my eyelids and face. Hershel Walker is my boy. He is a big, macho rogue who loves his mommy. Sara, my elderly lady cat, is subtle and shy. She stays nearby or comes to check on me to make sure I am all right, but she has never been a lap cat. Her show of affection is brief, sporadic, displayed when there are no witnesses and no distractions. Sometimes it is a little body rub as she silently slides by my leg. When she is very enthusiastic, she head butts me to insist that I pet her for a few treasured moments. It is our little secret that she loves me, but it is no secret that I always have and always will love her. Gracie is my shadow. Blind since birth, she has developed a singular bond with me. I am her security blanket; as long as she can hear me, everything is okay. She is so much an extension of my body that I hardly notice when she arrives in my lap—she is just always there. I am so accustomed to her closeness that I have difficulty falling asleep without her near me. And then there is Teddi. She is the purring machine, in perpetual motion, stopping only to gaze adoringly at me before scampering away. More and more she understands that "Ow!" means "no nipping"; and, in her quiet moments, she is learning to love me with her sandpaper tongue instead of her sharp, baby teeth. Happiness is living with cats.

Cats show affection in a variety of ways. Their fondness can be discreet and understated, or indisputable and simply sensational. Every cat has his or her own style of showing appreciation. It is determined, in part, by the cat's early exposure to people, inborn social inclinations, and the company the cat keeps. Cats, like people, can be socialized to show their affection or not. In some cultures public displays of affection between people, even family members, are inhibited or discouraged. How your cat displays affection toward you is partly determined by how you display your affection toward your cat. If you are remote and reject a cat's advances, your pet will learn to leave you to yourself. If you welcome a pussycat's affectionate displays, they will be reinforced and your cat will be free to lavish you with love. Cats have been divided into three categories: actively friendly, reserved friendly, and unfriendly. While this categorization is interesting, it may be overly simplistic. A cat's nature will depend on how the cat was raised and the current social context. A cat could be unfriendly because he or she: (a) has inherited few of the genes that promote "tameness," or (b) has been isolated from people during a critical stage of social development, or (c) has been traumatized in some way and become agoraphobic (extreme shyness of people), or (d) may not be compatible with you, or (e) is uncomfortable in the situation in which he or she is observed.

Feline facial expressions may be subtle compared to our own or the canine face, but cats do indeed have expressive faces. In fact, cats have the most mobile facial muscles of all carnivores! Watch their eyes smile at you, or flash in fear, or see the shadow of a temper tantrum creep in. Notice the position of their whiskers, the tension around their mouths. Are the ears pricked and alert, or flattened back with anxiety? Sometimes your cat will look at you with partially closed eyes and purr. This is a cat who is happy in your presence. You may be licked with a few brief flicks of the tip of the tongue or rub your skin raw with abrasive kisses. In a more blatant style, your cat may quiver his tail as he purposefully approaches you, rubbing his cheek, his forehead, and his entire body along you as he passes by. He may do this just once and be on his way, or he may perform this ritual over and over again in a sort of happy dance. He is marking you. You are his—be proud! Scent glands at the corner of a cat's lips (perioral glands) and on the side of the forehead (temporal glands) deposit chemical markers on you. The flank rub likely serves as a tactile or visual display, although an additional function of the flank-rubbing display may be the mutual exchange of scent. Your scents mingle as the cat presses against you. Other glands on the chin, cheeks, and tail may be more commonly used to deposit scent on inanimate surfaces, but I have seen many cats perform these marking behaviors on special people, too.

Cats, like dogs, treat their people as members of their own social group. Your cat might treat you like an equal or, perhaps, like a surrogate mother. Your cat's social behavior toward you depends upon inborn temperament but also on her lifestyle. For example, cats who are part of a multicat household may rub less than cats living as solitary pets. Juveniles rub more against adults, and submissive animals rub more against dominant ones. Also, cats who roam outdoors may rub more than cats confined as house pets. The underlying explanation for these observations is that the rubbing display is used as a greeting after a cat has been away from the group. My four exclusively indoor cats rub against me every chance they get, which seems to contradict these theories, so the tendency to rub is likely determined by many factors.

Some cats are not eager to mingle and prefer to be left undisturbed. This is a problem for owners who crave more open displays of affection from their pet. The solution is simply to let the cat come to you. Do not pursue a cat who is not in the mood for company. This will only teach your cat to run from you. Instead, let the little snob approach you on his or her own terms, when the mood strikes. Reinforce your cat with brief caresses, and stop before the cat has had enough of you. This way you will leave your cat wanting more. Perhaps your cat prefers to sit on the book you are trying to read, or knocks over the knickknacks on your desk when you are trying to work. He wants your attention;

he wants you to notice that he is there, near you but not *on* you. Does your cat stay close by, on the back of your easy chair just behind your head, when you read your newspaper or watch television? He wants to be around you. Every cat has his or her own style. Appreciate the subtle displays as much as the conspicuous ones, for they are equally precious. Whatever way your cat shows affection, you are lucky.

INTERPRETING A CAT'S TAIL

Sara enters a room with style. She doesn't just walk in, she makes an entrance. My little princess calmly crosses the floor with her tail at half-mast until just a few feet away, it is raised high as she meows her "Hello!" Closer to me, she waves just the tip of her tail from side to side, quickstepping her dainty feet and purring a song of love meant only for me—until she sees my husband, and then she is off to flirt with him, quivering her tail, pushing her head into his hand; I guess we both fell for him!

A cat's tail has several important functions. It communicates mood, helps the cat to maneuver at speed, and even serves as a toy. Watch your cat's tail. Held horizontally, it signals a friendly approach. Held high and vertical, it is as good as waving an enthusiastic, "Hi there!" The vertical tail posture is also seen during play and as a sexual signal. A tail tucked between the legs is an indication of fear or submission, much like a frightened or submissive dog. However, if a cat's tail is lowered and pointing to the ground in a concave arch, beware. This cat is aggressively aroused. The contrasting colors of markings on a cat's tail are a physical adaptation with social significance. Black cats with white tail tips or tabbies with ringed tail stripes, for example, may draw even greater attention to their tails, and the message or mood they convey.

It is not just the tail position that transmits information, but the nature of the tail movement as well. For instance, a cat crouching with the tail close to the ground may lazily wave just the tip or wildly thrash the entire tail. In the first case, the cat may be thinking about where to take her next nap; and in the latter case, she may be getting ready to cuff the new kitten for being annoying! Tails are interesting toys to kittens. If a kitten makes the mistake of playfully pouncing on an adult cat's tail once too often, the kitten will be reprimanded! A kitten discovers that her own tail is a handy thing to chase. Who hasn't laughed at a chubby kitten rolling off balance in an attempt to trap her own tail?

Is the hair on the tail smooth or is it puffed out? This is called *piloerection,* made possible by tiny muscles at the base of the hair follicle that allow the hairs to "stand on end." You will see this when a cat is frightened by something, or in kittens during peak forms of play, when their little tails get all bristly. Interestingly, cat's tails owe their flexibility to a unique muscle called the caudofemoralis muscle at the tail base. It is probably this muscle that enables them to thrash their tails. The average cat also has more tail vertebrae (between nineteen and twenty-eight) than the average dog tail (six to twenty-three), which further contributes to their greater flexibility.

The Manx cat, and other bobtailed breeds such as the Japanese Bobtail and the Cymric, are exceptions and have just a stump of a tail. But because they don't know what they're missing, they do just fine. Another of the major functions of the tail is as counterbalance. Cats, like other animals, use their tails as a rudder when changing directions quickly or for balance when they jump. However, cats rely on their tails to help run at ground level and when climbing elevated surfaces, and so their tails are even more complex. The tail also helps cats to right themselves when they fall from a height. Some cats may require a tail amputation because of severe injury or infection. Although they may seem a bit uncoordinated at first, they will soon adjust. We do fine without ours!

THE ADVANTAGES OF THE "INDEPENDENT" CAT

Snowflake's owner described her as "independent." From his perspective, this was far from a complaint. In fact, this was one of the things he liked best about his dainty yet confident white cat with luminescent, pale green eyes. Snowflake's "dad" was a busy young executive who was frequently detained by long hours at the office and a busy social schedule on weekends. A lap cat who shadowed his every move would have been a nuisance to him and might have made a more suitable companion for an elderly person. Snowflake was the ideal yuppie pet, just perfect for her owner's active lifestyle. She napped on her favorite easy chair, undisturbed by the big city symphony of sirens, trucks backfiring, or thunderstorms. She was satisfied to patrol her exclusive territory, savoring her view from each window as she made her daily rounds. Snowflake trotted happily to the door with tail held high to greet her guardian when he returned to the apartment they shared. After their tender reunion and a few moments playing together, however, she kept herself entertained with her favorite stuffed mouse and running from imaginary pursuers. At bedtime, she settled contentedly beside him and purred them both to sleep. Snowflake suited her owner to a tee. They were meant for each other.

Independence implies autonomy, confidence, and freethinking. It does not mean that an independent individual is unfeeling or incapable of forming a loving attachment. Up until quite recently, it was believed that cats did not need relationships with other living things, and interacted only to reproduce. Their reputed "independence" was attributed to the prevailing notion that cats loathe social interaction. We now know that this is completely untrue. Independence does not mean social isolation or emotional insulation. Although it is true that some cats are relatively untame or untamable, the asocial nature of *some* cats should not be extended to *all* cats.

Cats are masters of adaptation. Depending on their inborn temperament and their social context, they can become virtual social butterflies, or social introverts, or recluses. Some cats are dogs. They follow their owners around and become their "shadows." Many of these cats are lap cats and seek close physical contact whenever possible. Some cats will learn to perform a multitude of tricks (e.g., happily trotting up in response to their owner's whistle) that rival many dogs. There are also cats at the other extreme, who resent human handling, prefer to roam outdoors, and show only brief displays of affection, if indeed they show any at all. And then there are those who fall along the continuum between these two extremes.

Cats may not be "pack" animals to the degree that dogs or people are; however, in their own way they are social creatures, too. Depending on how they were raised as well as the social inclination inherited from their parents, some cats develop very close relationships with people and with other house pets. Occasionally, cats have even been known to cuddle with the family's pet guinea pig or bunny, or play with their frisky ferret. Sometimes the most unlikely cats form bonds that last a lifetime. Kitties that no one would have predicted could coexist become inseparable. Cats may show signs of separation anxiety when separated from their owners or pet companions. They may also be emotionally impacted by the death of their "friends" and owners.

Then again, cats are not dogs. They don't require obedience training or leash walks (although some cats enjoy going for a stroll with harness and leash). Cats are easily house trained and adapt well to a variety of lifestyles, such as living in urban, suburban, or rural settings. It is not that cats don't need their owners' attention or affection; it is simply that cats can thrive with abbreviated quality time, compared to the extended investment of time and energy required on a daily basis by the average dog. In a time when we are increasingly overwhelmed with juggling work, family, and play, many pet lovers are turning to pets who require less input or take up less space in a restricted urban residence. Cats now outnumber dogs in the United States. They are the most popular pets in America and are increasingly appreciated all over the world. Cats are the pets of the new millennium—sleek, self-confident, self-governing individualists, with the ability to connect to us on a spiritual and deeply emotional level.

So why did it become an insult to call a cat "independent"? I think the answer stems from the biology and perspective of human social behavior. Humans survived and excelled by virtue of our social cooperation. People need other people to survive. We are social beings, and very few of us would survive alone. Natural selection would have acted against individuals who did not interact well because sociability was and continues to be critical to the survival of the group and of each individual. It remains a deeply rooted human attitude to frown upon individuals who are not team players. Loners are outcasts, considered less trustworthy, and viewed with suspicion. This bias is probably an important defense mechanism, too. Some antisocial people do indeed show pathological behavior.

Interestingly, we tend to judge other species as if they were human, too. It is only natural for us to interpret the social nature of other creatures from our own unique perspective. For instance, dogs are pack animals, and like us, need to be part of a social group to thrive. Because their social behavior is so similar to our own, dogs and dog lovers have been characterized as more affable. In contrast, cats are social beings who can survive in groups or on their own (after weaning, of course). In a sense, sociability is an option for cats and depends in large part on their environment. It seems unfair to project our own values onto other species, particularly when their biological imperatives are so vastly different from our own.

I think independence is a good thing. It does not mean that cats are unsociable and apathetic. Cats are not attached to us, or to each other, by some invisible umbilical cord of neurotic overdependence or codependence. Independence is a healthy state of mind when it is founded on a healthy and happy life. A safe place to live, appropriate shelter, a nutritious diet, supportive caregivers, and quality time with compatible companions create cats (and people) who function independently yet still come together out of love.

CAT LOVERS WITH AN ALLERGY TO CATS

I will never know how I lived through veterinary school. I was allergic to most of my patients! I had asthma attacks moments after entering the stables or barns, and I broke out in hives from touching dog breeds with short, smooth coats such as Boxers and Dalmatians. Cats, however, triggered the worse allergic reaction by far. My eyes teared and I sneezed until my head hurt from close contact with one. I knew that over the years of my veterinary training, prolonged exposure to this massive onslaught of allergens was either going to kill me, or I would emerge with some acquired tolerance. I survived because of stubbornness, tenacity, obstinance, defiance, and my love for animals. I was totally devoted and completely determined that an inborn physical handicap (as I saw it) would not control the path chosen by my heart and soul. And so began my tale of how I came to know and love cats!

 Thank goodness for antihistamines! If you are a pet lover and have always wanted to have a cat, or are determined to keep your cat despite your allergy, help is available. These days there are so many antihistamines to choose from that you will certainly be able to find one that works to control your symptoms. Your doctor might recommend an over-the-counter medication or write a prescription, but you need not suffer from allergies to pets anymore. Ask for a referral to an allergy specialist who can help to control your discomfort with medications or specific treatment. Hopefully, you will find an allergist who is sympathetic to your love of pets and won't simply dismiss you by advising you to "get rid of the cat!" A commitment to a series of desensitizing injections that are tailored to your specific allergy sources could be the best solution. I followed this regimen for several years, and the quality of my life has improved dramatically because of it. In fact, we are up to four cats, all of whom remain exclusively indoors. Hershey comes to cuddle on cold nights; Sara comes to say good night before sleeping in her favorite spot downstairs; Gracie has always slept plastered to my side; and Teddi is a cuddler, too, often wrapping herself around my legs. And I can still breathe!

Like most people with allergies, I was allergic to more than just cats. Basically I am allergic to everything except rocks. I have varied sensitivity to pretty much everything that is alive (including many people!), but cats were high on the list. People with an allergy to cats are sensitive to a protein in cat saliva. Cats groom themselves by licking their coat to remove debris and tangles. In so doing they deposit salivary proteins on the entire body surface. When hair is shed, these proteins are then spread around your home. Salivary proteins can remain stable for extended periods and can trigger allergic reactions in sensitive individuals long after the cat is removed. For example, if you have an allergy to cats and move into an apartment where the previous tenant kept a pet cat, you may well have allergy problems for as long as six months!

The other major component of the cat allergy phenomenon is dust. The real culprit in dust allergy is the microscopic dust mite found almost everywhere. In addition to dust particles, these insects also thrive in mattresses, pillows, blankets, clothing, stuffed animals, books, upholstered furniture, carpeting, and even on the surface of your houseplants. Regardless of how meticulous a home you keep, dust and dust mites abound. A person who is allergic to cats is not necessarily allergic to dust mites; but when these two allergic sensitivities combine, the outcome is sure to be uncomfortable. All hair attracts dust to some extent, but cats may be even more effective dust mops because of their ability to get into cramped corners behind or beneath furniture or to climb onto the tops of bookshelves that are difficult to keep clean. Even if you cannot see dust on your pet's coat, believe me, it's there.

If you suffer from a pronounced cat allergy, it may be necessary to bathe your cat more often than would otherwise be necessary. This will remove some of the allergen; however, bathing will only stimulate your cat to self-groom more after the bath and thereby deposit more salivary allergen! Excessive bathing will strip away the cat's natural oils and cause dry skin and skin infection, among other problems. An alternative would be to wipe your cat's coat with an antistatic dryer sheet. Made to combat static electricity in the clothes dryer, this might be a simple and effective aid in controlling your allergy symptoms. This sheet minimizes surface dust and other allergy-causing particles and can be quite helpful. Some people with allergies to cats report that they tolerate such cat breeds as the Rex or Sphynx, who have only a soft undercoat. However, these cats still groom themselves the same way other cats do, and the salivary protein is still the source of cat allergy, not the hair quality itself. Allergies are an individual problem (individual to you as well as to the cat in question), and you may be allergic to one cat and not to another.

The major obstacle to having your cat and still being able to breathe is to find an allergist who sympathizes with your desired lifestyle. When I entered veterinary school nearly twenty years ago, the specific desensitizing injection for a cat allergy had not yet been developed, but it is now available. I was instructed by several allergists to either choose another profession or pursue veterinary medicine as a career and do without pets at home or at least to keep the cats out of the bedroom. Luckily, I was able to find doctors over the years who understood that I was not going to confine myself to a bubble or live in a sterile home without pets. In a sense I needed my pets more than I needed oxygen. In a deeply spiritual way, I simply had to be surrounded by animals both at home and at work. If you are driven by this same connection to your pets or to the pets you dream of having someday, don't be dissuaded by physicians who cannot empathize with your bond with animals. However, if you or your child are dangerously allergic and cannot be controlled by medication, I absolutely do not recommend that you ignore sensible medical advice. It may be inadvisable and unavoidable for people with severe allergic responses to keep cats or to allow them in their bedrooms. I am simply pointing out that many physicians will overlook your emotional need to have pets because it is such a logical solution to allergy symptoms to eliminate their source. If it is manageable and reasonable for your health, find a doctor who will work with you to help your body cope with the lifestyle that gives you so much emotional benefit. It can be done, with perseverance, and fueled by your love for cats.

COMMON AND UNUSUAL COAT COLORS IN CATS

I love black cats. They are like black panthers in miniature. Nothing else shines like a black coat on a healthy cat. No other coat color better features the sleek, sinewy, and sensuous form of a cat. It also makes them really hard to photograph because the camera can never quite capture what the eye can behold! My Sara is a black domestic shorthair. She has grayed a bit in the last years, but at twenty-two years of age she has earned her gray hairs. I am also very partial to milk chocolate and to my chocolate tabby. Hershey's coat is a mutation the color of milk chocolate. Hershey, like chocolate, is irresistible. He has white paws, a striped tabby pattern on his lower flanks, and chocolate spots on his white belly. But he doesn't show his spots to just anyone, only to me, when we are alone and no one is watching. Gracie is a domestic longhaired blue-cream calico. She is gray ("blue" if you want to be technical), cream, and white, whereas a regular calico coat is orange, black, and white. Some people call this a muted tortoiseshell, but I just call her beautiful. There is something so delicate about her softly shaded colors; she is my watercolor cat. Teddi is a shorthaired spotted cream tabby with white markings. Lovely, almost porcelain, she is the color of sand warmed by the setting sun. But she is still an impish kitten that only looks like she should be serene . . . well, maybe someday.

Color, pattern, hair length, and quality . . . the permutations of all these traits seem endless. Indeed, unique combinations of these traits have led to the establishment of many exquisite cat breeds. Some cat breeds have been developed from careful selection over generations and others have proclaimed themselves with the spontaneous appearance of unique variations from the norm. Mutations (such as the tailless Manx and Japanese Bobtail and the tipped ears of the Scottish Fold) occasionally emerge and sometimes lead to the foundation of a novel cat breed.

How are coat color and quality determined? What makes a flame point Himalayan different from, say, a champagne mink Tonkinese? Some of the genes that determine coat color and quality, long versus short hair for instance, are inherited as dominant genes. The coat quality may be short (about one inch or less, the oldest type) or long (e.g., Persians, domestic longhair), but that is not all. Some cats have inherited mutated genes for a curly (e.g., Devon Rex), wirehaired (e.g., American Wirehair), and even a hairless coat (Sphynx).

Did you know that the predominance of some coat colors in cat populations is geographically distributed? One explanation for this phenomenon has been traced back to the Vikings. It seems that wherever the ancient Vikings traveled, there exists today a predominance of white and sex-linked orange cats! In domestic cats the genes for coat color are inherited as a sex-linked characteristic. Male cats may carry the black or "red" (orange) gene, for example, but females may carry the black, orange, or tortoiseshell genes. The orange mutation is located only on the X chromosome. Because females have two X chromosomes, they can simultaneously have both orange and nonorange coats (calicos, creams, and torties). Males have just one X and a Y chromosome and so, in general, males are either orange or nonorange. Occasionally, a mutation occurs in which a male receives both orange and nonorange genes, and these males are almost always sterile.

In most mammals the hair is not uniformly pigmented but has gradations of color along each hair. This is determined by the "agouti" gene. Each hair may have bands of color along its shaft, for instance, giving rise to a brindle pattern. Most domesticated mammals are nonagoutis, meaning that each hair is uniformly pigmented (e.g., all black or all white). The cat is an exception because the agouti and nonagouti exist in a sort of equilibrium. The wild tabby coat has mutated into a variety of tabby types and is as common as nontabby cats.

Today, there are eight major coat colors in cats and many shades of each color. These are black, brown, red, chocolate, lilac, blue, cream, and white. Coat patterns also vary and include the following: *solid* (remember the nonagouti mutation); *tipped* (hair at the tip is a different color than toward the skin, for example, in Abyssinians); *smoked* (coats are black with gray closer to the surface); *piebald* (mostly white coat with patches of one or more color); *combination* (any usual coat pattern with white; for example, a tabby with white markings); *Himalayan* (also called *Siamese*; the face mask is in contrast to the rest of the coat: seal/blue/chocolate/lilac/flame/tortie/silver points with sable or champagne coats); *particolored* (more than one color; for example, black-and-white cats or calico). The *tabby* has at least five distinct patterns: the classic tabby (with swirls and stripes); the mackerel tabby (vertical stripes on the sides); the spotted tabby (spots with broken stripes); the ticked tabby (bands of distinct pigment on each hair); and the blotched tabby (patches of tabby with white).

Using the terminology to describe coat color and pattern, try to define your cat's appearance. Every cat is unique. Even when the resemblance is striking, no two cats are exactly alike. Pure breed or generic, every cat is distinctive, unequaled, and the only one of its kind.

RAISING A SOCIAL CAT

Sara was barely three weeks old when I rescued her. I fed her with a syringe until she gained a sincere interest in solid food. Jonathan, who was just six months older than Sara, helped raise her. Sara does not like to be held but is very friendly and easily handled when necessary. She has not changed in over twenty-two years. Hershey was a rugged little kitten, a bit of a bully but quick to back down. He had quite a temper when he was small, but he was a marshmallow most of the time. He was raised by Sara and me until Gracie came along about one year later. Gracie was a calm, quiet, shy kitten who quickly bonded to me, cuddled with Sara, and interacted only minimally with the rambunctious Hershey. Gracie prefers to be held if she instigates it and initially goes into hiding when she hears unfamiliar voices. We did not realize she was congenitally and progressively blind at first, and this must have shaped her social graces. Gracie was just over four years old when Teddi arrived. Teddi is an energetic, fearless kitten who gets a bit cranky when she is very tired. I suspect she will grow into a well-adjusted little girl with enough spunk to help her cope with three other cats and two dogs. She is the first of my cats to have been born into a family with dogs and has developed a real camaraderie with them, especially with Georgyanna, our Boston Terrier. My cats investigate visitors in their own time and are friendly, although they do have their favorite people. Can't fault them for that; I suppose I'm the same way!

Socializing your cat means raising them to behave in an acceptable way with people and other pets you may already have in residence. Kittens are most sensitive to socialization between two and seven weeks of age. In a way it is similar to imprinting in birds, although that results in a more inflexible relationship. The socialization period in cats is better described as an impressionable phase during which social exposure will have a lasting effect. This sensitive period may have more impact on some kittens than on others. Very timid kittens, for instance, may show a more dramatic improvement from gentle handling. In some cases adult cats can be rehabilitated to become more social. For example, stray cats who are nursed back to health can become quite attached to their caregivers.

It is possible to overdo socializing your kitten, too. In one study, kittens handled between one to five weeks and four to eight weeks were not as sociable as kittens handled during the optimal period (between two to seven weeks). Ideally, kittens should be handled for just a few minutes on a daily basis. More than fifteen minutes or so, and it may actually have a detrimental effect. Brief handling helps kittens to deal with stress better as adults and lays the foundation for establishing relationships later on. Handling should be minimal for the first two weeks when they can't see or hear you anyway! Introduce yourself gradually and keep your visits brief at first. There will be lots of time to get to know each other later.

Parental influences on cat temperament can be significant. If either parent had an unfriendly nature, it is possible that the kittens will be less than social. The paternal contribution to a kitten's temperament is primarily genetic because toms generally contribute little to raising the litters they produce. A friendly mother, on the other hand, contributes her genes and teaches, by example, to mold a sociable kitten.

No matter how friendly their parents were, many kittens seem to go through phases of social behavior. Like dogs, they will test other housemates to see how far each can be pushed. Dominance is somewhat fluid in cats, but it does exist. And because cats treat us as they would other cats, your kitten will likely be pushing your buttons at some point, too. Kittens that nip in play may simply need a more appropriate variety of toys and games. However, some kittens nip you to see if they can get what they want or just to see if they can get away with punishing you. Kittens can even have what is best described as a "temper tantrum," like my Teddi at bedtime. It is critical not to let this inappropriate behavior go unchecked. Immediately scruff your kitten by the loose skin on the back of her neck and firmly blow into the kitty's face (being careful not to get within range of little claws, of course). Without letting go, say, "Ow!" (as in "ouch") or "No!" Eventually, this word alone will replace any other punishment. If the kitten retaliates, however, blow again and repeat your verbal cue. If the tantrum persists, give the kitten one little flick of your finger on the nose, let the kitty go, and walk away. These are based on corrections the kitten would normally receive from other cats. Mama kitties normally scruff their kittens to transport them, and hissing resembles your blow of breath in the kitty's face. Your faint finger flick is not as severe as another cat's swatting paw, but hopefully it will make your point. Never ever shake, hit, or fling your kitten. The punishment, after all, should fit the crime. Don't be afraid to reprimand your kitten while he or she is young. Nip the nipping in the bud, before those adult teeth grow in!

The social nature of cats has only recently begun to be appreciated. It was previously thought that cats were solitary, independent, antisocial animals when, in fact, this couldn't be further from the truth. The complexity of their vocal, visual, tactile, and chemical communication implies a subtle yet complex interaction. Sociability in multicat households results from a tolerance of increased population density and an inborn predisposition toward social interaction. Cats who are raised with other cats are more accepting of newcomers than those who are raised in social isolation. This is additional evidence for a sensitive phase of development during which cats will be sensitized to bonding with nonmaternal companions. Genetics and learning are both important to a cat's sociability, toward people and toward other cats.

Cats, like people, have preferences in social partners. Outdoor cats can choose their companions, but indoor cats do not have the same opportunity. Their housemates will be imposed on them, although I have heard of outdoor cats who brought home their "friends" to stay. The best way to introduce new cats to resident pets is discussed in chapter 2. In most cases, housemates will learn to peacefully coexist although they may not become close. Still, peaceful coexistence is nothing to sneeze at. Perhaps our cats can teach us more than we know.

KEEP YOUR CAT INDOORS!

All my cats are indoor cats. They do not go outside, ever. Long ago, when my Jonathan was young, he used to come jogging with me. He loved to have his little leash put on and happily trotted beside me while I kept a slow but steady pace. His tail held high, he was quite a sight, and more than one person stopped to smile at this eager little soul who proudly escorted me during my workout. Sara did not want to accompany us and was perfectly content to stay at home. In the years since Jonathan's death, Hershey, Gracie, and Teddi have lived exclusively indoors. Gracie's blindness would have put her at an extreme disadvantage; she would probably not have survived had she been born as a stray. Teddi, the baby, is the first to grow up in our house rather than in an apartment. Sliding glass doors and doors of any kind are an invitation, beckoning her to explore what lies beyond. But the little bell on her collar reminds us she is ready to take advantage of any opening, and she is learning to stay within the boundaries, where she is safe from harm.

Some of you are cheering, I know, but not all of you. Some may be thinking, "But Dr. Cookie®, my cat loves to go outside! We live in a nice quiet neighborhood/dead-end street/wooded area/in the suburbs/ in the country, and it would be cruel to keep my cat indoors!" I do not dispute the fact that most cats would prefer to go outside. However, the fact is that you chose to accept the responsibility of caring for this creature and that includes keeping your cat safe from harm's way. Some of the potential dangers are natural, such as disease and other predators. But many of these dangers are man-made and include motor vehicles, hazards at construction sites, and people themselves. Your cat could even become the cause of car accidents as the driver swerves or brakes suddenly to avoid your pet. Your cat doesn't understand the risks, but you do, or you will now.

Consider your cat's risk of exposure to fatal feline diseases such as feline leukemia, feline immunodeficiency virus, and feline infectious peritonitis. Consider the menace of parasites such as fleas, ticks, tapeworm, roundworm, whipworm, heartworm, and other parasites that ravage your cat's kidneys and internal organs. Exposure to upper respiratory viruses can result in conjunctivitis and nasal discharge, bronchitis, pneumonia, and death. The rabies virus is alive and well almost everywhere in North America, causing pockets of epidemic in wildlife populations that may transmit the virus to pets who roam outdoors. Bacterial infections can be severe and fatal even from an injury inflicted by the cat next-door or a mouse killed by your cat. Your cat might not survive long enough to develop a bacterial infection from a dog attack. Someday, you might never see your cat again if the coyote, fox, or hawk sees them first.

Cats are the ultimate predator, adept at hunting day and night. In an age when we are increasingly aware of the fragility of our natural surroundings, consider the damage your cat can do to the environment. Many songbirds are already endangered by the effects of pollution or shrinking habitats because of real estate development. For every creature your cat kills, there may be babies who will starve waiting for it to return. You may not have pity for other prey animals such as mice or rats, but these also carry contagious diseases which could be transmitted to people and to your pet. Your cat does not need to hunt for supper when all you need to do is open a can or fill a bowl with prepared commercial diets.

Over the entire course of their evolution, cats were never meant to deal with cars, trucks, buses, or snowplows. How horrified will you be to find your pet lying in a tangled, mangled, bloodied heap on the side of the road? Perhaps your cat will survive the impact, only to crawl off into the trees to die an agonizingly slow death from internal injuries or be finished off by another predator. Human population is increasingly dense, and with it, the pet population is higher than it would have been in the days of our own ancestors. The social and physical pressures are far greater than your cat was ever meant to endure. Your outdoor cat struggles to control territory from other cats, competes with aggressive dogs, and flees from unkind people who see your cherished cat as yet another pesky stray. Don't be lulled into complacency by a fantasy of your cat romping blissfully through a field of daisies. It's a big bad world out there.

Not everyone is an animal lover, and in fact, some emotionally disturbed people see cats as prey. Satanic rituals are still performed with animal sacrifices, and cats continue to be a favorite victim. Particularly at Halloween, cats with solid black or solid white coats are in grave danger should they be captured by cult members. Cruelty to animals is not restricted to rituals of this kind. Children, too, can be very harmful to others who are more vulnerable. Young people with a history of family abuse can sometimes vent their own turmoil on any available target. These children may be crying for help, but who will be there to help your cat? Pathological behavior toward animals is a common denominator among those who commit violent crimes of many kinds. They are out there. Is your cat out there, too?

The emotional stress of being an outdoor cat is multiplied a hundredfold in modern times. It is no longer "natural" to let a cat outside, and it has not been for some time. No more do we dare let our young children play outdoors unattended, and the same should apply to our pets. Having convinced you, I hope, to keep your cat inside, let me give you some tips to make this lifestyle a satisfying one for you both. Feed your cat two meals a day and remove the uneaten portion once your cat has eaten his fill. This will help control the cat's weight and give him something to look forward to during his routine. Meals should be eagerly anticipated just as your cat would enjoy stalking prey in a natural setting. You could even sprinkle a portion of dry food in areas of your home so your cat really has to "hunt" for his supper. Or throw pieces of dry kibble for your cat to chase, one at a time, making it into a hunting game.

Until my Hershey was about one or two years old, it was important to keep him from bouncing off the walls. So we had time set aside for special games. He would retrieve anything I threw (except food), and I threw his kibble for him to chase, too! He loved those long, plastic sticks with feathers on the end, and continued to play with them long after he had plucked the feathers out! Indoor cats need alternative outlets for their energy. Interactive play with a playmate and a variety of attractive toys are important distractions. Enrich your cat's indoor environment with toys suspended from banisters, the backs of chairs, or even doorknobs. Be creative and make your own toys. Teach your cat tricks. If you want to, teach your cat to walk with you outside on a harness and leash (if your neighborhood is safe from mischievous dogs).

Keeping your cats confined to your home is not cruel when you consider the long list of hazards to which a cat is exposed outside. From my perspective, the cruelty (albeit unintended) occurs every time you open that door to let your cat out. Now, I know that some cats are intensely determined to go outside and that nothing, short of chains and barbed wire, will keep them in. But if you can manage it, you would do yourself and your cats a great favor by keeping them in. It may take some getting used to, but your cats can adjust. Alternately, a nice compromise to consider is to install a covered penned-in area just outside your back door. A chain-link fence beyond the pen will provide extra security by securing your yard from other animals. If you like, you can even install a cat door so that your cats can come and go to their outside pen to their heart's desire. This way, the cats cannot go farther and no harm can come to them. Your pets will never be too cold or too hot, wet, dirty, hungry, thirsty, lost, frightened, or alone. Your cats will be safe and sound, at home with you where they belong.

TAKING PITY ON STRAY CATS

Smurf was a stray, a huge black-and-white longhaired tom who lingered around the back porch of a multicat household. Despite his fleas and his matted coat, he was a big teddy bear of a cat. He must have appreciated the scraps the homeowners left for him faithfully every day, yet despite their invitations, he did not enter their home. Through snowstorms and deep freeze, the freshness of spring rains, blazing summers, and the chill of many falls, Smurf hung around, waiting. Months and years later, the last of the resident cats died of old age. As if he knew that his way had been cleared, Smurf nonchalantly entered through the cat door the very same day. He has not strayed from his new home since (except for visits to the veterinary clinic, of course) and has become the pasha of his palace. If he could speak, I know he would simply say, "It was worth the wait."

It is so very tempting to want to take in every pitiful little stray cat that comes to your door. If you manage to capture them, do a good deed and have them neutered immediately. This will help to control the ever-increasing numbers of cats who live on the edge, desperate for food, shelter, and denied a quality of existence that most will never know. It will also improve the quality of life for those who are neutered and released should they be too wild to make good pets. Females will not have to provide for litter after litter of kittens at a tremendous cost in energy and time, nor will males be as inclined to instigate or participate in cat fights.

Every stray in your custody should be tested for the contagious viral diseases that devastate the outdoor cat population, strays as well as pets. The two types of feline leukemia as well as feline infectious peritonitis are the worst of these. A simple blood test can confirm exposure to these viruses. If exposure is confirmed, you should explore the options with your veterinarian. Euthanasia may be the kindest thing for these infected strays who might otherwise die a miserable death. An alternative might be to place the carrier in a home without other cats or with other cats that are carriers, too. It may be many years before signs of disease appear; and if you understand that you could have higher veterinary bills along the way and still lose them in the end, you might still commit yourself and make the remainder of their lives the best that it can be. If, however, your own cats are free of these deadly diseases, your loyalty must be to them. I have known some determined cat lovers who keep two distinct populations of cats by sectioning their homes into two completely separate zones of infected and noninfected cat territories. It must be tricky, but it can be done.

If your little stray tests negative for contagious diseases, you still must check for other transmissible problems, such as fleas. These are easily treated with a new wave of flea-control products. A stool sample to check for the eggs of internal parasites is advised; but because these may not be present in the sample selected even when parasites are present (a "false negative" result), I recommend that your stray be treated for the most common parasites anyway, just in case. Many of these parasites, including tapeworm, which is transmitted by fleas and mice, are transmissible to people, so it makes sense to treat any stray in your care.

Stray cats are a mixed group. Some have been born in the wild and some are pets who, for one reason or another, did not return to their homes. People often assume that a friendly feral cat must have been a pet who got lost or was abandoned, but this is not necessarily the case. There is a wide range of social behavior in cats, even among those born wild. Their sociability is a function of inherited genetic inclination and the essential contribution of experience. Many pet cats become quite aggressive in some circumstances, even toward their owners. And many strays are born with a very tame and mild temperament. These are, indeed, diamonds in the rough.

If you cannot keep your stray, try to place him or her in a good home. A friend, neighbor, or relative might appreciate the company. The staff at your veterinary clinic may know a client whose pet has recently died and might be ready to fill the void. Adult cats are always more difficult to place than kittens, but it can be done with a little perseverance. I believe that while we can't save the whole world, each of us can save our own little part of it. Thank you for helping even one little lost soul to live happily ever after.

HOW TO NAME AND RENAME YOUR CAT

I will now tell you, not without a little embarrassment, how I came to name my cats. Jonathan, my first cat, was playful but not obnoxious, sensitive but not anxious, social but still selective. His name means "gift from God" in Hebrew, and that is exactly what he was. Sara Lee is a very prim little cat with the patience of a saint, who perched on my shoulder when she was small.

Her full name, inspired by the baking goods company and her birdlike ways, evolved into Sara Lee Angel Food Chocolate Cake Bird, but I usually just call her Sara Bird. Gracie just looked like the portrait of grace. She became Gracie Allen because, like her namesake, she is just a bit silly and sweet, but very smart. Hershey was named because of his chocolate coat. His full name is Hershel Walker, after a professional football player who also studied ballet. I have danced most of my life (perhaps to stave off my recurring fantasies of cake and chocolate) and liked the idea of naming my sturdy boy cat after this impressive athlete. And Tiadora. Well, I looked through a name-your-baby book and found nothing that fit her, so I made it up. Tia is "princess" in Greek, dora is "golden," but it could also mean "I adore you" in Italian. We just call her Teddi anyway, which suits her best after all.

Naming your cat can be quite a challenge. You may be inspired by the cat's appearance (Bob, Snowflake, or Blackie); your alcoholic beverage of choice (Brandy, Kahlua); the location where you found your cat (Freeway); a favorite novel (*Emma, Beau*); astronomy (Orion); or your favorite snack food (Peanut). Some people let their children name the family pet and end up with a name from their favorite movie (*Rambo*) or cartoon character (Simba is very popular still) or just a word they like (Squishy).

I've always found it interesting to learn what someone has named a pet. My theory is that what you name your pet is a reflection of you. Your choice of pet name reflects not only your originality and creativity, but also what that creature means to you, what your cat symbolizes to you on an emotional level. I suspect that people who give their pet a person's name relate differently than those who name their pet after something trivial (Spot). This doesn't mean that people who name their pets with goofy or bland names do not love their pets. Lucky, for example, is a very common pet name. However, if you pour over a book with 35,000 baby names for weeks before selecting the perfect name for your new cat, it seems to me your cat is clearly more than "just a pet." Some pet owners seem to fixate on one name and give it to successive pets. This results, for example, in a series of Fluffies. Does this reflect a simple lack of imagination or perhaps a failure to value the uniqueness of every cat? In the end as long as a cat is loved and well cared for all its life, the name hardly matters. A pet's welfare, emotional and physical, is all that really counts.

If you have adopted an adult cat from a shelter or acquired it with a name that you would not have chosen, are you stuck with that name? Don't worry, you can rename your new friend; but there are simple ways to avoid any initial confusion. If you don't know your cat's previous name, simply choose whatever name you'd like. With time, repetition, and reward for coming or paying attention to you when you call, your kitty will eventually learn the new name. However, if you do know a cat's given name before his new life with you began, simply say the old name together with the new name you have chosen for a few weeks. Essentially, your cat will temporarily become a "hyphenated cat." For example, if you have a new cat named Kitty but want to change it to Angela, call her Kitty-Angela for a week or so (get her attention with her familiar name first), then use Angela-Kitty for a while. When she is responding reliably to this name, just drop the Kitty.

If you care to be introspective, ask yourself why you selected the name you did for your pet cat. You might learn something about yourself and the nature of your bond to your pet. Have you ever thought about what your cat's name inferred about you, your sense of humor, your emotional attachments, spirituality, or personal preferences? It's not that your cat really cares what her name means in Lakota Sioux or why you named him Stinky, but it will tell other people something about you. So choose wisely, grasshopper!

2

General Stuff About Cat Behavior

Let Hercules himself do what he may,
The cat will mew and dog will have his day.

—WILLIAM SHAKESPEARE, *HAMLET*

INTRODUCING A NEW CAT

Jonathan was six months old when I brought the abandoned three-week-old Sara home. Jonjon was already established in my little apartment in the student ghetto. He liked having me, and his space, to himself and did not want to share either. I kept the tiny kitten in a cozy basket lined with soft towels and left her closed in the bathroom when I could not be there. They did not meet for the first week, although he knew she was there. At their first meeting, Jonjon was incensed. He fumed, stomped around, snorted. She simply gazed up at him with her sweet baby eyes in total adoration. He responded by using her head like a basketball, bouncing it between both his paws. Surprisingly, she did not seem concerned. He looked at her, stunned, and walked away in a huff. The next day they were cuddling, playing, and grooming each other. Sara followed Jonathan around for the rest of his life. He didn't mind, not one bit.

The most important tip I can give you about introducing new pets to each other is to take your time! Better to take things too slowly than not slowly enough; the damage could be irreversible. Let them discover each other gradually from a safe distance at first. Spend time

alone with each of your pets, including the new one. Seclude the new-comer in a private room (with fresh food and water every day and his or her own litter box) for at least one week without ever seeing the other pets of your household. Let the new cat adjust to one location where the cat can develop a sense of security and begin to form a bond with you. Make frequent visits to feed, pet, and play with your new friend. Over the following two to four weeks, give the newcomer brief moments to explore his or her new home under your supervision. Your other pets initially should be isolated elsewhere in your home while their new housemate becomes familiar with the new territory. Your new cat can explore one new room a day during these brief outings before returning to confinement.

If things are a bit rocky when the cats begin to socialize, time their initial encounters to coincide with mealtime. Feed them by placing their food dishes at a comfortable distance from each other (e.g., opposite ends of the kitchen), then return the new cat to his or her private quarters until the next scheduled mealtime. Over the next few days, let them spend progressively longer periods together following meals. Eventually, you should be able to move their food dishes closer over successive meals as they grow accustomed to each other. Above all, be patient. If, after several weeks or several months, the cats are persistently or increasingly antagonistic, you may need more help. It is occasionally necessary to use psychoactive medication for brief periods to facilitate the introduction and adjustment period. Medication should be preceded by blood tests to make sure there is no underlying medical disorder. Your veterinarian should be able to refer you to a veterinarian specializing in pet behavior in your area.

The good news is that most cats learn at least to tolerate each other in the end. Every so often, there are exceptions. Some cats simply cannot bear any other cat in their space, or there is a basic personality conflict between them. If this happens, you could create a permanent time-sharing territory whereby one cat is alternately confined while the other is allowed to roam, and vice versa. Or you could divide your home into two separate spaces and set up each cat in his or her own exclusive territory. Your final option, of course, would be to find another home for the new cat. After all, your allegiance should be to the resident cat.

If your other pets include dogs, remember that a dog is more likely to do serious injury to a cat than the reverse. Details on how to introduce cats and dogs are discussed further on in this chapter. If you are introducing a new cat to other pet cats and dogs, the new pet actually needs to adjust to both species on slightly different terms. Review my suggestions for both situations and you should all settle in just fine!

INTRODUCING A NEW CAT TO A MULTICAT HOME

Monroe was a funny-looking little kitten with big yellow eyes and a red-and-white blotchy coat. What he lacked in looks he more than made up for in charm. His introduction to a household of four other cats was abrupt. He was simply plopped down in the middle of the living room. He froze as the other cats descended upon him. They hissed, swatted at each other, spit at him, and then they all scattered. Tempers flared for days, and days became weeks. After several months things seemed to stabilize, more or less. The original four cats remained nervous and startled easily, especially if Monroe came racing down the hall in a kitten frenzy. Two of the cats had taken to hiding under the bed in the guest bedroom and virtually ignored their owner. The eldest of the cats, an eleven-year-old Siamese cross named Willow, had lost weight since Monroe discovered she was the most fun to chase. Monroe was more than they had all bargained for. His owner called me in desperation when Monroe had been with them for about three months. He hoped to be able to salvage his formerly happy relationships with his pets and to stabilize the dynamics between the five cats of his household. It was quite a mess.

The social behavior of cats is complex. They are, indeed, social creatures, or at least they have the potential of being social. Their acceptance, or rejection, of a new cat depends on the social nature and dynamics of the cats already in residence, the individual newcomer, the territorial nature of the resident cats, and the degree of socialization of all concerned. The more cats are involved, the more complicated are the dynamics because each cat will have his or her own individual history, social attitudes, tolerance of population density, and preference for territorial sovereignty. The relationship between two cats can be intricate enough. The permutations of interaction in a multicat household can be phenomenal. One thing is certain. The introduction of a new cat to an established feline household will upset the dynamics of the entire colony. The presence of any new cat sends ripples through the social waters and forces all cats to reestablish territorial boundaries and rank. In other words, even if Monroe had been introduced in a more ideal fashion, the other cats would still have been upset, although perhaps not as critically insulted.

It is nearly impossible to predict how cats will get along. The most unlikely cats sometimes become the best of friends in an instant. In other cases, their intolerance of each other is immediate and enduring. Most of the time, an initial period of conflict typically evolves over time toward a steady state of mutual tolerance. My recommendation to Monroe's dad was to start over, as if Monroe had just arrived, so that the other cats could regain a semblance of the equilibrium that his arrival had so acutely unbalanced. A gradual integration allows house cats to slowly discover and investigate each other in a more natural way. Take your time! Here are my guidelines, so successful for Monroe and his family, for integrating your new cat or kitten:

- For the first few days, confine the new cat to one room with food, water, and litter box. This room should be neutral turf, in other words, not the favorite space of your resident cat. Make frequent visits to play with your new kitty, bring special food tidbits, and spend time just petting and holding the cat. Remember, your new pet is under a lot of stress. The cat needs to get to know you, a new home, and the other cats, so try not to mix the issues! Give the newcomer time to adjust to just one room, to feel emotionally and physically secure, and then build from there.

- Meanwhile, spend extra quality time with your resident cat(s). Engage them in favorite activities to minimize their anxiety. Your resident cats will be fully aware that there is an intruder in the house and deserve reassurance that your preexisting relationship will not suffer.

- Feed your resident cat near the door of the room in which the new kitty is confined. Gradually move the confined cat's food dish toward the inside of the door. They will be separated only by the closed door but feeding should help to distract them from each other. Eventually, they will equate each other's presence with something good (food). Do not progress to the next step until the cats are comfortable being this close to each other. It may take days or it may take weeks. The best relationships take time to build, and you need to build on a firm foundation.

- Confine your resident cats to their favorite room, perhaps your bedroom, which is so strongly associated with you. Then, let your new cat out of confinement for brief expeditions to investigate your home. Stay with him so that he will feel less overwhelmed by this new territory. Exploring one new room every other day will help to pace the discovery.

- When your new cat seems comfortable in the rest of the house (spontaneous play or self-grooming are good indicators of a relaxed cat), you are ready to introduce them face-to-face.

- You must be present when the new cat is finally revealed to your resident pets. Some hostility and hesitation are to be expected from any of the cats. I have found it helpful to introduce them at mealtime at opposite ends of the same room (the kitchen is fine). Place their food dishes at a comfortable distance. If any of the cats become aggressive toward the other, remove the food bowls and confine the new cat to the "safe" room. Wait a few minutes and try again. In some cases, it may be helpful to restrain a cat that lunges at or threatens the other. A harness or collar and leash will help to teach the assertive cat to remain more passive during the introduction process.

- If a second attempt is met with more hostility, separate them again and feed them in separate quarters when they've calmed down. Try the same introduction at mealtime on the next day.
- As the cats grow accustomed to seeing each other at feeding time, let them spend gradually longer periods together after they have finished eating.
- When things seem to be calm, inch their food dishes closer to each other over successive meals. Leave the leash on in case you need to control a sudden confrontation. If the cats are comfortable being about three feet or so from each other at mealtimes, you should be ready to let the new kitty out of confinement.

In some cases aggressiveness can persist for longer than anticipated. In these cases the option of psychoactive medication becomes more attractive to help ease the transition. These medications are best pre-scribed by a veterinary behaviorist, who can also offer additional sug-gestions tailored to your cats. In exceptional cases, there are cats who simply cannot be integrated into an established feline territory. If so, you can keep the cat confined to his or her own exclusive part of your home so that the new cat never interacts with the others. Another option is to alternately confine the cats who don't get along; while one cat is confined, the other is free to roam. You can always try to reintroduce them later on. If things seem hopeless, or if you have lost patience, it is probably better off to find another home for your new kitty. At least you tried!

INTRODUCING A DOG AND A CAT

Hershey was so insulted when my dog Aliya came home to stay that he refused to sleep with me for a month. He was grumpy toward Sara and

Gracie (Teddi had not yet arrived on the scene) and skulked around the apartment. Hershey was in a funk for the first few weeks, but then he decided to take matters into his own paws. One day I heard the puppy scampering in the hallway and looked up just in time to see Hershey chasing the puppy at top speed. I stood there paralyzed by an indescribable mix of amazement and hysteria as I watched the cat chase the puppy back and forth, and back and forth. This scene repeated itself sporadically for weeks. Hershey was empowered by his campaign of harassment. Meanwhile, Aliya's confidence (and legs) grew until one day she had a flash of insight and suddenly turned to face her formidable foe. Hershey screeched to a halt and stared up at Aliya's long nose. And then the chase began again, this time with Aliya in hot pursuit. Hershey's life had changed forever. Four years later Aliya still chases him whenever the mood strikes her, and Hershey has begrudgingly accepted her dominance. Sometimes we get used to change and learn to live happily ever after, even when life is not perfect.

Cats and dogs always fight, right? Wrong. Some of the most touching relationships I have ever seen exist between the most unpredictable partners. Hershey and Aliya, my Saluki dog, learned to tolerate each other, but they have never become close companions. Hershey was about two years old when this puppy arrived. I think they both enjoy each other (I know Aliya does!), but neither would admit it.

Their relationship is in contrast to the one between my Teddi and Georgyanna. Teddi grew up in a home with two dogs. Georgie, our Boston Terrier, was just six months old and Aliya was over three years old when Teddi came. Teddi's first reaction to the dogs was to bestow upon each head a firm and well placed "thump" with a tiny paw. As comical as it was to witness the defiance of a runt who weighed less than a pound, it appeared to be very effective. Aliya gained an immediate and healthy respect for this diminutive hellion, and Georgie's ongoing fascination began. Today, Teddi and Georgie are best buddies. They take naps together, with Teddi curled between Georgie's paws. Sometimes, they take turns using each other as pillows. They play constantly, with Teddi playing "lion" and Georgie as the "zebra." They chomp on each other's cheeks and paws, and chase, wrestle, and roll around. Never a dull moment here. They grew up together and had a better chance of developing a special bond than did Aliya and Hershey.

Pets who are introduced later in life evaluate each other with a natural and healthy defensiveness. Cats who have known and loved (or at least tolerated) dogs during their kittenhoods will be more open to welcoming a new canine member of the family. On the other hand, I have also known many cats and dogs who were introduced as adults and became lifelong and constant companions.

The most important thing to determine when introducing a dog to a cat for the first time is whether the dog will hurt the cat. Unless the dog is considerably smaller than the kitten or cat, the dog can do far more harm to the feline. The misperception that a cat will "scratch a dog's eyes out" is grossly exaggerated. Yes, a cat might injure a dog if the dog's face gets too close for comfort, but a cornered and frightened animal lashes out at anything in order to make a quick escape. The panicky cat is not going to hang around to wait for the dog to recover from the surprise attack. The cat is not necessarily aiming for the dog's eyes; however, if the dog's eye is scratched, a corneal injury heals quite well with appropriate treatment. On the other hand, any damage that the dog can do to a cat will be far more serious.

Just because a dog has never seen a cat does not mean the dog will necessarily be aggressive toward cats. It depends on the dog's predatory instinct and hunting opportunities, prior experience with other dogs and animals, the specific context in which they are introduced, and the leadership provided by the dog's owner. If you are thinking of adopting an adult dog, ask the previous owner or shelter staff about the dog's history with cats. With or without prior friendly experience with cats, dogs can react explosively and with little warning when presented with an unfamiliar cat. If a dog has a history of injuring other small dogs, behaving aggressively toward cats, escaping, hunting, and behaving disobediently, the chances of integrating the dog into your feline household will be slim. The new cat, or new dog, you would like to take home is better off going home with someone else.

Whether you are introducing a dog to your resident cat or a new cat to your own dog, hold that dog firmly on a very short leash and keep the cat beyond the dog's biting range. Pups younger than three months are not likely to pose any serious threat to the average cat; however, it is always wise to supervise unfamiliar animals until you are completely certain that all is well. Animals are unlikely to injure individuals with whom they have grown up. Other housemates are probably regarded as pack members to the dog, even if the housemates are cats. Keep your dog on a leash at first until the dog recognizes the new pet as part of the pack. Do not leave them unattended unless you are certain your cat is safe. If your dog has a history of aggression toward cats or small prey animals, it might be wise not to introduce a cat to your home. Although some dogs will learn to accept a cat despite ongoing aggression toward cats outside your home, it is still a gamble that the cat could lose, and the cat's stakes are highest.

If you have decided to proceed with the introduction, firmly restrain your new dog or puppy on a very short leash. Instruct the dog to *down* and *stay* when the dog sees your cat for the first time, and repeat this command at every supervised meeting. Reward the restrained dog with a tasty tidbit. Be very cautious of your dog's intent to hurt the cat. Do not try to restrain a panicky cat! It may take several days, several weeks, or several months to make certain that your cat and dog can be safely left together. Keep your cat confined to one room when you are not at home. Remain vigilant of your dog's moods and your cat's physical frailties, such as an inability to jump onto elevated surfaces to escape danger. They may never become inseparable pals like Teddi and Georgie, but at least they may become friendly rivals like Hershey and Aliya.

UNPREDICTABILITY OF PET CAT COMPATIBILITY

For his first year, Hershey and Sara had me to themselves. They also had each other, but with over fifteen years between them, it was definitely a spring-winter kind of relationship. I kept Hershey busy at first, but he began to play more and more roughly with the elderly cat. I made the decision to add another cat to the household who would be closer to Hershey in age and provide him with a more appropriate playmate. Gracie was meant to be a playmate for Hershey, unfortunately, that's not exactly how it worked out. It was not immediately apparent why she was such a shy and withdrawn kitten, rarely playful, and clinging either to me or to Sara. Hershey tried to play with her, but she did not respond to his invitations. Within several months, it was confirmed that she had congenital retinal atrophy and was almost completely blind. Hershey did not understand why she walked into him, and he, of course, took this as an insult to his dominance. Instead of becoming her companion as I had hoped, Hershey learned to resent her some of the time and tolerate her most of the time. During cool weather, however, he will briefly snuggle up to her and allow her to groom him. Cuddling, even for brief moments, can be an important part of living happily ever after.

Unfortunately, it is almost impossible to predict compatibility between cats. With so many contributing factors to consider (such as size, gender, age, individual temperament, early life experience, and health status), it all comes down to the luck of the draw. Each pet will bring his own genetic and psychological "baggage" to the mix, and predicting the response to another cat seems remote. Still, the fact that most cats will at least learn to coexist is a tribute to their behavioral flexibility and intelligence. Chances are that introductory difficulties will subside. Your cats just might become inseparable friends! Time and again I have seen the most unlikely pairs become instant and lifelong companions. Only occasionally is an initial negative response by one or both cats the sign of enduring antagonism. On the other hand, even stable relationships can degenerate months or years later for a variety of reasons. A change in health status or redirected territorial aggression, discussed elsewhere in this book, can bring about tension between housemates.

Choosing a new cat of the opposite sex of your resident cat does not guarantee they will get along. A male and female cat do not necessarily form a pair bond. There is an element of choice, particularly by females, when cats are free to choose their own mates. Their preferences as individuals do not vanish because of neutering, only the sexual outcome is altered. Our pet cats do not choose their housemates. We impose our choices on them and leave them to adapt and overcome. We have all occasionally heard stories of an outdoor cat who brought a friend home to stay. These stories are true and such relationships often do develop between and within the sexes. In almost all cases, however, your cat population will expand by the pets you acquire without your resident cats' input. The addition of any new cat to your colony will send ripples and even tidal waves into the social dynamics between all cats present. The only question is the degree of upheaval and how long it will take to return to a calm, steady state. I have found that it might take several days, if you are very lucky, or as long as six months to a year for cats to learn to live with each other. A gradual and intentionally delayed introduction will benefit everyone involved.

Here are some very general guidelines to help minimize any major mistakes when introducing new cats to each other:

- *Don't* introduce two intact adult males (or two females in heat). Sexual tension will interfere and complicate things unnecessarily. *Do* have adult cats neutered right away (e.g., before you bring them home from the shelter and attempt an introduction).
- *Don't* introduce an assertive cat (male or female) to a home containing a single cat who has been raised alone. *Do* understand that cats raised alone do not adjust as easily to other cats on their turf!
- If you are getting one kitten, get two! I often advise getting two kittens at a time because they will have more fun and because it will be a smoother transition to adding another cat down the road. Even if one of the original pair is gone, the remaining cat will adjust better to a new housemate. Besides, you will be doing the good deed of rescuing not one but two cats!
- A male kitten or young adult will play more roughly than a juvenile female in most cases (although some females can be quite *macha*!). In general, if you have an aging or ailing cat, you might be better off with the addition of a female (or two kittens who will focus on each other rather than on the resident cat). Either way, you must create constant entertainment for any new kitten so that your vulnerable resident cat is not the sole target of the kitten's playful enthusiasm. Past the crazy kitten year, however, many males become big marshmallows—a placid, adult, neutered male might be a perfect choice.
- *Do not* base your choice of a new pet on looks alone. *Do* make

your selection based on health and temperament with less emphasis on your partiality to a certain coat color or pattern. Tips on pet selection are discussed at length in chapter 8.

- *Do not* forget that quality is more important than quantity. Your love of cats could turn your home into a place where the quality of life for all is impacted by the quantity of pets! *Do* consider the size of your home when you are thinking of adding another cat. This is particularly significant for indoor cats. Although there is no hard and fast rule of how many square feet any cat will require to feel comfortable (there will be individual differences for this preference, too), avoid overcrowding. I would suggest one or two cats for every floor of livable space (don't count an unfinished basement) of your home. Given the great variability of floor plans, floor area, and cat temperament, even this could be too much! If your cats are used to roaming outside, your home represents only a fraction of their territory. However, I would still caution you to minimize complications by restricting the number of pets. Interestingly, in homes of high cat density (say a dozen or more), the population may seem even more placid than with only several cats (although there is an escalating risk of other unwanted behaviors, such as urine marking). This is a phenomenon which, again, attests to the flexibility and intelligence of cats. With such a squeeze for space, these cats might realize that they simply have no choice but to get along!

THE SOLITARY CAT AND NEW HOUSEMATES

Marlena was a six-year-old tortoiseshell domestic longhair. She was purchased at a pet store at the age of six weeks and had been raised as an exclusively indoor cat. Her life was perfect. She had the whole place to herself, and she was completely pampered. At some point her owners decided that she was lonely. In fact, if they had been able to ask her, she might have replied, "I want to be alone!" Coincidentally, she had been named for Marlene Dietrich, and they may have had more in common than just the name! Well, Maya arrived and everything changed. Maya was a two-year-old gray domestic shorthair who had been turned into a local shelter. She was one of ten cats belonging to an elderly gentleman who had died. Maya was used to living with other cats. She stayed in the guest bathroom of her new home for the first week and was then allowed to make several short field trips a day into the rest of the house, while Marlena was confined to her owners' bedroom. Marlena hated Maya from the moment they met, despite this gradual introduction. Maya tried to make friends, but when she gently touched noses, Marlena recoiled and spit at her. Maya tried to cuddle next to her in the sun, but Marlena swatted and hissed. Marlena withdrew from her owners, refused food, and was easily irritated. Everyone was upset. Marlena was a cat on the edge.

Marlena was adopted as a young kitten and had grown up isolated from others of her kind. During the sensitive formative stage between two and seven weeks when the foundations of her social attitude toward other cats might have been formed, she had only been exposed to people. It is not that she did not know she was a cat; she had just not had the opportunity to develop social skills that might have helped her interact with another cat.

Cats who have not been exposed to other cats while growing up often adjust less readily to a new housemate. This does not mean that they will never accept a new housemate. It might mean, however, that the road could be bumpy for a while. Marlena had become clinically depressed. She was anxious, socially withdrawn, and her appetite was poor. We decided to medicate her with a short-acting antianxiety medication for approximately eight weeks. Meanwhile, Maya was confined to the bathroom, and her integration was begun again at an even slower pace. Things went more smoothly this time, and within six months Marlena allowed Maya to shyly rub noses. By the end of the first year, they were seen lying side by side in the bay window and they lived happily ever after.

To avoid conflict when introducing cats, carefully prepare for the first encounter. If one of the cats has been raised as a solitary cat or if you are uncertain of their backgrounds, you should aim for a minimum of four to six weeks before the new cat is allowed to roam freely in your home. For cats with greater social experience, a gradual integration over two to three weeks should be fine. The cats will sense each other's presence by odors that travel through your home and on your clothing. They will also hear each other moving about. It is always better to proceed too slowly than too fast. The damage done by a bad first impression can be harder to undo and make living happily ever after just a fairy tale.

THREE-DIMENSIONAL TERRITORY IN CATS

Teddi is hanging over the top of my computer monitor. Her delicate paw is dangling over the screen and making it difficult to see what I am writing. She is having a dream. Her little pink nose is twitching, and her eyeballs are rolled back. The monitor is warm from working hard with me as I write this book, so Teddi must be cozy. What will she do when I get my new laptop, I wonder? Many of you must have cats who "help" you while you work at your computer or try to read. Teddi's position is not that unusual. Hershey, my lion king, lies regally atop his tower. One of his strategic perches is on top of the refrigerator in the pantry. He has a great view of the adjacent rooms and can guard the food, too. Hershey rules with an iron paw.

Cats use every inch of space. To them, it is not just the square footage that counts. The floor area is just the beginning. Cats climb. Cats jump. Cats use horizontal and vertical space. Humans are tied primarily to the horizontal. After all, how many of us are actually driven to climb Mount Everest? For dogs, territory is also mostly on the horizontal plane, although some of you may know or own dogs that insist on sleeping in your bed or on the kitchen table! Cats, on the other hand, use every elevated surface within reach. Bookcases, the top of fish tanks, the top of your television or entertainment unit, kitchen counters, the top of kitchen cabinets, tabletops of every room, windowsills, ceiling fans . . . When my Sara was a kitten, she used to jump from the sink in the bathroom to the top of the shower stall and walk along the shower curtain rod. She had already shredded the toilet paper roll, of course. Cats are creative explorers. They will analyze how to get from point A to point B. By trial and error (called *insight learning*), they will get there.

Exploring every part of their territory, indoor and outdoor, is intellectually stimulating. It is also very good exercise. Jumping and climbing makes use of all of their considerable athleticism and balance. Cats climb because they can. This ability allowed them to expand their hunting targets, to seek refuge from other predators, and to find shelter from the elements. The feline territory is very three-dimensional. If, however, you fail to admire the vertical inclination of your cat because of the potential nuisance it may cause, please refer to the discussion of how to deal with your little Tarzan in chapter 5, "Destructive Behavior."

TERRITORIAL TIME-SHARING

Gracie lives in my bedroom. She is either on the bed, under the bed, or in a comfy basket under my dressing table. She comes downstairs only when she is hungry or to greet me when I come home. If I am working in my home office, she will join me in a basket placed under the desk or knead in my lap before settling in for a nap. Sara follows the sun. In the morning she lies in front of the living room windows, but by the afternoon she has picked up the sun's trail in my husband's office. In between, and in the evening, she can be found curled up on either one of two favorite dining room chairs. Teddi goes where I go when I am home. She has found the bookcase of my desk and the top of my computer monitor to be her favorite perches thus far, although cuddling under my sweater is even better (unless Gracie is already on my lap!). She also likes to sleep in the sun in front of the balcony doors of our bedroom or on the kitchen chairs. Hershey's core territory is the dining room and the adjoining kitchen. No surprise there. He lives to eat! He has a soft bed in the corner of the dining room that no one else would dare to use (except Georgyanna, our Boston Terrier, but only if Hershey isn't looking). And on cool nights, he shoves Gracie aside to get closer to me.

Cats claim favorite resting perches. Typically, these are in quiet corners of a low traffic room or on elevated surfaces. During daylight hours, most cats will choose to sleep in a sunny spot, which might be in the middle of your living room carpet. Cats sleep out in the open only when they are very confident that they are safe. At night cats will usually snuggle in a cozy spot of their core territory. This might be your bedroom, but if you have more than one cat you may notice that they can each be found in a particular place at different times of day. If you pay close attention, this will tell you where each cat feels most comfortable and at what time of day. And therein lies the secret. *Territorial behavior in cats is a function of place and time of day.* For instance, one of your cats might use your living room chair during the morning, but another cat might use it in the afternoon. And they both might share your bed with you at night! I have at least six cozy baskets scattered around our home to minimize arguments over any particular choice spot.

Dominant cats tend to prefer elevated perches or strategic locations from which they can command the flow of feline traffic and supervise the household's activity in general. Hershey's preference for the dining room is not accidental. From here, he can survey the front door and the kitchen. His priorities are quite clear; however, he does allow Sara to share the room as long as she confines herself to her favorite dining room chair.

Cats use space on a time-share scheme. For instance, if your neighbor's cat is not allowed out at night when your cat roams, they are time-sharing the same territory. Outdoor cats might patrol the same route but at different times of day. Dominant animals have priority in choosing what time of day and what range they use. For this reason, the term *spatiotemporal dominance* (referring to the key elements of space and time) is used to describe how cats will come to share their territory. This applies to cats who are confined to your home or those who roam outdoors. The major difference in their lifestyles is that confined cats live in a finite territory. Territorial behavior in cats is complicated and based on individual strategy and social ambition for dominance, the value of the space in question, and the time of day they are allowed to use it.

THE FEAR RESPONSE

Ashley was terrified of the doorbell. When she was three years old, her mom had tripped over her on her way to answer the door, sending a potted plant crashing to the floor in the process. Ashley decided the doorbell was to blame. The doorbell was evil. When it rang, her eyes opened wide, her ears went back flat, her hair stood on end, she hugged the ground, and she piddled urine as she raced to her safe place in the back of the linen closet. Just once her worried mom had tried to calm her down and had reached into the closet to pet Ashley where she huddled on a neat stack of towels. It took a year for the scars of those scratches to fade from her arm.

Ashley had developed a phobia to the doorbell. She had been exposed to a single and intensely traumatizing event that was enough to make a powerfully negative association. To her, the doorbell was a sure sign of impending doom. In reality, it triggered a conditioned fear response that was excessive in view of the actual danger present. This is the definition of a *phobia,* an excessive fear to a relatively benign situation. Some phobias develop gradually over successive exposure to a frightening event. This is what occurs, for instance, when your cat becomes more and more afraid of trips to the veterinary clinic. If a single event is sufficiently horrifying, however, a phobia can develop after a single exposure to the trigger.

When the doorbell rang, Ashley displayed the physical signs of extreme fear. Her pupils dilated, she lost control of her bladder, her ears flattened against her head, and her body flattened against the ground. Then she fled in terror. The famous "fight or flight" scenario summarizes Ashley's behavior. She could not fight the doorbell, so she ran. Still in a panic when her owner reached for her in her closet refuge, she could not run from the outreached arm so she scratched it.

Rule number one: *Do not try to pursue a terrified animal.* Rule number two: *Do not block the path of a frightened animal* who is running from a real or imagined threat. Always consider your own safety first. A frightened cat will strike out in an attempt to flee danger. It is the most primitive instinct that is common to us all. Panic and defensive aggression can be an explosive combination, and you are better off waiting until things calm down.

I asked Ashley's mom how often the doorbell rang. She mentioned that the family usually entered the house by the back door. The doorbell at the front door rang once every two or three months when a package was delivered, and more often around the holidays when visitors were more common. In other words it was used only occasionally and always associated with something less than great, at least from Ashley's point of view. I suggested that Ashley's family ring the doorbell on a daily basis. Between five children and two parents each ringing the doorbell at least twice a day, every day, on an unpredictable schedule, Ashley's exposure to the doorbell was significantly increased. By having the bell rung this often, she began to respond less. It was less and less of an unusual event because it was happening so often. We helped her along by medicating her with an antianxiety medication for the first three weeks. Once she calmed down a bit, we also gave her special treats when the doorbell rang. Within two months Ashley ran to the kitchen for a treat when she heard that bell! Eventually the treats were discontinued, and Ashley ignored the bell. Six months later the doorbell broke; and rather than fix it, they used the doorknocker instead!

"HALLUCINATORY" PLAY IN CATS

Mutt, a ten-month-old brown tabby, was having "fits." Over the telephone, I could hear the deep concern in his owner's voice. We scheduled a house call to investigate his strange behavior. Was he having seizures? Mutt seemed like a normal cat otherwise (when he was not having a "fit"), and his veterinarian had given him a clean bill of health. His owner wondered if he was seeing ghosts. Was her home haunted?

Play is serious business. Play functions to improve motor control and the development of muscles and response time, which are so important for detecting and capturing prey or for evading a predator or rival. It also contributes to cognitive training as young and adult animals maximize their senses and the use of their environment. Play also has an important social function and allows kittens to learn about their individual limitations, to practice sexual behaviors in nonsexual contexts, and to develop bonds between individuals to maintain social stability in their territory.

Mutt was fine. We soon determined that Mutt was engaging in a peculiar form of solitary play, called *hallucinatory play*, which seems to erupt spontaneously. The cat will begin to thrash his or her tail violently, freezing as if to listen to or look at something and race away at top speed. The cat seems to be chasing something or running from something or both. Some cats will bound off furniture, ricochet off walls, and vocalize loudly all the way. And then it is over as quickly as it began. The cat will plop down, groom him or herself to make sure they aren't too disheveled (actually, the cat is probably just getting ready to have a snooze), and look at you as if to say, ". . . and just what are *you* looking at?"

Hallucinatory play is a common variation of normal play. It is not associated with any documented seizure activity, and it occurs in perfectly normal cats. They do not harm themselves or anyone during these silly episodes. In fact, kids and puppies can be seen to engage in similar playful bursts of energy, racing up and down as fast as their little feet will go for no apparent reason! I remember doing it myself! With cats, play should not be confused with *feline hyperesthesia syndrome*, which is a much more extreme case of agitated and compulsive overactivity. This pathological behavior requires psychoactive medication. Mutt's goofiness was normal and did not require treatment, although I did suggest to his owner that she play more with him and provide a wider variety of toys. She gladly complied. His new toy was named Jeff, a boisterous female brown tabby who beat Mutt up on a regular basis. He loved her. I never could tell if the house was haunted . . .

TAIL CHASING

Zorro was a white domestic shorthair kitten with a black mask. At five months of age, Zorro's favorite games were jumping from dining room chair to dining room chair and tail chasing. Actually, his favorite game was to try and catch moths through the screen door when they fluttered close by in the evening, attracted by the patio lights. But during the day his favorite game was chasing his tail . . . when he wasn't intentionally knocking things off his owner's desk just for the fun of hearing the "thud" or "crash." And if he wasn't stalking the fractured rainbows of light set off by the dancing prisms hung at the window, his favorite thing was definitely chasing his tail. Of course, he really loved to ambush the dog from under every bed in the house, nipping on his leg then sauntering away in cocky triumph. Best of all, he loved to chase his tail. Once he tried to catch his tail when he was sitting on the back of the sofa. He rolled off and actually seemed embarrassed, but not for long. Sometimes when he did capture it, he sucked and chewed on it, but only for a second. He had far too many other things to do.

Social play between kittens in a group peaks by the ninth week of life. From that point onward, kittens tend to pair off as opposed to playing in groups. This developmental sequence makes sense when you consider that it is safer for babies to remain in the nest and entertain each other. In fact, this early stage of social play has been compared to an invisible "playpen" in preparation for the day when they will roam farther and farther away toward their individual independence. By the age of four months, self-directed play will predominate as environmental exploration overlaps with locomotor play (running, jumping, climbing). Most kittens go through a phase of self-discovery. They seem to solicit play from their own reflections in the mirror, but this eventually stops, we think because they come to recognize themselves in the mirror and are no longer intrigued. The discovery of his or her own tail is an exciting event in a kitten's life. It is an ever-ready playmate, always there when they need it. Tail chasing usually fades as the kitten matures and looks to more stimulating objects with which to play.

Tail-chasing behavior in and of itself is harmless. However, some cats get a bit carried away. In a minority of cats tail chasing becomes tail sucking, and tail sucking turns into tail chewing. Self-mutilation of the tail is uncommon, but it can be difficult to treat when the cat has become obsessive. A kneading motion of the front paws may accompany tail sucking. It is almost as if the kitten or cat has redirected nursing behavior onto his own tail. Because tail-chasing play can evolve into more problematic behavior, I prefer not to encourage it in young cats. Rather than encouraging your cat by teasing him with his own tail, wriggling the tip into his mouth, dangle a stuffed mouse from a long cord or throw a ball for him to chase instead. Your kitten needs substance, challenge, meaningful interaction, and intellectual stimulation, not just a piece of tail!

SYNCHRONIZING YOUR CIRCADIAN RHYTHMS

Waldo was a black-and-white neutered male who lived alone with his dad, who worked a split shift and long hours. He complained that Waldo, his only pet, was pushing him over the edge. This four-year-old cat got frisky by pouncing on and leaping across his dad's waterbed while he tried to sleep. Waldo was disrupting his owner's much needed sleep and making him very grumpy. He was falling out of love with his cat. Poor Waldo couldn't possibly understand that he was living on borrowed time.

The normal pattern of activity for cats is to show peaks of activity at dawn and dusk. This type of circadian rhythm is called a *crepuscular* pattern. Pet cats are not nocturnal (active during the night), although some cats may gravitate toward this rhythm depending on their owner's schedules or when they are put outside. For example, some cats are let out at 10 P.M. and return (hopefully) the next morning. In most cases, however, our pets synchronize their schedules to our own daily rhythms. You may notice that your cat is most playful when you are hustling to get to work in the morning. He probably sleeps most of the day and then has a burst of energy when you return in the evening. We are tired by the end of the day and take our pets for granted. We pet them absentmindedly while they cuddle up to us as we watch TV. Then, by our bedtime, they want to play! Waldo was raring to go when his dad was trying to shut down. Their sleeping schedules were out of synch. The solution was simple.

Play with your cat before you go to sleep. You *both* need to be ready to collapse by your bedtime. Waldo's dad made some toys, bought some toys, and played with his boy every chance he could. I suggested he even wake Waldo up to play with him during the day or early evening so he would be more tired by his owner's bedtime. In no time the two pals were once again curling up together on that waterbed and floating off to a deep and restful sleep.

NUISANCE PLAY

Skyler was a one-year-old Russian Blue with an aristocratic air. Her behavior, however, was less than ladylike. According to her sleep-deprived owner, Skyler threw "tantrums." Each morning, at the crack of dawn, she woke her owner by deliberately pushing items off the top of her dressing table onto the hardwood floor below. Several treasured items had been damaged, and Skyler was becoming more of a nuisance than a pleasure. Could Dr. Cookie® teach this kitty some manners?

Skyler was pushing her owner's buttons. She wanted attention. She wanted to play. She found a way to get both! Mischievous attention-seeking behavior is often self-reinforcing. Your cat quickly learns what will get your attention, and this behavior is sure to be repeated! Playful mischief rapidly becomes nuisance behavior. Skyler's owner was increasingly frustrated with her and, because of this growing resentment, she played less with her cat and paid less attention to her. This, of course, only made things worse.

The solution began by letting bygones be bygones. I suggested she take a deep breath and start fresh with Skyler. Skyler's mom could have closed her bedroom door, but she preferred not to shut her pet out. More playtime overall, playtime before bedtime, and a wider variety of toys were advised. Breakable items were removed from every surface to make her home more pet proof until Skyler was a bit older. We cleared the dressing table surface and suspended soft toys from strings attached to the back of the chairs in her bedroom. This gave Skyler something to do while she waited for her owner to get up. In case Skyler discovered some other way to wake her owner up, such as vocalizing, I warned her owner to be prepared. Under no circumstances was she allowed to respond to any of Skyler's attention-seeking mischief. If this meant burying her head in the pillow to ignore her, so be it. Any attention, positive or negative, would have reinforced Skyler's attention-seeking misbehavior. Fortunately, this was never an issue. Skyler was thrilled with the extra interactive play; and because she got to play later in the day, she woke up later, too. But when that alarm clock went off, all bets were off!

SLEEP-WAKE CYCLE IN KITTENS AND CATS

Panda was black with white boots and white whiskers. Recently spayed, she was a very happy six-month-old indoor cat. Her owner thought she was a bit too happy, however, particularly when she kept her awake at night. Panda loved to play. She loved to play all the time. During the night she bounced across her sleeping owner, pouncing on her in the middle of some very nice dreams. When Panda was sure her mom was awake, she would bite at her toes. In the morning Panda would stalk her as she came out of the shower, playfully swatting her bare legs as she scampered away in triumph. Panda's owner was getting pretty tired of her tomboy. She called me on a Monday morning after a sleepless weekend, determined not to lose anymore rest because of her cat.

Kittens are born with a highly developed sense of smell but cannot see or hear until they are between nine and fourteen days old. Walking begins shortly thereafter and by four weeks they are up and running. Social play between kittens in a litter begins at around four weeks of age, and by eight or nine weeks they tend to play in pairs or by themselves rather than in one big fuzzy group. By four months of age, kittens become more focused on playing with objects in their environment. Object play is a stronger trend in male kittens (it doubles that of females by the time they are five months old), but every kitten's favorite toy is another kitten (or a dog's bushy tail) so it does depend on the household in which they are raised. Locomotor play (jumping, running, rolling, leaping, bouncing off walls, flying through the air . . .) peaks by four months and coincides with more courageous environmental investigation. By five months of age, males play more roughly and display sexual components during play with other play partners. On the other hand, kittens sleep for up to 70 percent of the time. By eight weeks of age, their sleeping pattern is the same as an adult cat. Adults tend to be more active during the daytime, with peaks at dawn and dusk. They sleep up to ten hours a day, in short stages, with frequent periods of drowsiness in between.

I explained this to Panda's owner so that she could begin to understand her kitten's daily rhythm of activity. Panda was behaving as any normal, healthy teenage kitten would. She slept peacefully during the day while her owner was away or preoccupied with other tasks at home. Come bedtime, she entertained herself briefly with a few toys that were left around the house, but these did not hold her attention for long. She cuddled with her mom at bedtime, but by 4 A.M., she was raring to go!!!

Panda's circadian rhythm was not synchronized to her owner's daily activity pattern. In addition she was not getting enough interactive playtime. Not surprisingly, aggressive play toward owners is more common in solitary pet cats. Because she was Panda's only playmate, it was up to her owner to make certain the young cat was truly tired by bedtime. I advised her to wake Panda up if she dozed before it was time to retire. Panda needed to play for at least thirty minutes each morning and longer, if possible, in the evening. I also suggested she throw a toy for Panda to chase when she emerged from the shower. Panda needed stimulation, but it had to be appropriately channeled toward toys rather than her owner's legs and toes! A variety of attractive toys, many of which can be made with common household items (such as string, aluminum foil, paper bags), is important in entertaining your cat. Don't leave them lying around, however, because your cat will grow tired of them. Keep them in a box or basket and rotate them on a weekly or even daily basis. Novelty is key. Young cats don't need to play for long, but they need to play and play hard.

Once you are in bed ignore any attempts to get your attention, and your kitty will eventually stop disturbing you. This can be quite challenging since young cats can be very persistent. If necessary, close the door to your bedroom to keep your cat out and put a pillow over your head! Your kitten will mellow with age. Understanding when and how much your cat needs to play will help you both to live happily ever after!

CATS ARE DOGS THAT PURR

Some cats, like Hershey, are actually dogs that purr. His intelligence and facial expression are uncanny, even for many dogs. As a kitten he would retrieve objects tirelessly. Almost anything I could throw, he would "fetch" and return to me. Proudly he would parade with his captured prize and then drop the object before me. His favorite things to chase and retrieve were long, skinny, plastic sticks stripped of the feathers that had once been fastened to the tips. Over and over, he would pursue his stick. On his way back to me, he would hold one end of the stick in his mouth and run around and around as if trying to touch his own tail. Then he would jab the stick into other surfaces or under pillows and doors, just to see how far it would disappear. The best trick was to slide the stick under the refrigerator, go around to the back of the fridge, retrieve the stick, carry it back out, and return it to me. He's some kind of guy, my Hershel Walker.

Not all cats are equally playful or interactive. But if your cat has boundless energy and focuses much of his attention on you, you too might have a dog who happens to look like a cat. He needs challenges and lots of playtime with you. Invent new games and provide a variety of interesting toys. Build him an "agility course," a little playground for him to enjoy. Teach him to climb a little ladder, walk across a ramp, crawl through a bag, jump through a hoop. Cats may need a bit more coaxing to keep their focus, compared to a real puppy dog, but most kitties will do almost anything for a taste of their favorite treat. You'll be amazed at what your cat can learn to do! Remember, your cat will only be a kitten for about fifteen years. What are you waiting for? Get up and play with *your* purring puppy!

3

Hissy Fits: Stuff About Feline Aggression

The cat in gloves catches no mice.

—BENJAMIN FRANKLIN (1706–1790)

GROWING UP ALONE AND
THE SOCIALIZATION OF KITTENS

Skittles was a red-and-white domestic longhaired cat who had been raised alone and indoors. She had been found, bewildered and alone, at around six weeks of age near the town dump. She was prima donna of her domain for several years until that terrible day when Scooter arrived. Skittles's owner had been walking down the street minding her own business when she came upon two little boys with a basket of kittens for sale at five dollars each. One of the kittens was a little male with long red-and-white hair just like Skittles. Scooter fell hard for Skittles, but it was spite at first sight for Skittles. Even after a gradual introduction over two weeks, along with extra attention and treats, Skittles was not at all pleased with her new housemate. I was called in to help a very concerned mom who dearly hoped to keep both pets.

The domestic cat is now considered a relatively social species, at least when compared to many of its "wild" relatives. Nonetheless, most cats would rather not share their territory at all, indoors or out, or would prefer to do so with a select few. Cats can be truly gregarious and seek

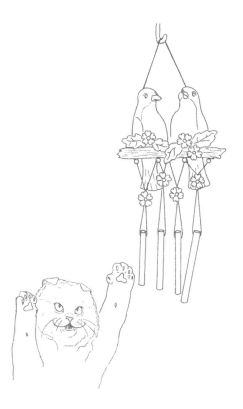

the company of favorite playmates. Some cats are more inclined to share space and to socially interact with other cats. A cat's social nature is an inherited predisposition that may be additionally shaped by learning and experience. In fact, there is a critical phase during which a kitten's social behavior will be indelibly influenced. This sensitive interval occurs between the ages of about two and seven weeks. Negative interactions with or isolation from other cats (and people) during this phase could leave a kitten with a less than friendly attitude. Like Skittles, this kitten could have more difficulty accepting a new feline housemate later on.

Cats do not always fight when they meet. In fact, they would much rather avoid bloody battles and usually perform elaborate rituals in order to circumvent direct contact. When they see each other, they evaluate each other from a distance and may approach cautiously to gather more details at closer range. Do I know you? Do I like you or did you beat me up the last time we crossed paths? Are you a kitten? A male or female? Sexually receptive? Are you confident and healthy, or are you defensive and submissive? At closer inspection, tensions rise. A fight could result if both cats are prepared to challenge each other or defend territorial priority. Even if just one cat is prepared to do battle, a fight (or at least a chase) could ensue. Feline social conflict like many other species, is directly proportionate to population density. In general, the more crowded the area becomes, the greater the risk of tension between individuals. A given territory may be shared by many individuals who either try to share the space or drive rivals away to reach a dynamic equilibrium. Cats confined as housepets in a multicat household live in a finite space. They can't move to another territory, but they can try to avoid each other or perpetuate the social upheaval or learn to coexist.

Skittles needed more than just a few weeks of introduction and adjustment. Every cat is an individual, and she needed more time. She was unused to living in the company of other cats and probably had some unhappy memories of cats, other than her mother, during the sensitive weeks of her socialization period. Other cats encountered back in her days at the dump could have been aggressive toward her or, at least, must have seemed to be formidable threats to the abandoned kitten. We took Scooter's integration back to square one and alternated the use of their home by confining one to a familiar room of their own when the other was exploring, and vice versa. They did not get to see each other for another four weeks. At that point Skittles and Scooter were brought together on neutral ground in a room where neither had been confined. Skittles was given a piece of her favorite treat (olives!) to reward her tolerance and then returned to her favorite room. Over another two weeks she spent longer periods of time enjoying her treat, a meal, gentle grooming with her owner, with Scooter playing or eating nearby. Skittles gradually associated Scooter with positive elements of her life. Over the next six months, Skittles warmed up to her new housemate. They were not best friends, but at least she did not have conniptions every time she saw him. Sometimes, peaceful coexistence is the best you can hope for with cats. In this case a reliable truce between Skittles and Scooter allowed them both to enjoy a happy and loving home.

INTOLERANCE TO HUMAN HANDLING IN KITTENS

Marco was a two-week-old brown tabby kitten with enormous, luminescent, blue-green eyes. He was truly one of the most beautiful kittens I had ever seen. He had been rescued as a stray by a lovely young couple who completely adored him. By the time he was about twelve weeks old Marco began to change. He suddenly resented being handled and had little tantrums during which he bit any fingers and hands within his reach. Marco bit hard. He didn't just nip and scamper playfully away. He actually seemed to frown as he bit hard and harder still. His owners were worried about this "personality change." They wanted their kitten back, not this tiger!

Almost all kittens go through a nipping phase, beginning as early as two or three weeks of age. This inhibited biting is a natural and normal part of how kittens play with each other and eventually with other cats. They learn to inhibit their bites by feedback from playmates. If one kitten bites too hard, the other screams or hisses and pushes back at him. Eventually, they learn who is toughest, most persistent, and most cunning. These interactions between littermates provide the basis for each kitten's social attitude, and the confidence gained or lost at this stage will remain with kittens, as they make their own way in the world. Kittens try to play or push around their own mothers, too, but she swiftly teaches the unruly kitten that she is not to be tampered with. In this way, at least, kittens are like puppies. From valuable interaction with littermates and their queen, kittens learn to inhibit their play bites. They discover, too, that biting sometimes gets them what they want or what they don't want at all. Kittens soon realize that aggression is a useful tool to intimidate others, and this contributes to the emergence of an assertive temperament. Eventually, many of these confident kittens will mature into the aggressively dominant cats we know and sometimes love!

By the age of two or three months, lucky kittens will be placed in a loving home. But all they know how to be is a kitten and they can only relate to people as they would to other kittens, unless you teach them otherwise. I have found it useful to say, "Ow!" in a loud and stern tone when my kittens have nipped too hard. At the same time, I give a little push away, just enough to throw them off balance. You need to respond right away, within a second or two, or the punishment will lose its impact on the behavior you want to discourage. If the kitten retaliates, I say, "Ow!" again and repeat the gentle push. If the kitten persists, I pick him or her up by the scruff, grasping the loose skin at the back of the kitten's neck, and give a quick blow of breath (like blowing out a birthday candle) into the rascal's face before I set the kitten down and walk away. Never ever shake your kitten; this is dangerous! Scruffing mimics the way the mother cat carried the kitten and thereby reinforces submission. Abruptly blowing in the kitten's face resembles a hiss. For some cranky kittens, like Marco, it might be necessary to use the "finger flick" in the nose. This is the sternest form of punishment you should ever use. Using your thumb and index finger, flick the naughty kitten lightly but firmly on his nose and say, "No!" or "Ow!" This is a controlled punishment so restrain your efforts; it is meant to injure your obnoxious kitten's pride, *not* to injure the kitten physically. The kitty's mother or sibling would have punished any persistent impudence with a firm swat or box of a paw; a light finger flick from you should have the same effect.

Marco had been collected off the streets and had not grown up in a litter of kittens. He had not interacted with other cats his own age and had not been exposed to the valuable social lessons that they could have taught one another. His "parents" were very indulgent, and tolerated his nipping until it grew too painful. The nasty side of Marco's temperament had begun to emerge. He was an assertive and bossy little boy who had learned that biting was fun and that it got him what he wanted—attention, or to be left alone, to be picked up, or to be put down. Marco was a tyrant in training and needed to be reminded that he only weighed three and a half pounds! His parents followed my progressive plan of pairing the verbal cue "Ow!" (which should eventually be enough to discourage any nipping) with a gentle push, to a scruffing combined with blowing in the kitten's face, to a finger flick and walking away. The punishment should escalate if the kitten retaliates; you must respond to the little tiger's challenges. Be as persistent as the kitten is. Some kittens take several weeks or several months to grow through this rebellious stage. Don't back down, and don't give up. Your cat needs to know that (a) *you* are the dominant "cat," and (b) nipping or biting will bring swift retaliation and is not acceptable. That little tiger, Marco, it seems, turned out to be a pussycat.

CONFLICTS BETWEEN HOUSEMATES

Naida and Namir were Turkish Vans who had been raised together. They were the best of friends and played together daily, took many naps curled side by side, and often groomed each other. They got along, until around four o'clock in the afternoon when Namir followed the sun streaming through the windows to Naida's favorite spot on the sofa. As the sunlight fell on Naida, so did Namir. Naida protested his assault with an angry hiss, but Namir did not care. He had already settled into the cozy spot conveniently warmed by Naida and the sun. He was oblivious to Naida as she walked off, with head lowered and tail dragging, muttering to herself.

Just like our own relationships, the interaction between feline housemates evolves over time. Conflicts can occur for any number of reasons between cats who have calmly coexisted. Kittens reaching physical and behavioral maturity, for example, discover their own sense of territoriality, and this can launch a new social rivalry. During play, kittens and cats learn about their playmate's temperament and physical ability as well as vital feedback regarding their own talents. Playful games of chase and ambush are among the ways that dominance status and territorial priority are established in a relatively peaceful way, without resorting to actual catfights. Still, playtime can abruptly end with an angry chase if one cat subtly challenges the other's dominance or territoriality.

Minor territorial or dominance-related disputes between cats are frequently misinterpreted by human observers as overly enthusiastic play. The more cats there are in your household, the greater the likelihood for conflicts over food, your attention, and use of space. Namir was the dominant cat. He was simply exerting his rightful claim to the best resting spots. Naida didn't like being expelled, but she knew it was his privilege.

A fascinating aspect of feline behavior is the fact that dominance and territoriality are intimately connected. The dominant cat has control and claims preferential use of the territory. Feline dominance in an established territory is a function of time and place. Namir had use of the sun-drenched sofa, but only after around 4 P.M. Up until then, it was Naida's spot. He deferred to her in the morning when she napped in the kitchen window seat, and he obligingly moved to another part of the house. Each cat used his or her shared territory slightly differently throughout the day. Sometimes they napped together and then parted to patrol the territory on their own.

To resolve territorial aggression between cats, the first order of business is to identify the factors that contribute to the conflict. The daily pattern, location, and major instigator of the confrontations are all significant. If conflicts erupt more often at certain times of day, it might be helpful to briefly confine one of the cats, perhaps for an hour or two, prior to this period to prevent the opportunity for clashes. This promotes a more peaceful "time-share" of the same space. (A similar technique is incorporated into the gradual introduction of new cats to the household as described elsewhere in this book.) If one cat waits in ambush for another or if conflicts occur in specific areas of your home, it would be important to neutralize these locations. For instance, additional litter boxes placed at various locations give a victimized cat more options to evade habitual ambushes at a single box shared with his or her tormentor.

If the quarrels are brief and cats are not sustaining real injury, it is probably wise not to interfere. These minor outbreaks are normal and just part of living together in close quarters. Naida and Namir had worked out their own relationship, and it was a healthy one. They had an occasional quarrel, but who doesn't? If, however, the disputes had been escalating in intensity, it might have been necessary to separate the cats, confining each to his or her separate quarters to prevent ongoing opportunities to provoke each other. Gradual reintegration into the household could then follow, just as if they were newly acquired cats, after tensions subside. Treatment, with or without psycho-active medication, recommended by a veterinary behaviorist, usually brings good results. In rare cases cats can be so hostile and determined to drive each other off their joint territory that it becomes necessary to find a new home for one of the unforgiving rivals. Ultimately, every-one will live happily ever after, although not necessarily in the same place.

REDIRECTED AGGRESSION BETWEEN CATS

Raoul and Renata were littermates. A lovely pair of ruddy Abyssinians, they had lived in bliss for five years. One night Raoul was looking out the window into the backyard. He seemed to detect something and became increasingly agitated. The hair on his back and tail stood straight up, and he hissed and moaned. Suddenly, he turned toward Renata, who had come to see what the fuss was all about. Without further warning, he unloaded all his wrath upon Renata. An innocent bystander had become the target of all his fury. He flew after her, pursuing his screaming victim in a wild chase around the house. She finally found refuge on a bookshelf in the den. Luckily, neither was seriously hurt, but their domestic tranquility had been shattered. From then on, Raoul chased Renata whenever he saw her. She became a recluse, and because he ambushed her on her way to eat, she began to lose weight. Things were going from bad to worse when their frantic owners invited me to their home to help them restore the peace.

Redirected aggression occurs when an animal is unable to reach the appropriate source of aggressive arousal. Many types of aggression can be redirected toward the closest available target. For example, one of two companion cats in a cage is frightened by someone staring into the cage. The cat cannot run away or hide and so lashes out at a buddy sitting innocently nearby. This is called *redirected fear-induced aggression.* We don't know for certain what Raoul saw when he looked out the window, but chances are he was reacting primarily out of a sense of territorial invasion to another cat or some other animal in his backyard. This is an example of *redirected territorial aggression* (which includes an element of fear). Raoul could not reach what triggered his rage, and so he blew up in his housemate's direction. His unexpected outburst led to a destabilization of the social order between them.

Redirected aggression is often intense and explosive. More often than not, it launches a literally vicious cycle between the victimized cat and the aggressor that can persist for several days or many weeks. In some cases the relationship can be permanently altered without immediate professional intervention. I believe that one of the things that helps to maintain the ongoing unrest is the persecuted attitude of the "victim." The unfortunate target is conditioned by a single, swift surprise attack to behave submissively, fearfully, and defensively. In anticipation of an attack, the victim's defensive posture becomes a powerful cue that triggers an attack long after the initial context is forgotten. Over time it often seems to me that the dominant cat chases the other as a kind of game. Occasionally, the initial attacker can become the "victim" if he or she redirects aggression toward a cat with an even bigger attitude. Their roles can be dramatically reversed, but the antagonism is launched nonetheless.

Here are my recommendations for coping with feline redirected aggression, even when, more often than not, a trigger can't be identified:

1. Your first response should be to separate the cats *immediately following* the initial explosion. Do not rush in to separate the cats in the middle of a flurry of claws and teeth. Wait until they have each gone to their own corner and gently approach one at a time. If necessary, reach for them with a towel or blanket to protect yourself from injury. Remember, you are approaching two very frightened and aggressively aroused animals who could turn their redirected aggression on you!

2. Confine each cat to a private room or enclosed space where the other is not in view for at least seven days. Don't be tempted to reintroduce them earlier than this. Provide the cat with a litter box, food, water, and some private time alone with you every day. The biggest mistake is to attempt a premature reintegration of the cats in conflict. This could easily turn a relatively minor altercation

into lifelong resentment or war. For indoor cats, your home could become a permanent battlefield where neither side can retreat!

3. If either cat does not appear calm and eager to be released from confinement, you may need more than seven days. Wait an additional day or two from the time both cats are completely relaxed before the next step. We want to give them time to forget why they were confined to begin with! When they are ready, alternately release one cat at a time for a few minutes to readjust to life outside the "safe" room. During this period, cats should be placed on a feeding schedule of two daily meals with no food between meals.

4. Eventually, both cats can be allowed out at the same time, under strict supervision. Mealtime is a good time because they might be more interested in eating then in each other. If either or both cats hisses, lunges, or shows any resentment toward the other, remove their food and confine them to their respective rooms for at least five minutes before trying again. If either of them behaves aggressively this time, remove their food and return them both to confinement for an additional twelve hours until the next scheduled meal.

5. If one or both cats remain anxious, antianxiety medication may be useful. Speak with your veterinarian about a referral to a veterinary behaviorist in your area who can direct and monitor your case closely.

Aggression between cats is common, and mild cases generally resolve without intervention. Even when things settle down to normal, it is important to realize that conflict can erupt for the same or for unrelated precipitating events. Aggression is a part of life for all animals, and it is no different for pet cats living in the same household. Interestingly, feline redirected aggression is not exclusively directed toward other cats. Remember, the key is that the aggressive cat lashes out at any available target, and the nearest scapegoat could turn out to be your Cocker Spaniel or your husband or you. If your cat is intensely focusing on something or someone, keep a safe distance. The secret to living happily ever after is sometimes as simple as giving each other a little extra space and time to regain composure.

AGGRESSIVE PLAY DIRECTED TOWARD OWNERS

Oliver was an eight-month-old Ocicat kitten who tormented his owner. He amused himself by ambushing his elderly owner whenever she walked down the hall or simply shifted her feet as she watched television. He would jump at her long housecoat, wrap himself around her leg with all four paws, and bite. The poor lady had the scars to prove it. Oliver's behavior was not just troublesome, it was painful and dangerous. His owner was diabetic, and the risk of these scratches and bites was compounded by her disease and advancing years. Oliver was always on the prowl, pouncing on anything that moved. If a leaf flew by his window perch, he would fling himself against the pane. He was a sleek and athletic kitten, looking for any excuse to rumble. Oliver wanted more while his owner wanted less.

Oliver's story demonstrates normal feline play aggression, but his choice of target was unfortunate. His owner was the only available playmate, moving target, and entertainment he had. He was an indoor cat. This meant that his owner needed to provide substitute activity for what he might have had outdoors. Cats are naturally drawn toward moving objects and must be directed away from your moving body parts. Oliver needed a variety of stimulating toys to distract him from his owner. Games and toys direct a cat's normal playfulness toward appropriate targets. Many cat toys can be manufactured at home from common household items. One option is to crush aluminum foil into small balls the size of Ping-Pong balls. These shiny, lightweight balls catch the cat's interest, are inexpensive and lightweight, and can be sent sailing across the floor with little effort. They are easily tossed up or down a staircase for a more animated quarry, which is great exercise for a healthy cat. String, heavy yarn, or ribbon can be attached to toy mice or other small, stuffed animals (remove any accessories that could be swallowed!). You can also suspend toys from "fishing poles" made from plastic sticks or even wire hangers that have been carefully unwound. Toys can be hung from any kind of clothing hanger. Dangling a toy suspended from a string is often within the physical capacity of elderly owners who may be unable to engage in more interactive play. In fact, dangling a toy while seated in a favorite easy chair is good upper body exercise for an older person with physical limitations.

There is a definite tendency among solitary pet cats for increased aggressivity toward their owners. Solitary cats are limited in their choice of social partners and can only interact with people. In most instances this is normal play behavior that has not been channeled toward more appropriate toys and games. After nineteen weeks of age, play behavior in male cats is increasingly sexual toward females. Males play more roughly than females in general. Males play with objects twice as much as females do. It is important to direct cats toward appropriate targets and to invite them to play *before* they pounce on you! Encourage their play by tempting them with fun toys at least twice a day. Cats are sprinters by design, which means that they have bursts of energy for relatively short periods. Playtime should continue until the cat is tired. For a young cat, this might be as long as sixty minutes, but playful exuberance will mellow as the cat matures.

Oliver's owner did not want a second cat, and I would have hesitated to recommend one as a solution to the problem. The addition of a second cat could have backfired and complicated the problem she was already experiencing. Oliver's owner was very upset and did not have the patience to gradually integrate a new cat in a manner that would have minimized any incompatibilities. It seemed reasonable to resolve the problem at hand without further complications. I initially recommended that Oliver's mom wear long slacks rather than her long housecoat. The movement of the fabric fascinated Oliver as she walked and triggered his playful assaults. I noted that his sneak attacks occurred at around 9 A.M. and 8 P.M. and indicated that he really needed more playtime, particularly nearing these predictable peak activity periods. Oliver was a healthy young Ocicat, one of many breeds noted for their beauty as well as their high energy. His owner admitted that she often did not feel strong enough or well enough to give him what he seemed to crave.

As we talked things through, I helped Oliver's mom to understand that as much as she loved him, he might be better off in another home. Sometimes, love really does mean letting go. Fortunately, her son offered to take Oliver into his home on a trial basis. Oliver was slowly introduced to the resident Singapura, a lively young female named May Ling, and they were a perfect fit. Oliver's original owner visited him often and was comforted to see him so happy. Coincidentally, I knew of an adult Persian cross named Marjory whose owner had died suddenly. She was being held for adoption at a veterinary clinic owned by a friend of mine. It seemed like a match, and indeed, it was. Marjory was quiet, calm, and docile, the perfect companion for her new guardian. They both lived to a ripe old age and enjoyed every moment they spent together. Sometimes, things happen for a reason. The trick is to recognize and act on the opportunity to facilitate changes that improve the world around you.

TERRITORIAL BEHAVIOR DIRECTED AGAINST FAMILY

Lucy was living the good life. She was a sweet, gray tabby who loved her owner, and he loved her. All was well in their little world, until his fiancée moved in. Suddenly, three was a crowd. Lucy was mildly piqued with the intruder, although they had known each other for over a year. Lucy's stepmom-to-be had spent many nights and weekends on Lucy's turf. They all seemed to get along; however, things changed when the fiancée's presence became permanent. Lucy was not happy. She ignored her owner's fiancée, except to sulk in her general direction. In a dramatic shift, Lucy began stalking her owner whenever he went to change her litter box. As he knelt down, she would pounce on him, wrapping herself around his arm and biting hard. He was being harassed and pursued by his seven-pound cat, and his fiancée (I don't know how much she weighed!) was threatening to force him to choose between the two loves of his life. Could Dr. Cookie® help them to live happily ever after?

Cats can be very particular about sharing their space. Having an occasional houseguest or visitor is not the same as adding a new member to your household. Just as cats must be gradually introduced to the idea of a new feline housemate, a new human housemate takes getting used to.

Territorial behavior functions to define, control, and defend the area in which the cat lives. Valuable resources, such as food, water, and shelter, are important to cats, even when the instinct to govern core parts of the territory is not as vital to survival as it would be for an outdoor cat. Lucy was guarding her litter box. It was important to her sense of territory. The upheaval in her home had left her unsettled, and anxious cats often feel compelled to reassert their territorial claims. Some cats do this by marking with urine and stool (see chapter 4!). In Lucy's case, she behaved aggressively toward her owner when he entered her last territorially exclusive space. He had crossed the line she had literally drawn in the sand.

We had two problems. We needed to help Lucy accept her stepmom-to-be, and we needed to reestablish her relationship with her dad. I recommended that her dad's fiancée take over the responsibility of feeding Lucy. This would help Lucy develop a positive association with this lady. Lucy enjoyed being briefly petted as she ate. Meanwhile, with the door to the room closed, Lucy's dad went in to take care of her litter box! In no time at all, Lucy relaxed and realized that, although change is stressful, it is not worth holding a grudge against people you love!

TERRITORIAL AGGRESSION TOWARD VISITORS

Lamont was a stocky, orange tabby who was adored by his owners. They were a fun-loving couple and enjoyed having friends over. It was summertime, and they were in the mood for a party. Apparently Lamont did not share their enthusiasm. As more and more guests arrived, he became noticeably agitated until he suddenly lurched toward one of the guests who happened to be standing near his favorite chair. He bit her and raced away. She was not seriously hurt, but it put a damper on the carefree mood of the crowd for a while. After the guests left, Lamont's owners realized that this antisocial attitude had been growing in their compact but solid cat. It was time to get some help before the next party was planned.

Lamont was acting out his territorial aggression. His aggression at the party had been building for quite some time. He had never been a particularly easygoing or social kind of cat. He remained cautious and distant when small groups of guests came by. A visitor once commented that he seemed to be giving her dirty looks for sitting in his favorite chair by the window, strategically placed for a full view of the birdbath outside. His tolerance to repeated territorial insult was lowered each time visitors came, and the last party completely overwhelmed him.

Territorial aggression is not just reserved for other invading cats and is often directed toward other animals, including unwelcome people. Visitors may be perceived as intruders or rivals and injured by a territorial cat immediately upon their arrival or later on during the visit. Some cats actually stalk a selected individual, or they may resent everyone who does not belong on their turf. Cats with a territorial sensitivity should be confined when guests are expected or intentionally exposed to them under direct and careful supervision. To teach your cat to become more tolerant of your guests, invite a few cooperative visitors over for a quiet visit and restrain your cat by your side on a harness and leash. Keep your greetings calm, and when everyone has settled down, ask each guest to call your cat over to offer him or her an extra special food treat. Your cat should be offered this treat only when you have visitors. Your guests should not touch your cat unless it is in response to the cat's solicitation. Remain vigilant to ensure that an apparent invitation to be petted is really a friendly gesture.

For large social gatherings, most pets should be sequestered for their own protection even if they are friendly under normal circumstances. Crowds can be frightening to everyone, and even the best-natured cat might misbehave. In addition, with so many people coming and going, your cat could run outside without you realizing that he or she is missing until hours later. Keep your cat in a quiet back room or board the cat for the day if you are expecting many guests. It will take a lot of pressure off you and your cat.

CATFIGHTS AS TERRITORIAL CONFLICT

Rex wasn't the biggest or the heaviest cat of the "hood," but he cast a long shadow that left the other cats meowing like eight-week-old kittens. Rex was

the king. He hadn't gotten into fights in years because all the cats in the area knew him and respected his stature. Things changed when Cameron moved in with his owners about two blocks down the road from Rex's house. Cameron was an enormous black cat with a piece of his left ear missing. He had scars on his head, and he walked with a swagger. Cameron must have been a pirate in his last life. He was fearless, ruthless, and determined to make his presence known. Rex's parents did not know about Cameron, but they soon began to see his handiwork, or paw work, so to speak. Rex began coming home with puncture wounds, abscesses, and scratches that required veterinary care. After the fourth round of antibiotics, Rex underwent a change. He refused to go out in the evening and began to meow by the door in the morning. His owners complied with his new request, and his injuries stopped. Rex knew what they did not; Cameron went out at night and came home in the early morning. Rex's problems were solved until about a year and a half later when one of the young toms came into his prime and decided to go for the crown. By then Rex had decided to stay in his own backyard for a few hours a day. He was ready to abdicate his throne and stepped down graciously and with great dignity.

Cats fight for many reasons, but a major concern is the determination of territorial size and priority. Cats' use of territory is determined by the space in question and the available resources it contains. Territory is also a function of individual temperament, the cat's willingness or ability to fight for sovereignty, and the other cats in the mix. Rex was not willing to leave his territory when Cameron and he clashed. Instead, he used the same space but at a different time of day. When he became less able to defend his turf, he settled into a smaller territory that was more cost-efficient to maintain. After all, castles are expensive real estate to maintain these days, even for kings.

Indoor cats frequently have territorial struggles. The difference is that the boundary of their kingdom is finite. The walls of your home don't move. In most cases these cats learn to patrol their territory (your house) at different times of day. Housemates might share favorite perches, or the dominant cat might push the lower-ranking cat away from a favorite window seat. One of your cats might remain in just one room of your home and leave this core territory only at specific times of day. My

Gracie, for example, stays close to my bedroom and home office, and comes into the kitchen only around mealtime. Hershey rules the downstairs and reminds the other cats with a hiss and spit when they congregate at feeding time.

Territorial behavior is complex in cats. I find it fascinating to watch them work out the intricacies of territory. It is almost like learning the steps to a new dance. There can be a bit of stumbling around, stepping on each other's toes, twirling accidentally into a wall or another couple on the dance floor . . . you get the picture. As long as no one is getting hurt, it is best to let them sort out the details. Chances are good that the dance will be performed smoothly, with an occasional glitch, before the music ends.

IRRITABLE AGGRESSION IN PET CATS

Spike had a short fuse. He was an orange tabby with an attitude. He didn't mind being petted, for about ten seconds, but he scratched and bolted if anyone tried to pick him up. Spike was a cranky cat. He had always been cranky, although he did have brilliant moments of adorability when he redeemed himself for his bad behavior. His owners were disappointed that Spike was not a cuddly lap cat and couldn't understand why he rejected their affection.

Pet cats come in quite an assortment. Sort of like what Forrest Gump might have said: "Cats are like a box of chocolates . . . you never know what you are getting until they take a bite!" Some are attentive and demonstrative and seek out contact with people. Others are anxious and guarded and avoid human handling. Along the continuum between these extremes is the average cat, who balances an interest in social contact with an individual need for space and solitude. Your cat, for instance, might love being petted but hates to be held for long. Your friend may have a cat who seeks out contact until you touch her belly. My cat Gracie is glued to my side or on my lap until I shift into a position that no longer suits her, and then she slips away. Sara, on the other hand, has never been a cuddler. For her, a deeply felt show of affection is a brief head butt and rub, a few seconds of allowing her neck to be scratched, and she is away. Teddi and Hershey are usually too busy to be held for long, but they have days when they just can't get enough.

Every cat is different; just like that box of chocolates, there is usually something for everyone to enjoy. Like people, cats have preferences for where, when, how, and by whom they are touched or held. Their likes and dislikes with regard to handling are generally an inborn predisposition. An animal who resents or resists human handling was probably just born that way, although a few may have had unpleasant experiences with people somewhere in their past. Although a history of physical abuse may cause some cats to avoid human contact, many cats who have been abused become gentle and demonstrative pets, and many more cats who have never suffered at the hands of people are irritable or shy.

I suggest that you accept your cranky kitty for his or her good points and try to make do despite your cat's less desirable traits. If your cat can endure only one minute of petting, then stop petting after thirty seconds and leave the cat be. If your cat tolerates being held for just three minutes but lashes out at you if you move the wrong way after that, push the cat off your lap after two minutes. In other words, avoid re-inforcing the context that puts your cat in a position to tell *you* to stop. Stop the interaction *before* it becomes uncomfortable for your cat and leave it at that. By building upon a positive association with your handling, your cat might learn to seek it out and enjoy you for longer periods of time. You could squeeze the chocolate square in that box and find out you don't like what's inside, or you could just pick one, let it melt in your mouth, and enjoy the surprise filling! Don't put the squeeze on your cat. Cats should be accepted for who they are and related to within their own boundaries. Chances are you and your cat will be happier for it.

HIDDEN RISK OF AGGRESSION AND
THE OUTDOOR CAT

Tambo was a large gray-and-white tabby who had not been neutered because his owner feared this would change his personality. He was allowed to roam outside because his owner wanted him to have a "full life." Tambo's owner was stunned to learn that the rugged cat he so admired had contracted feline immunodeficiency virus (FIV). Tambo faded slowly at first. His owner wanted him to enjoy his life right to the end and continued to let him roam free. Tambo was a fighter and came back with his usual scratches and small bite wounds at first. After a while it was clear that he was losing more fights than he was winning. His weakened immune system could not cope with the onslaught of infection, and Tambo began a steep downward spiral from which no antibiotic could save him. He died that winter. They found him, quite frozen, under the back porch, all curled up as if he was trying to keep warm.

Some cat owners live in denial, choosing to believe that their outdoor cat will somehow live an idyllic existence. Nature, however, is not all butterflies in a field of wild daisies on a sunny day. Tambo was a prime target for trouble. An intact male in his prime, he roamed far and wide to patrol a large territory. The size of a cat's territory is dynamic and expands or contracts according to population density, availability of natural resources, the receptivity of females in heat, and pressure between aggressive rivals. In general, males roam over greater areas compared to females, and younger cats tend to patrol wider areas compared to aging cats. Intact males have the greatest territorial imperatives. Ultimately, Tambo's chances of encountering rivals who would challenge his claim to territory as well as to sexually receptive females were high. I have already discussed the very real risks of allowing your cat to roam outdoors (see chapter 1 about keeping your cat indoors!). Tambo's story gives me the opportunity to discuss more of these risks in greater depth.

The feline immunodeficiency virus is one of two types of viral feline leukemia. It is transmitted by direct contact between cats and is not contagious to other animals, including humans. One of the ways that a cat can contract FIV is from his or her own mother, either before birth (*in utero*) or during lactation. The virus is transmitted via contact with a carrier's body fluids, i.e., blood, saliva, milk, and urine. FIV distinguishes itself from the feline leukemia virus by an additional mode of transmission. Among adult cats, like Tambo, FIV is also transmitted by aggressive contact through the bite of an infected cat. FIV has a lot to do with feline aggression between outdoor cats.

Neutering will reduce your cat's urge to escape the safety of your home. Like children, cats cannot be the judge of what is good for them because they are not aware of the dangers in the world. Many young kittens and cats who have been reared indoors from birth become interested in going outside and attempt to escape. Neutering alone, however, will not deter any cat with a strong predisposition to roam. It is up to you to block your cat's path, close the door more quickly, put a collar with a bell on it so you can hear the cat running for the door . . . your cat will eventually learn that going outside is simply not an option. If you are unable or unwilling to keep your cat inside, then neutering will minimize the size of your cat's territory outdoors and will reduce the frequency of catfights. And catfights don't just cause cat abscesses and systemic bacterial infection, which are bad enough. They also cause FIV. Unlike the feline leukemia virus (FeLV) for which a preventative vaccine exists, there is no prevention for FIV short of keeping your cat inside.

Make sure to request that your new kitten or cat be tested for both FIV and FeLV with a simple blood sample drawn at the veterinary clinic. If the test result is positive, the cat should be confined indoors to enjoy the best life for as long as possible with supportive veterinary care as necessary; or the cat should be humanely put to rest. If your cat is positive for any contagious feline disease, do not allow the cat to roam outside—period. It is bad enough to know that your cat is carrying a disease that will eventually take his or her life, but to knowingly allow your infected cat to continue to roam and transmit a fatal disease to other cats is unforgivable.

HUNTING INSTINCT IN CATS

Out of the corner of my eye I saw Sara pounce. With her back turned to me, I could see two little pink feet dangling from the corner of her mouth. We were then living in a sixth-floor apartment in a nicely maintained build-ing. I swiftly crossed the room to where she crouched, motionless. A mouse! Where it came from, how she saw it, and most of all, how she knew to catch it, I will never know. I grabbed her by the scruff of her neck, and she dropped it. I snatched Sara up and closed her in my bedroom along with Jonathan, who watched with mild amusement but little interest in joining her game. The little mouse was trembling terribly and paralyzed with fear. I could see one small puncture wound on her side but no other apparent injury. With a little feather duster I gently pushed her into a paper bag and, clutching the bag in the elevator to the basement level, released her outside. I knew that Sara was doing me a favor by capturing the little creature, but I could not stand by and watch her finish the kill. Sara was well fed and did not need to kill that mouse. Secretly, I was very impressed with her skill despite her sheltered life with me. Now, years later, we have moved to the country where her skills are more practical, and I have become more pragmatic. Each fall, tiny field mice who cannot afford a ticket to Florida for the winter, attempt to set up residence in our home. Sara, as matriarch of the cat clan in our home, diligently discourages them, and we are glad of that.

The feline predatory instinct is legendary. Hunting is probably why their wild ancestors first dared to approach early human settlements, attracted by the rodents that fed from grain reserves. Their small size is probably why their presence was tolerated by our own ancestors, along with the obvious service they provided. Cats continue to earn their keep, in rural, suburban, and yes, even urban homes around the world.

Not all cats are adept hunters. A cat's predatory instinct is what un-derlies the skill, but learning is a major influence on hunting behavior. A mother cat will teach her kittens to hunt if she has the opportunity and the instinct herself, of course. The lesson begins at around the age of three weeks when she will present dead prey for the kittens to investigate and consume. By the time the kittens are about six weeks old, the mother cat (or queen) will bring home live prey for the kittens to practice on. She will teach them how to hunt when they follow her out to the fields and watch her stalk and capture her prey. Mama kitty will not just teach them *how* to hunt but *what* to hunt. She will actually teach them her own preference for prey, which shows some individual variety among cats.

Sara's mother never taught her to hunt (I rescued her when she was three weeks old), and she had never seen a mouse in her life. Her predatory skill was instantaneous and completely inherited. Jonathan, who had lived in a barn until he was about three months old, stood idly by and contributed nothing to her effort. Perhaps he thought it was beneath his dignity, given the fact that he now enjoyed a life of luxury. Or perhaps he was deferring to her obvious prowess. Deep in every cat are the experiences of millions of years of evolution. A superb carnivore, a swift hunter, a tireless tracker, a patient stalker, a lover of laps, an expert at naps, your cat.

PREY PRESENTATION

Wilson was a big cream-and-white longhaired cat who was adopted by a veterinary colleague and very dear friend, who is married to another fine veterinarian. In exchange for agreeing to keep yet another unexpected pet, her husband was granted the privilege of naming their new addition. Wilson was named for a professional baseball player, whose first name I cannot recall. Fortunately, it is a good name for this cat, who quickly ingratiated himself with his new family and is living the good life in rural Massachusetts. Wilson is an indoor cat but takes pride in his job as faithful defender of his domain. He happily deposits many half-eaten mice on their bed or on little bedside rugs, where bare feet can step on them on the way to check on the baby in the middle of the night. Wilson is thoughtful that way. Yup, Wilson is that kind of a guy.

Okay, what could be worse than a half-eaten mouse in your bed? A live one, of course! Or perhaps part or a whole chipmunk, squirrel, or bird.

Prey presentation is a behavior that has impressed, perplexed, and disgusted many cat owners. Cats who are inclined to hunt and have the opportunity to execute their plan, indoors or out, do not always completely consume their prey. In fact, studies have shown that cats will kill again and again even when their bellies are full with a recent meal. Does this make them cold-blooded and wasteful killers? Hardly. Cats do not hunt only when they are hungry. If prey is plentiful, cats will practice to keep their skills sharp and probably for entertainment as well. It is simply the way their brain is wired. The instinct to kill a recognized prey animal never really evolved a mechanism to inhibit it. Bountiful prey was probably not all that common in the evolutionary scheme of things. It also made sense to kill prey when it was available and store it for a short time, in case fresh prey would not be so easy to come by. In particular, the prolific reproductive female had a very good chance of either being in the middle of weaning a litter or preparing to deliver the next one. Extra food would come in handy.

If your cat presents prey to you, it is not really a gift or a token of gratitude for your warm hospitality and loving care. Instead, it may be a form of redirected maternal behavior (females) or food-storage behavior (females and males). Your cat returns with prey just as a cat would return to a favorite territorial location to store excess food. Males rarely contribute much, if anything, to rearing their own kittens, and so it is unlikely that a male cat is acting out of parental concern. The queen normally brings dead prey back to the nest, first regurgitating half-digested food for her young kittens and then returning with live prey to educate her kittens. The next time your cat vomits up half a mouse, we can only hope it's not Mickey!

PREVENTING UNDESIRABLE PREDATORY ACTIVITY

Deven was a puckish, chubby, gray tabby who did not stray from his own backyard. Deven had a hobby. It was not, unfortunately, a hobby such as knitting or crocheting, of which one could boast. Deven's hobby was hunting. He specialized in the capture of songbirds at the birdbath that his owner had thoughtfully provided. The lovely little visitors came to take a quick sip of cool water, perhaps a brief dip to refresh themselves on a hot summer day. Deven hid in the bushes nearby then slowly inched his way forward like a commando in the jungle. Within pouncing range, he made his move, and it was all over before a last, beautiful feather drifted to the ground, a lonely afterthought to the bright little life and cheerful songs that had been needlessly silenced.

You may be amused, perhaps even pleased, by your cat's hunting abilities. I would ask you to consider the toll of this behavior on the wildlife around you. Songbirds are not pests. They are lovely to behold and help us by controlling the insects that attack you and your flower or vegetable gardens. Many of these songbirds are becoming endangered as their habitats are squeezed by construction and pollution. Your cat is well fed and hunts because that is what feline instincts drive cats to do. In habitats all around the world, such as the Galapagos Islands, where cats have been accidentally or intentionally introduced, they have wreaked havoc on defenseless birds and other species and pushed them to extinction.

In the beginning of the new millennium, we are called upon to become responsible caretakers of not just our own domestic pets, but all the creatures of this planet. Native Americans put it best in their tradition of living and loving the Earth: This Earth is not ours; we merely borrow it from our children. This planet is our ark, and we are called upon to take the role of Noah and his family; we are responsible for the preservation of all living things.

The only practical way to prevent undesirable predatory activity in cats is to deny them the opportunity to hunt. Once a cat has acquired hunting experience, the drive to hunt is persistent and virtually insatiable. Simply stated, as long as a cat *can* hunt, a cat *will* hunt. It is a safe bet that almost all outdoor cats will learn to hunt, regardless of how well they are fed at home. Indeed, some cats are picky eaters at home because they are successful predators with distinct prey preferences. Preventing your cat from learning to hunt is best accomplished by keeping the cat indoors. There will still be some opportunity to hone predatory skills with houseflies and other bugs that dare to enter your home. Any other small pests that have the misfortune to cross your threshold are also fair game. I have not used a fly swatter in over twenty-two years, since Sara came into my life. The other cats gleefully help control any uninvited "guests."

If your cat is determined to go outside, or if you are determined to let him, here are some simple suggestions to undermine your cat's successful hunting. Attach a breakaway collar with at least two bells. Cat collars can be purchased at any pet supply store and typically come with one bell. The idea for two or more bells is so the cat will have more difficulty in controlling the tinkling of multiple bells. Many cats learn to control their movement so that a single bell remains silent and does not warn their unsuspecting prey. Don't forget to attach an identification tag on your cat's collar. Replace the collar whenever it is lost.

To prevent your cat from returning home with any prey, install a cat door that allows the cat to exit freely but requires you to permit reentry. This is usually a magnetic system, with a special collar for your cat, that enables the regulation of uninvited guests. If your cat is hunting near your birdbaths or birdfeeders, remove them. At least put them in a location that does not provide vegetation or other cover for predators. Better to have a bird that leaves your yard a bit thirsty or hungry than one that stays behind dead. Finally, remember that hunting is not just hazardous to the wildlife population. Your cat can be injured during attempts to capture and subdue prey and is vulnerable to any infectious organisms it carries.

AGGRESSION AT THE VETERINARIAN'S OFFICE

Simba did not like to go to the veterinarian's, and she made this abundantly clear. Every year it was the same, only worse. At first, she seemed to shrink into herself, curling into a tight ball. Then a muffled, gurgling sound in her throat turned into a low growl, which became a hiss and then a spit. And then all bets were off as the leather gloves of the veterinary technicians were put on in a hurry. The silver-blue Korat cat's panic escalated to a frenzy. She became a wild creature convinced she was in a battle for her very life.

Her rage filled the room, and only sedation could blunt her fury. Everyone needed to calm their frazzled nerves after Simba's visit was over.

I have often tried to put myself in my patients' paw prints, trying to empathize with what they must be feeling or thinking. A trip to the veterinary clinic must be something quite horrific. I imagine it must be similar to the experiences described by folks who say they've been abducted by aliens. Imagine being transported from a warm and comfortable bed, against your will and with no chance to escape, to an unfamiliar place filled with strangers who do not speak your language. The room is permeated with smells, some unpleasantly familiar and others unidentifiable. Strangers come at you from all sides as you are placed on a cold table. They push things into you, take samples out of you, all the while babbling to each other in foreign tongues. If I were on that veterinary table, I do believe I'd be as bad as Simba, or worse. What has always surprised me is not the Simbas of the feline patient population, but those cats who remain calm, stoic, and even affectionate in the midst of an unpredictable and frightening environment.

It is not surprising that most cats are at least a little perturbed by their second veterinary visit. Less common, but far from unknown, are the phobic responses and panic attacks that evolve over the course of a single or series of veterinary examinations. Phobias are fear responses that are out of proportion to the actual danger present. Excessive fear of the veterinary experience is probably the most common phobia of cats. When a frightened animal sees no way out of danger, the result is the classic "fight or flight" of a cornered and panicky cat. Cats who become uncontrollably aggressive risk injuring themselves, everyone around them, and exacerbating whatever problem they were brought in for in the first place. Their behavior also makes them very difficult to examine and treat. With the supervision of a veterinary behaviorist, your pet can learn to disassociate these deep, dark emotions from the clinic. With a step-by-step plan, along with the possible use of psychoactive medication to ease a reintroduction to the clinic, your fraidy cat should come out with a renewed tolerance for those who have only the best intentions for your pet's physical and emotional well-being. Ask for a referral to a veterinary behaviorist in your area.

If your cat is not quite as bad as Simba, your veterinarian can carefully immobilize the patient. This might require physical or chemical restraint, and your veterinarian will discuss the options with you as necessary. It may be helpful to remove your frightened kitty from the exam room so that procedures can be performed in another part of the hospital. Some cats seem to relax when they are separated from their anxious owners. If you are asked to sit in the waiting area, for example, while blood is drawn from your frazzled feline, trust your veterinarian to know what is best for you and your cat.

PATHOLOGICAL AGGRESSION IN CATS

Tommy was a smoke domestic shorthaired cat who had always been a good boy. One day he suddenly began to lunge and chase his owner. Tommy was frenzied and wild; in fact, his owner later told me that he thought his cat was "possessed." Tommy chased his owner into the bedroom and continued to attack a pillow that was held up as a shield. Tommy's attacks continued for over twenty-four hours until his owner was able to capture him in a gym bag and transport him to the veterinary clinic. He was kept sedated and under observation there for forty-eight hours and released when he began to return to normal. By the time I saw Tommy several weeks later, he had gradually settled down and had almost returned to his calm and friendly self. During my visit, I took a very detailed history of Tommy's life and the events preceding the attack. I learned that he had been playing with a new toy the night before the attacks began. It was a small, stuffed toy attached to a spring that was anchored to a carpeted base. Tommy's owner had seen him sucking on the carpeted base of his new toy for a long time and thought he was just enjoying the catnip applied to the toy's base by the manufacturer. Was there a link between this new toy and Tommy's erratic behavior?

Blood work drawn by his veterinarian the day after Tommy's episode was normal. Tommy could have had an unusual seizure, which can sometimes appear as any type of mood swing or strange motor pattern.

Catnip does not cause this type of extreme response. Tommy's owner was certain that his cat had not come in contact with any poisons, such as household cleaners, in his home. I had a hunch, however, that Tommy had ingested something on the surface of the toy that had triggered his attacks. Unfortunately, his owner had discarded the new toy in question. Undaunted, we purchased six more of the same toys made by the same manufacturer from the same store as the original toy.

With the cooperation of an intrigued scientist at the Environmental Protection Agency, I had the toy samples tested for environmental toxins and, in particular, lead and organophosphates. I also brought samples of dust from under the owner's radiators to test for any suspicious particles. The house dust had a small amount of lead, but this was normal for older homes in the Boston area and would not have been enough to harm Tommy. However, the carpeted base of several of the toys tested positive for spots of an organophosphate called Diazinon. This toxic compound is soon to be withdrawn from production. One of this chemical's many uses is as a surface fungicide, insecticide, and preservative on new carpets. Tommy's original blood sample had been stored by the laboratory and was forwarded to another laboratory for an organophosphate screen. Tommy's blood was negative for everything, except for one compound. At the time of his attacks, his blood contained more than one hundred times the "acceptable" concentration of Diazinon.

The mystery was solved. It became clear that the catnip on the base of the toy had enticed Tommy's licking and sucking. This normal element of the catnip response was likely the mechanism by which Tommy ingested the poison that subsequently triggered his attacks. Organophosphates can cause a variety of physical problems. Aggressiveness and mood changes are among the recognized psychological effects occasionally reported in people and other animals. The chemical enters the fatty deposits of the body where they are slowly metabolized over several weeks. Tommy's blood was redrawn and retested. He showed a trace amount of Diazinon, indicating that his problem was resolving and was unlikely to recur.

Tommy's case was exceptional and, from a scientific perspective, it was very interesting. It serves to make an important point. Most cases of feline aggression are variations of normal behavior. However, if you feel that the frequency and/or intensity of your cat's aggression are unusual or abnormal in any way, you should notify your veterinarian immediately. There are many physical and psychological conditions that are associated with mild to bizarre behavioral changes, aggressive or otherwise. If your veterinarian feels it is appropriate, you might be referred to a veterinary behaviorist in your area. Furthermore, even if your cat does not go outside, he should be vaccinated against the rabies virus, which is known to cause acute episodes of unprecedented aggressivity. We knew this was not Tommy's problem because his vaccines were kept current, his symptoms were fading, and he was not allowed to roam outdoors. Tommy's recovery was complete, and his story had a happy ending. The veterinary community is available to help you and your pet have a happy ending, too.

AGGRESSION AND YOUR CAT'S COAT COLOR

Temper tantrums, at least that's what Billie's owner called them. According to him, Billie's tantrums were to be expected, given the cat's coat color. Billie was a calico (red, white, black) cat with a grumpy disposition. Her dad seemed to actually enjoy her mood swings and called Billie his "feisty girl." She liked to be petted, for a while. She stayed near him, but not too close. And she was friendly, to a point. If you crossed the fine line between what she tolerated and what she didn't, she growled and hissed and swatted to let you know you were out of line. Billie was not known for her patience. I was called in to consult on her crankiness when Billie's dad became serious about his new girlfriend and realized, for the first time, that Billie's deficit in social graces was impacting his own social life.

Although many folks insist that calico cats are inclined to be hot tempered, the truth is that their coat color has nothing to do with it. There is no evidence of any relationship between coat color and a cat's temperament. Calico cats are no more ill-natured than gray or black or purple ones. Reputations are easily damaged and rumors remain in circulation for a long time, even when they are unfounded in truth. This rumor is a form of what I call "feline racism" (there are many cases of canine racism, too), generalizing about a group of cats based on a given characteristic, in this case, coat color. It is unfair and undeserved to condemn (or applaud) any animal based on a suspected or perceived physical or behavioral deficiency without significant clinical data to support it. The calico cat has a genetic predisposition toward a particular color; her temperament is unrelated to her appearance.

Cats of any color can be irritable and for a number of reasons. Cats have individual preferences for how they like to be petted, and how long they are petted. Some are more easily handled than others. Part of this is situational, of course, but a good part of a cat's basic nature is based on inheritance and early socialization. Some cats are cranky, in other words, because they were born that way. Early handling will help make a more easily manipulated kitty, but the nature and timing of the early handling is also very important.

Another reason that some cats are more irritable than others is that they learn early on that being just a bit cranky gets them what they want. A cat who wants to be left alone could quickly learn to behave aggressively in order to terminate interaction. This is usually pretty effective given the speed with which claws can be unsheathed and teeth bared! Dominant cats tend to "punish" insubordinates with an impatient swat or nip. It is likely that many assertive cats treat their owners as they would any other cat for unwelcome attention.

So what were my recommendations for Billie's tantrums? I advised her owner to minimize petting and handling in general. We knew that she would tolerate being petted for just a few minutes, so I advised him to stop petting her after about one minute, long before her anticipated complaints. I also suggested that he interact with her only when his new girlfriend was present. This allowed Billie to associate her "rival" for her dad's attentions with an extra something special rather than with something less than she wanted. His girlfriend fed her a few tidbits of Billie's favorite cheese treat and then petted her briefly (just a few strokes) while she savored her snack. Identify the limits of your cat's tolerance and then reinforce that tolerance by stopping *before* the cat lets you know it's enough. Otherwise, you end up reinforcing the intolerance, and that is not what you want! Sometimes, less is more. Billie did very well. She became more sociable and solicited petting from her dad and his girlfriend. Billie was never going to be a lap cat, but she was the perfect cat in her daddy's eyes and that's all that counts!

4

Your Cat and the Litter Box

In privacy I crouch
Tail quiver, I shake my paw
Dig, dig, done, gone.

LITTER-TRAINING YOUR KITTEN

Bettina was a tiny, longhaired calico kitten. She was just six weeks old when she was brought home. She was a fluffy, frazzled baby whose mother had been killed by a car. She was overwhelmed by a lot of things, including the jumbo-size litter box that was used by the other family pet, a very large Maine Coon appropriately named Sir. Fortunately, he was the least of Bettina's worries. One look at Bettina and he was smitten. Her owner, however, was confused about how to integrate her new kitten into this giant's world.

Cats are not born with the understanding that we expect them to use a litter box. When you stop to think about it, it is a miracle that any of them use the box at all! It is unnatural for them to void in a single container on manufactured litter filler. Their natural choice is to eliminate in sand or soil and to distribute their scents at strategic points in their territory. So why do cats and kittens use the litter boxes we provide? They use the boxes because the litter filler mimics the loose substrate they would have chosen outdoors in the wild. Cats use boxes because their own scents attract them to return to refresh odors as they

fade. Ideally, they use the boxes because they are in locations that are in keeping with locations they would have chosen themselves. Hopefully, the litter box is preferred to other substrates in your home, such as plants or carpets, that your cat could have selected as alternatives. The popularity of keeping cats as house pets has grown in recent years, thanks in part to the invention of cat litter and litter boxes.

Your new kitten will rapidly discover what a litter box is for. Just place your itty-bitty kitty in it the first time and scratch gently in the clean sand with your own fingers. This will trigger an interest in digging and the instinct to void. There are many styles and sizes of boxes to choose from at your local pet supply store, pet supply catalogs and magazines, as well as on the Internet at pet-related sites. Some are open pans, others are covered with an entry door in the front, and still others are hooded. Most boxes are rectangular, however, square and triangular models are made to fit into compact corners. The majority of litter pans are manually cleaned by scooping. One variation is sifted with stacked pans. Another product is even mechanized and marketed as "self-cleaning." Actually, any container you prefer will do as long as your cat agrees with your selection.

In my experience simple choices are usually best. The box should be comfortable for the cat to enter, stand, and turn around in. The sides of the pan should be low enough to allow easy access for a kitten or an ailing or aging cat. For example, for very young kittens I often recommend using a simple aluminum pie plate or small baking square with just enough litter to cover the bottom of the plate. The walls of this shallow pan do not discourage an awkward kitten from climbing in. The container is easily cleaned by dumping its contents daily, and it is disposable (and recyclable!) when your kitten is big enough for transition to a larger box. Aluminum foil pans are available in a variety of sizes that can accommodate your kitten or cat.

The choice of litter filler is equally confusing, but here again there is really just one criterion that should dictate your choice; use the litter your cat prefers. Remember that cat litter is marketed to you, the owner. You may find the notion of perfumed or scented filler appealing; however, many cats are put off by perfumed or deodorizing filler materials. Some products contain more dust than others, and you should take care that your cat does not approach the box until the dust settles. Cats may prefer sand filler to regular clay or even shredded newspaper. You could test your cat's preference by offering several boxes each with a distinct filler to determine which box gets the most use. Once your cat is using the box consistently, try to avoid making any changes. I really believe that "if it ain't broke, don't fix it!" Why tamper with a winning combination? If, however, you decide to try a new brand or if your favorite brand is no longer available, try to mix the old with the new litter filler so that your cat can make a gradual adjustment.

CARE OF LITTER BOXES

Jonathan had severe chronic inflammatory bowel disease that did not respond to medication. He had frequent daily bouts of diarrhea that ranged from pasty to explosive. Even with two covered boxes, which helped to control the splatter, things were messy. They were messy from the time he became ill until the day he died five years later. Many pet owners might not have tolerated this for as long as I did, but Jonathan was a special boy and I loved him completely. Sara, my second sweetie, was very particular about her litter box hygiene. Unfortunately, the litter boxes were impossible to maintain according to Sara's pristine tastes. She began to defecate just next to the boxes, although she continued to urinate in them. I suspect that hygiene was a major part of it, but I also think she was anxious because her best friend was so ill. After Jonathan died, and I was able to keep the box up to Sara's standards, she slowly returned to its regular use. Her continued litter box use is a reflection of her state of mind. Life, even following great personal loss, can be happy and even happier than you ever dreamed possible.

Litter box hygiene is the first cardinal rule of keeping a pet cat happy. Cats instinctively avoid malodorous and heavily used latrines. They don't like the smell, and they certainly don't like putting their paws in stinky places. It is not what *you* consider to be clean that counts, but what your cat finds satisfactory. Anything less will not do.

Every cat has his or her own standard of what makes the box tolerably clean. I have known cats who consistently use the box even when it is contaminated by many days of waste. I have also known cats who would refuse to use a recently cleaned box merely because a housemate had looked at it. I know because I have lived with both of these types of kitties. There is a wide range of tolerance in cats for what is, and what is not, a suitably clean litter box.

So here is an important tip to help you and your cat live happily ever after. As a minimum, provide *one litter box for every cat* in your household. Moreover, *a minimum of two boxes* should be provided even for a single pet. This will give your cat an alternative latrine, perhaps satisfying the feline tendency to mark a territory and distribute the waste (and odors) at more than one location. Although a clean and dry box is critical, I have also known cats who are offended if the box is excessively clean. Some owners become overzealous in cleaning, disinfecting, and deodorizing the box. This can distress a cat who finds it comforting to have a baseline of familiar odor and who may be offended by the scent of the cleanser's residue.

If you already keep more than one litter box, you may have noticed that some are used more than others. This is important feedback about your cat's preferences for location, style of box, type of filler, or standards of hygiene that should not be overlooked. A box that is attracting consistent use should be maintained as is. A box that is getting less consistent use may need to be revised because it is somehow less than ideal according to your cat's preferences. In multicat households, where litter boxes are shared, it can be more challenging to determine something that pleases everybody, but it is not impossible. With a little trial and error, you will find what works, even if that means offering a variety of covered or uncovered boxes with a selection of more than one litter filler. Listen to your cats. They are trying to tell you what they want. Make them happy, and you will all be happy!

CHOOSING A LITTER BOX

Phil was quite a performer. The chubby, white Oriental Shorthair made such a fuss digging in his box that his owner was thinking of selling tickets. He was enthusiastic and vigorous, sending so much sand flying that the room where his box was kept began to look like a beach. Phil was a slob. His owner found his pet's personal habits exasperating because it was in such contrast to his own meticulous ways. Phil was a challenge.

Here's the scoop, pardon the pun, on litter boxes. The box and its contents, placement, and hygiene should suit the cat. You might like the idea of a covered box because these control the circulation of odors. They also retain odors in the box and can discourage a cat with a sensitive nose. Even if you cannot smell anything, clean the boxes regularly. Remember that cats have a much more developed sense of smell than we do, and some cats prefer uncovered boxes regardless of your efforts.

There is an additional advantage to a covered box. They help to keep sloppy cats under control. Phil did not like covered boxes, which is why his owner had turned to an open box. I suggested several alternatives. The top portion of a covered box can be turned upside down and becomes an instant box with a front door (the bottom portion of the upside down door can be partially blocked with a sheet of plastic to prevent spillage) and high walls. Another option is to purchase a box with a detachable rim, which helps to keep in the sand. We also reviewed the types of filler available. Sand filler has fine grains that are easily sent airborne and can be tracked throughout the house without regular sweeping. An inexpensive sisal or straw doormat or place mat adjacent to the box is helpful to trap the grains. Regular clay litter has larger particles but is not as easily scooped from the box. Litter made from recycled newspaper is not easily scattered, and although the odor of wet newsprint takes getting used to, it works well for fastidious cat owners who change the litter frequently (and those who feel that recycling is important!).

Phil's dad and I discussed the options and decided on a plan. Phil did well with the rimmed box. His owner liked the idea of using a mixture of clumping sand and recycled newspaper litter to further minimize the effects of Phil's flinging style. Phil was still a slob, and his owner was still meticulously neat, but they lived happily ever after anyway.

LITTER BOX LOCATION

Nola was a cream-colored Manx about eighteen months old. Her litter box was in a quiet corner of the kitchen and was scooped every day. Nola was an only cat, and this was the only box in the house. Nola's owner called me in total frustration because her beloved cat had been eliminating intermittently in a corner of the basement for over a year. She could not understand it, she explained. The box was clean, and Nola was not ruffled by any change in her routine or her owner's lifestyle. I was invited to make a house call and took a detailed history of Nola's life and daily habits. When I discovered that the litter box was placed just two feet from Nola's food and water bowls, I knew the mystery was solved.

When it comes to choosing the perfect spot to put the cat box, you have to think like a cat. If you were a cat, you'd prefer to eliminate in a box that is placed in a quiet out-of-the-way location. Uncluttered corners in a relatively low-traffic room or a closet are best. It is important to place the box in an accessible location. The door to the room or closet must never be allowed to close and block the cat's access. This would, of course, force the cat to hold his or her urine or stool or to find an alternative latrine. If there is no backup box, you are both in trouble.

If you were a cat, you would also never void where you eat or drink. The litter box must be at a considerable distance from food or water bowls. The functions of the two locations must not overlap or the cat will be confused. And because there is no other place to eat, the cat is essentially forced to find another place to urinate or defecate.

I suggested that Nola's box remain in the corner because she was used to finding it there. The food and water bowls were moved to the opposite corner of the kitchen. I also recommended that a second box be added to the basement corner. Nola had already indicated a preference for that location, and we wanted to apply this information to reinforce her use of the litter box. It was also a good idea to have an alternative location even though Nola was a solitary pet. Two boxes gave her a controlled way to mark the boundaries of her territory. It also redistributed the use of the box placed in the kitchen and, therefore, the amount of daily time and effort to keep a single box clean. Nola appreciated this new arrangement and was quick to cooperate with our plan.

MOVING THE LITTER BOX

Charmin was a chinchilla Persian kitten about ten months old. She slept on satin pillows in a home filled with period antique furnishings and antique Persian carpets. She was surrounded by exquisite works of art from her owners' private collection. Charmin had even inspired a new collection of cat figurines. Charmin was leading a "charmed" life, or was she? I was summoned by an emergency call when it was discovered that Charmin had begun to void behind the baby grand piano. I arrived for the home visit, and as I asked about the details of Charmin's life, I learned that Charmin's litter box had been moved to a new location. Until recently the box had been in a guest bathroom that was rarely used. But it was holiday time and guests were expected.

Cats can become quite attached to their litter boxes. And rightly so! It is a special part of their territory in which they must feel sheltered and undisturbed. Cats develop an affinity for the location, orientation, and texture of the box and probably for the view surrounding them when they use it! Moving the litter box to a new location can be quite upsetting.

If the litter box must be moved, it should be done gradually and in keeping with the cat's preferences. There are two options to minimize offending your cat. In the first method, place an alternative box at the new location you have selected. Then, slide the original box a few inches each day toward the new location. Your cat is bound to discover the new box at the designated location, and once use of the replacement box begins, it is probably safe to remove the original one. The second method is to place several additional boxes in a variety of potential new locations and observe which of these most appeals to your cat. Both methods are appropriate, although there may be an advantage to allowing your cat the opportunity to indicate any partiality for location. Although you may not agree with what your cat considers an ideal placement, you are not the one who has to use it!

Charmin was disturbed when she went to use her litter box only to discover it had disappeared. She was probably not too pleased with its new placement near the door to the garage. She was obliged to select another latrine and chose the quiet corner behind the piano. To discourage her repeat visits to this location, we sprinkled some dry cat food in the corner. This changed her marking target into a feeding area. We placed a number of litter boxes in quiet corners around the house that were all good possibilities for box placement. Soon enough, Charmin began to frequent two of these. The third box received little attention and was removed. Charmin's bathroom issues were resolved in time for the arrival of their houseguests. She was, once again, everyone's little darling.

HEALTH CONCERNS UNDERLYING
INAPPROPRIATE URINATION

Checkers was a large, seal point Snowshoe with vivid blue eyes. He lived in a happy little cottage by the sea with two dogs, a cockatiel, and several pet turtles. His owner was upset with a recent development in his behavior. Her frustration began when Checkers decided to urinate every few days in the bathtub. This turned to concern when, after a few weeks, his urine took on a bit of a pinkish hue. He seemed anxious and uncomfortable and spent part of his day under the bed, which was also something new. Was Checkers urinating in the tub because he was ill?

We are all creatures of habit. Routine is what helps keep us healthy, and it is also a reflection of our inner state. When an apparently healthy individual suddenly breaks routine, it is always important to consider the possibility of an underlying medical problem. When a cat urinates out of the litter, the first thing that must be determined is whether there is any underlying health-related explanation. In order to be certain, your veterinarian will want to perform a thorough examination. Blood samples should be drawn to evaluate kidney and liver function, as well as to pinpoint the presence of anemia, for example, or an elevated white cell count, which might suggest infection. A urine sample is critical to the diagnosis of any problem associated with the urinary tract. Inappropriate defecation should prompt the collection of a stool sample in addition to relevant blood tests. In more serious recurring cases, your veterinarian may also recommend a variety of additional tests, which could include radiographs (X-rays) and ultrasound.

Among the most common conditions associated with inappropriate urination in cats are cystitis (infection or inflammation of the urinary bladder), diabetes mellitus, and kidney disease. However, virtually any illness can cause inappropriate urination. In many cases the symptoms are subclinical, meaning that you cannot really notice anything obvious. In early stages of a bladder infection or inflammation, for instance, the urine may appear a normal or deep shade of yellow. It is only when the problem worsens that you might see the color change to a pink, or a cider tone, or even wine red, suggesting the presence of blood in the urinary tract. As long as your cat continues to void in the litter box or outdoors, you may not notice a thing until behavior changes indicate a worsening problem.

If all tests are normal and there is no apparent physical explanation for your cat's behavioral disruption, you are probably dealing with a problem that is behavioral in origin. Even if the problem is health-related, however, inappropriate elimination can persist beyond medical treatment and resolution of the physical condition. Once acquired, bad habits tend to linger even when the initial cause is removed. Checkers had a bladder infection secondary to bladder crystals. Cats who experience pain during urination are inclined to avoid the box, which they may associate with their discomfort. The bathtub and sink are common choices for these cats, although we are not sure why. It may be that they have a similar rectangular or basinlike resemblance to their litter box. Checkers was placed on an antibiotic to treat his infection with a low dose of anti-inflammatory medication to make him feel more comfortable. We also left the bathtub filled with about one inch of water to discourage any return visits for about two weeks. By then Checkers was back to himself and enjoying the view from his cottage by the sea.

See your veterinarian regularly so that physical problems can be detected early, and do not hesitate to report even the slightest problem. Ask for a referral to a veterinary behaviorist for lingering behavior problems. Work with your cat's caregivers to form a strong team that is committed to keeping you and your pet living happily and longer.

MARKING NOVEL ITEMS

Austin was a Havana Brown who seemed to shy away from his owner's houseguests. He was a magnificent mahogany cat with pale green eyes. By the time he turned two years old, however, he apparently lost his shyness. Opened suitcases became a fascination, and he was particularly drawn to luggage belonging to visitors. Unattended open suitcases beckoned to him as he gleefully hopped in and deposited a fresh urine sample. By the time I was called in to help, he had been urine marking for at least a year, and his repertoire of targets had expanded to plastic bags, gym bags, dirty socks, open briefcases, and anything interesting that was left on the floor. Austin was in serious trouble with the whole family, not to mention the houseguests. This was definitely a case for Dr. Cookie®!

Marking behavior is a normal element of territorial behavior. It is essential to the emotional well-being of cats. In fact, marking behavior tends to increase when a cat feels anxious or emotionally unsettled or physically ill. Cats mark with urine, stool, scent gland deposits, and scratching. Luckily for the majority of cat owners, their pets generally refrain from urine or stool marking indoors. However, when a cat feels threatened in his or her home turf (e.g., by a new pet, a new roommate, or houseguests), the cat may become more inclined to marking with bodily waste. In such cases, litter box hygiene may not be the impetus toward inappropriate elimination, but if box hygiene falls short of the cat's ideal it will certainly contribute to the misbehavior.

Austin's case allows us to explore a common kitty ritual of marking novel items in the environment. "If it's new and it's in my space, I'll mark it for future reference," is probably what Austin was thinking to himself. Austin was a slightly nervous kitty, who was even more anxious because of unfamiliar intruders. Marking behavior is a cat's primary anxiety-releasing mechanism. Austin relieved himself in the open suitcases and thereby deposited his scent on top of the guests' clothing. He was proclaiming his territorial priority by covering their scents with his own, and he felt immediately empowered. It is also possible that the rectangular shape of the suitcase reminded him of the shape of his own litter box, and this could have been a secondary visual cue. Once cats learn that marking with urine or stool is such an immediately gratifying experience, the pattern is incorporated into their repertoire. Austin quickly learned to urine mark in a squatting position whenever he felt anxious about something. Sometimes, he was a little concerned or curious about an unusual object left lying about. So he marked it and felt better. From there he got into layering his scent on top of familiar scents just to identify himself with that individual, especially if they weren't around and he missed them. Well, you can see how the problem escalates.

We needed to add several more litter boxes in virtually every room in which Austin had urinated so he had no excuse not to use a box. His litter pan had always been well maintained, and his owner continued to keep all the boxes very clean. I advised Austin's mom to instruct all members of her family to pick up their belongings, their laundry, and other personal objects. Gym bags and schoolbags were also to be kept closed and out of the way.

When she realized that there was hope for her cat's problems, Austin's owner was able to see the comical side of the situation. She commented that her kids would not pick up after themselves if she asked them, but they sure were listening to Austin! Because Austin targeted such a wide variety of items, it was decided that psychoactive medication would be part of the treatment plan. After blood and urine tests proved that he was physically sound, we started him on medication. Within weeks he had stopped his restless pacing, and everyone in the household was more relaxed. Medication was continued for about six months and then gradually withdrawn. I advised Austin's owners to warn house-guests to keep their bedroom door closed during their visit and to safely stash their luggage in the closet or under the bed. The less temptation, the better!

ELIMINATION IN POTTED HOUSEPLANTS

Mitch was probably a gardener in his last life. He loved plants, which is something that he and his owner had in common. The problem was that Mitch loved to dig in the houseplants and then deposit his urine and stools. He eliminated in the huge fan palm in the living room, the geraniums wintering in the sunroom, and the sansevieria in the den. There were three boxes that Mitch and his housemate shared, although Mitch had not used them much recently. The boxes were scooped daily and changed completely when the sand got low. Mitch's predilection for houseplants was becoming a thorn in his mom's side.

It is not natural for cats to use the litter box. They are really just doing us a favor! Their natural instinct is to dig and deposit their waste in sand or soil or even a pile of dead leaves. When you look at it this way, the question should be, not why Mitch voided in the houseplants, but why should he void anywhere else?

If your cat has shown an interest in gardening by watering and fertilizing your houseplants, your solution should include two approaches. First, you need to make absolutely certain that the litter boxes are immaculate and conveniently located according to your cat's preferences and standards (not yours!). These points are discussed elsewhere in this chapter. Second, you will have to deny your cat access to the potted plants so that the pattern is not reinforced further with additional practice. For example, hang your plants or place them on an elevated shelf. Put all the cat's favorite targets in a room to which he has no access.

If you would like to preserve the integrity of your décor and would rather not relocate your plants, you will need to cat proof the plants. Cover the soil with wire mesh or aluminum foil. Leave the center at the base of the plant uncovered so that air can circulate and so you can water it. You may need to place upside down mouse traps (they will not hurt the cat this way) on top of this cover to further discourage your little gardening buddy. If your cat tries to disturb the plant, the mousetraps will snap shut and fly off the plant. This is enough to scare me away (yes, Dr. Cookie®'s younger kitties are gardening enthusiasts, too, although they just like to dig in the soil, chew on the leaves, or play with the branches) so it should work on your cat! If you don't like the idea of the mousetraps, even though your kitty will not be harmed, you can scatter a few mothballs on top of the surface cover. Finally, to direct your cat toward a new hobby, plant a patch of cat grass (sold at local pet stores) or plant a small patch of grass seed purchased from any garden center. Your cat can use the turf to graze or to void and it will be a desirable alternative for either behavior.

Well, we did all this, and Mitch still tried to get to his favorite palm. After using the houseplants for so long, he had developed a preference for voiding in soil. To increase the attractiveness of his litter boxes, I instructed his owner to sprinkle potting soil on the top of Mitch's litter box every other day. This did the trick! Six months after Mitch had recommitted himself to litter box use, the mixture of soil was slowly phased out over an additional six months until he was back to using

100 percent litter filler. Mitch was happy, his owner was happy, I was happy, but happiest of all were the plants!

LITTER BOXES AND THE TERRITORIAL CAT

Rocky was a mischievous Japanese Bobtail. He kept himself entertained by torturing his meeker littermate, who was, of course, named Bullwinkle. One of Rocky's little games was to play "king of the castle" atop the hood of the covered litter box. He waited patiently until Bullwinkle approached the litter box and then pounced. Bullwinkle's terror was Rocky's reward, and Bullwinkle fell for it every time! Rather than a direct retaliation, which was not Bullwinkle's style, he internalized his anxiety. Bullwinkle began to spray urine against the potted ficus tree in the dining room. This progressed to spraying under the windows along the walls of the living room, the mat at the front and back doors, and the door to the linen closet. Rocky was unphased and continued to stalk his brother at the litter box. The atmosphere during my visit to their home was tense. Their veterinarian had recently prescribed a psychoactive medication, but it had not helped. The boys had been misbehaving for over a year, and their mom was beginning to wish they really were in a TV cartoon so she could turn them off!

Territorial urine marking is one of the most common reasons that cats are referred to a veterinary behaviorist or put down. At least 10 percent of all cats mark inside their homes with urine or stool at some point in their lives. Territorial marking is a normal feline behavior, yet it is understandably undesirable when it is expressed indoors and by the deposit of urine (or stool). Urine marking is performed in one of two positions. Urine can be voided in a squatting position, or it can be expelled in aerosol (sprayed) against vertical surfaces from a standing position. Both males and females mark with urine using both techniques, although spraying is more common among males. Neutering will help to control the problem if marking occurs in an intact cat; however, some cats begin to urine mark long after they have been surgically sterilized. Hormones, it seems, can't be blamed for everything.

Territorial conflict between cats in a multicat home is a common finding in cases of inappropriate elimination. In this case, Rocky's little game at the litter box had a serious goal. He was announcing his control over an important territorial component. He was proclaiming that the litter box, and the room it was placed in, was his. It was just another excuse to remind his less confident brother that Rocky ruled. And yet poor Bullwinkle could only keep his little legs crossed for so long. He was able to access the box when Rocky was napping in the middle of the afternoon; but at other times of the day, Rocky was not so sympathetic. Urine marking is a primary territorial and anxiety-releasing behavior, and Bullwinkle could only take so much abuse from his brother.

This little feud had been going on for over a year by the time I was called in. Their veterinarian had tried to help by prescribing medication, but as I explained, there is no such thing as a "magic pill." Medication can be very helpful in the treatment of a variety of behavioral problems; however, there is no substitute for going to the source of the problem rather than chemically subduing the symptom. It was clear to me that we needed to evaluate and restructure the social and environmental issues that directly impacted Rocky and Bullwinkle's emotional states.

Bullwinkle's acts of spraying near windows and doors were not accidental. He was marking strategic locations along the periphery of the territory he shared with a dominant cat. The walls of your home represent concrete borders and house cats are restricted by these boundaries, despite social tensions. The windows are strategic vantage points from which the outside can be monitored. Every door is an entry to or exit from the cat's territory and takes on added significance to a territorially anxious cat who has been put on the defensive. Bullwinkle's fondness for the visual trigger of doorways had extended to other less strategic doors, such as the closet.

To defuse the situation, I requested the addition of at least two or three more litter boxes. Rocky was successfully controlling access to a single box, but he would have found it nearly impossible to monitor three or four or more of them simultaneously. Multiple latrine locations would give Bullwinkle a fighting chance to use one of them in peace. I generally recommend a minimum of two boxes for a single cat, if possible, and at least one box for every cat in your household. In cases where a litter box problem exists, it is better to provide at least two or more boxes per cat. Even when a young kitten playfully harasses a housemate near the box, you should be aware of any situation that discourages future use of the litter box. Prevention is often easier to institute than a cure.

We placed one of the new boxes next to the ficus plant, which had become a favorite scent post, and at other preferred targets around the house. We placed lemon-scented room deodorizers at other locations (wedges of fresh citrus are another easy option) and sprinkled dry cat food at others. Covered boxes were placed at areas where Bullwinkle habitually sprayed to contain his aerosol. However, the cover was removed from the original box so that Rocky could no longer use it as a perch from which to pounce! Within days, Bullwinkle was using the new boxes at his marking targets, and within weeks, he had indicated his favorites among them. Several months later the boxes that he used infrequently were replaced by bowls of water for a few more months to discourage regression to old urine marking habits. I advised that at least three boxes be maintained. I also recommended that the owner spend extra time playing with Rocky so that he was less focused on other games that had undesirable consequences! Rocky and Bullwinkle were pals once more.

AVERSION TO THE LITTER BOX

Groucho was a chocolate point Birman with deep violet eyes. His whiskers were very long and white, and he was really quite spectacular. His owner had lived with cats before Groucho and had never cleaned the box more often than once each week. He called me because his cat, as he described him, was weird. Groucho did not step into his box like other cats; he was different. He balanced precariously on the side of his jumbo box. When he was done, he ran off as if something was chasing him, stopping only to shake his paws in apparent disgust. When I saw the state of his box, I had to agree.

 A dirty litter box is repulsive and can teach a cat to avoid the box instead. The cat's devoted use of the box hangs as precariously as does the cat who tries to balance disgust with the need to use the box. Hygiene is often the source of an acquired aversion to the litter box. There is a wide variety between cats with regard to preference for litter box hygiene. One cat may faithfully use a box that is cleaned just once or twice a month, but another cat might be insulted if the box has been used just once. There are, however, other reasons that a cat will learn to dislike the box.

Any negative experience associated with the litter box could deter even the most fastidious of kitties. An ambush at or near the box by a playful or proprietary housemate could do it. Scolding your cat in the vicinity of the litter box could be traumatizing and establish an unfortunate association. Pain coincidental with litter box use, due to urinary tract disease, intestinal disorders, or arthritis, could discourage a return visit. Cats are sensitive creatures and litter box use is a tenuous habit at best. If you want your cat to use the litter box religiously, you must keep the litter box sacred!

Groucho was showing several behaviors that are typical of acquired litter box aversion. He performed awkward maneuvers to avoid stepping in the contaminated substrate. He shook his paws vigorously as soon as he stepped out, and he could not get away from the stinky place fast enough! Hygiene was an obvious factor, but so was the placement of the box. It was located in a back room that was used for storage. The walls were lined with piles of unused sports equipment, boxes, old mattresses, toys, and luggage. It was cluttered and dusty. As if this was not enough, precariously placed items had fallen near and even into the box when the poor cat was nearby. This room was a problem and not just for the cat's litter box use. Someone was going to get hurt by falling objects, and this room was a fire hazard! Groucho's box was placed in the middle of the mess.

Once the room was cleared out and cleaned up, Groucho's fresh litter box was placed in the corner to the right of the door. We did not want him to feel obliged to cross the full width of the room, and this was a nice compromise. We placed a second box immediately adjacent to this box so that Groucho had a choice. Some cats like to urinate in one box and defecate in another, alternating from box to box according to how the mood strikes them. Groucho showed his appreciation by happily stepping into the boxes, briefly digging, and strolling away. Groucho was not one to harp O on past grievances, and he was happy to turn the other cheek O!

INAPPROPRIATE DEFECATION

Ruffles was a shy, cream-and-white cat who had lived in the same apartment with his dad for all of his six years. When they moved across town to a spacious new home, Ruffles became a bit unruffled. He began to defecate at various locations, such as on the area carpet next to his owner's bed and on the bath mat. Ruffles was having a hard time adjusting to his new home, and his dad was having a hard time understanding the unexpected shift in Ruffles's behavior.

Inappropriate defecation can be accidental but it can be an intentional behavior, too. Felines have the option to mark their territory with the strategic deposit of feces, and marking with waste is often the hallmark of a cat's expression and release of nonspecific anxiety. In Ruffles's case, he had been transplanted to a new territory for the first time, and he was quite unnerved by the experience. By defecating outside the box, he was identifying himself with his new space. This anxiety-releasing behavior made him feel much better about the move.

Inappropriate defecation, like inappropriate urination, can also be triggered by a dirty litter box, fear, and a variety of medical problems. Aversion to a malodorous box can cause inappropriate urination or defecation if there is no clean, alternative litter box. Fear, an extremely anxious state of mind, has physical symptoms that include an increased heart and respiration rate as well as the release of bowel and bladder contents. Medical problems associated with inappropriate defecation include constipation, diarrhea, and health issues that are unrelated to the intestine, in other words, anything. Some cats mark with urine when they are upset, others mark with stool, and some do both.

Inappropriate elimination, whether urine or stool, is not an intentional act of malice or revenge. Your cat can only behave as a cat, and these are human traits. It is essential to try to determine the underlying source of your cat's troubles and to resolve them. As always, it is important to begin by evaluating your cat's physical health. Your veterinarian will want to thoroughly examine your cat and will advise appropriate blood, urine, and fecal tests. Consider the state of your cat's litter boxes. Are you scooping them every day? Have you recently changed litter brands or the location of the box? Have you added or removed a cover over the box? Have you bought a new box? It is important to keep the box clean, but sometimes it can be too clean. Your cat could be repelled by the scent of the cleanser you used to disinfect the box. It might be best to avoid strong-smelling cleansers and to leave some of your cat's scent in the box. It is one of the things that make it a familiar and appealing place.

In Ruffles's case, his pattern suggested an additional issue. He had acquired an apparent preference for voiding on small area rugs. Part of the solution was to remove these visual triggers that also retained his scent so effectively. One of these little mats was sacrificed for the good of the cause. It was cut into strips and placed vertically inside the box to line the sides. Several boxes were prepared in this way and then filled with Ruffles's favorite litter filler. Ruffles could scratch at the carpeted sides while he became reacquainted with litter box use. Over the ensuing weeks, the carpet fragment lining each box was cut into smaller and smaller strips until it was simply discarded. It had served the purpose of reinforcing Ruffles's renewed interest in his litter boxes. We considered psychoactive medication to alleviate some of Ruffles's understandable anxiety since moving to his new home. Instead, I asked Ruffles's dad to spend some quality time with his boy, despite the fact that he was devoting much of his spare time to unpacking boxes and settling in himself. He set aside about forty-five minutes each evening to play, groom, and pet his cat. They both needed to relax and unwind. Ruffles appreciated all our efforts. He and his dad finally agreed that their new house really felt like home.

URINE-MARKING CATS AND HUMAN TARGETS

A Bombay beauty with an inky black coat and copper eyes, Griffin was a happy boy until his mom started to date a new man. He thought nothing of it at first, but his attitude changed when she began to spend several nights a week at her boyfriend's home. He soon became a frequent overnight guest at her home as well. During one of her overnight absences, Griffin urinated on her bed. The following week he anointed her neck while she and her boyfriend slept. Griffin's mom called me in a panic, terribly worried about her cat's happiness and how this might impact her own.

We have already discussed the function of elimination to mark strategic territorial locations and to decrease a cat's level of anxiety. Some anxious cats groom themselves excessively, vomit their food repeatedly, stop eating, hide, become aggressive, or scratch at new targets. However, if your cat displays anxiety by voiding out of the box, there are an endless number of markable surfaces from which to choose! Not unusually, cats layer their scent over the surfaces most strongly identified with you, such as your favorite chair or your bed. For a minority of these marking cats, this means marking the source of their greatest comfort and possibly their greatest anxiety—you.

We needed to reintroduce Griffin and his mom's new partner so that they could all let bygones be bygones. I suggested that the boyfriend take over feeding Griffin, and that he hand feed the cat as much as possible to promote even greater familiarity. Griffin needed some extra playtime to give him an additional outlet for his nervous energy before bedtime, and this provided another opportunity to interact positively with the new man in his life. On overnights away, Griffin's mom had the choice of either keeping her bedroom door shut or sprinkling some dry food on the cover. In addition, we decided to put Griffin on medication that would lessen his separation anxiety. He had become a bit overly dependent on his owner, and he was unused to being alone and lonely for her. After a few months things settled down to a cozy routine, and Griffin's medication was gradually withdrawn. I understand that his owner and her boyfriend eventually were married. I was not invited to the wedding, but then again, neither was Griffin. He was at home, sleeping on their bed.

SOILED HAIR IN LONGHAIRED BREEDS

Lucifer was an enormous black Himalayan hybrid with long, soft hair. He was a docile, sweet guy who was loved by all; however, he had an occasionally embarrassing problem. Sometimes his soft stools adhered to the long hairs on the backs of his thighs. This was most unbecoming to his normally dignified self. His dad would try to clean him up, but Lucifer found this uncomfortable. Lucifer would break away and run off with his tail held high like a flag waving above the debris that stuck to his bloomers. Lucifer would try to remove the stools himself when he could by scooting on his behind. His owner could not decide if this was a devilishly amusing or hellish experience and asked me to help.

Cats with long, luxurious coats, such as Persian or Himalayan purebreds or hybrids and domestic longhaired cats, can unintentionally soil themselves. This is not really a behavioral issue (although it can present as one) but a sort of silly side effect to the fluffy coats they bear. The anus, underside of the tail, and the long, soft hair on their thighs can be easily soiled. Stool segments can adhere to their long hair or are found elsewhere in random spots around the house. This is sometimes confused with inappropriate defecation; however, it is more likely that the dried segments eventually drop off or are finally removed by the cat during grooming.

Try not to be upset about your cat's less than polished appearance; remember that it is not the cat's fault! If you want to clean your cat up, make sure you are not angry, upset, or in a rush. The cat will just learn to avoid you when you approach. I find the easiest solution to this sometimes sensitive issue is to make an appointment with a professional groomer or veterinary technician. The long hair beneath the tail and at the back of the thighs can be clipped away to minimize soiling and to make maintenance grooming a breeze.

The diet can also influence the consistency of stools. Lucifer was fed canned food and this can sometimes produce a softer, stickier stool. I suggested that they gradually introduce a quality dry food, which was more likely to produce a firm stool. This, combined with keeping his bloomers a more manageable length, resolved the "sticky" problem. It seems, after all, that Lucifer was not really a bad boy, just a fallen angel.

FAILURE TO COVER WASTE

Jezebel was a sassy gray tabby with golden yellow eyes. Her owner complained that Jezebel did not bury her urine or stools in the box. She had tried a variety of litter fillers to see if Jezebel would cooperate, but no luck. Jezebel used her box religiously and was a lovely kitty, but her owner was concerned that this could signal the beginning of a serious problem.

The instinct to deposit waste in a loose substrate, such as sand or soil, is strong in most cats. Kittens who have never watched their mother use the litter box will quickly learn to use one. Digging before and after waste is deposited is also a genetically programmed behavior sequence. In fact, kittens will develop their own distinctive patterns of digging by the time they are just four weeks old.

The amount of digging associated with litter box use is highly variable among cats. Some cats hardly dig at all before or after eliminating, while others are extremely enthusiastic! In addition, the amount of digging can vary each time a cat uses the box. Your cat might send the sand flying after he or she has defecated but give a quick sniff and walk out of the box after having urinated. The next time the cat might perform an elaborate digging ritual prior to urinating and just a few quick digs after defecating. The important point is that *you should not be worried about whether or not your cat digs in the box.* The failure to cover urine or stool does not make your cat abnormal. It is simply a matter of style together with an underlying predisposition to dig—or not.

Cats could just make their deposit and walk away, but why don't they? One plausible explanation is that covering or burying waste helps to decrease the transmission of intestinal parasites. It is also possible that covering their waste helps to minimize the attraction of predators. On the other hand, urine or stool that is strategically voided to advertise a cat's presence is not covered. Presumably, the importance of territorial marking must outweigh the risk of parasite transmission and detection by intruders. It remains a mystery as to why cats dig and why other animals don't! Dig it?

5

Destructive Behavior

"It is a very inconvenient habit of kittens," said Alice,
"that whatever you say to them, they always purr."

—LEWIS CARROLL (1832–1898)

CLIMBING ELEVATED SURFACES

Mercury was a silver mackerel tabby American Shorthair with emerald green eyes. At one year of age, he was an active kitten whose favorite game was to climb on top of the kitchen table and leap onto the hanging plants. Spider plants, with their long, thin leaves and shoots from which were suspended baby spider plants, were Mercury's favorite prey. These plants tantalized him with their hanging branches. But those "vines" were not strong enough to support his weight and he often came crashing down, along with a portion of the shredded plant. His owner was considering changing his name to Tarzan. Still, he was appropriately named, for you had only to gaze in amazement as he streaked through the house like quicksilver.

Cats climb. It is an inborn gift that enables them to evade predators or to pursue prey or, perhaps, to seek shelter from the elements. Cats climb because they can and also because it is fun! Territory for most earthbound creatures, such as dogs and people, is primarily a horizontally oriented space. Cats, however, use a very three-dimensional area. A cat's territory is horizontal, vertical, and everything in between.

Territorial exploration is an essential part of a cat's daily routine. This allows the detection of uninvited visitors, such as rivals or predators, and allows a young cat to discover hiding places from unexpected danger. Learning all the details of the territory is important, even if it is less critical information, such as where the dog's biscuits are kept or simply to find an inconspicuous hideout for a nap. This investigation is an intellectual exercise as well as a good physical workout. And it is just as important, or more so, for indoor cats to explore their territory than for outdoor cats. Cats who are confined indoors must rely on fewer outlets for entertainment and, like Mercury, they must often make their own fun.

Feline anatomy provides cats with speed and agility. Powerful muscles in the hind legs thrust a flexible and lightweight skeleton forward or upward. Keen eyesight allows them to focus on prey or other objects of interest that are just out of reach, and their athleticism gives them the ability to attain it. From your cat's perspective, that hanging plant is too attractive a toy to pass up. Spider plants are nontoxic to cats, but a cat that falls in an attempt to reach one can be seriously hurt. Cats get broken bones or worse without ever leaving their homes. They are not invincible, but their curiosity is legendary. That is another reason why it is so important to pet proof your home.

Part of being your cat's guardian is to provide your pet with a safe environment as well as an entertaining home. When he was a baby, my boy Hershey loved to explore and discovered the bulletin board hung over my desk. He soon learned to amuse himself by pulling out thumbtacks from the bulletin board. He could have punctured a paw or swallowed them. Some of the tacks fell to the floor where I might have stepped on one with my bare feet. I put the bulletin board away during his Tarzan phase. If you notice that a particular object, such as a plant, is irresistible to your cat, *move it so that it is unattainable.* If that means placing it in another room, a higher shelf, closing the door, or giving it to your mother-in-law, remove the temptation. It might even be helpful to rearrange the furniture to prevent your cat's route of access to an attractive object. If a plant is on a tabletop, suspend it high and away from your little Tarzan.

Hanging drapes or curtains, for instance, are an invitation to kittens in particular. Climbing curtains can be a special treat to little Tarzans in training. Most will respond to a stern, "No!" but your decor could be easily damaged in no time and the behavior must be quickly controlled. You might have to lift draperies off the floor or remove them until your kitty is older. It helps tremendously to keep their little talons well trimmed!

Cats also climb to look out a window, which gives them a strategic view of the yard and outdoor cats or the birdbath. This becomes a problem if the window is at the kitchen counter, and you do not approve of your cat on kitchen surfaces. If your cat is drawn by the view, pulling down the shade or drawing the curtains may not be enough because these are easily pushed aside. Cats can be quite determined to reach elevated surfaces when they are rewarded for doing so. An important territorial perch, an entertaining view, a few crumbs of food, or unwashed dishes to lick . . . it should come as no surprise to you that part of the solution must be to remove the reward. Keep countertops clean, remove tempting tidbits, and wash your dishes!

Another element of keeping your cat off surfaces such as kitchen counters, or any other undesirable location, is to make it an unpleasant experience. This doesn't mean that you should be there to yell at your cat or squirt him or her with water because the cat will simply learn to wait until you are not around to enjoy the perch. The cat could also learn to be afraid of you, and you would not want your pet to avoid you. It is also not possible for you to be around twenty-four hours a day, and your pet will be reinforced even more strongly for every successful trip. So what to do? The countertop itself must be the one to "punish" the cat! Make jumping on the elevated surface an unpleasant experience by booby-trapping it. Here are some suggestions for "remote" control for you to try:

- Stack a dozen or more empty soda cans into a pyramid so your cat will knock them over on the way to that attraction. The stacks should be at least three rows or more in height to leave a real impression. The sound and movement of the tumbling cans will scare the daylights out of most kitties and are often enough to dissuade their return.
- One of my favorite solutions is to crisscross two-sided sticky tape on the countertop (if you prefer, you can place the strips of tape on a heavy-duty plastic sheet for removal when you need to prepare dinner). Your cat will hate stepping on a sticky surface! And your cat won't know for certain when those sticky strips are gone because they can't be seen from ground level. When the sticky sheets have done their job, don't remove them too quickly. Wait at least a month before removing them, strip by strip, over another few

weeks. (You can also use a sheet of contact paper placed sticky side up.)

- Another trick is to fill cookie sheets with water so that your cat jumps into water when he or she jumps onto the countertop. Unless your cat likes getting wet, this is an easy and effective solution.
- Motion detectors can be set up on the counter so that your cat gets blasted with a terrifying sound when the sensor is crossed.
- Upside-down mousetraps make a loud "snap!" and pop up when disturbed but will not harm your cat. You will need to put down as many as necessary so that your cat can't step over or around them.
- Block off the window by obscuring the view with adhesive sheets of frosted plastic that give privacy from outsiders and make it uninteresting for an indoor cat in the mood for a little sightseeing.

Be creative; come up with some ideas of your own!

DESTRUCTION IN YOUR ABSENCE

Rhett was a restless, nine-month-old Norwegian Forest Cat kitten, who was left alone during the day while his owners worked. They often wondered how he kept himself entertained in their absence until one day they returned home to find the shattered pieces of porcelain bird figurines. His mom's collectibles were not the only items the rugged young cat had damaged. Glass vases and pitchers, part of another prized collection, were out of place, teetered on the ledge, or had crashed to the floor. Display shelves in the bookcase were tracked with dirty little paw prints made muddy by stepping in the potted plant on the way to knocking over the crystal candlesticks. Rhett's parents looked around the room and thought that perhaps Rhett might be better off living in the Norwegian forest.

Pet proof your home! Before you welcome your new kitten or cat into your residence, look around you. Lie down on the floor to see the world from the cat's perspective. Many temptations and hazards are clearly at ground level, but don't forget to look up, too. A healthy kitten or cat is an amazing athlete motivated by curiosity. Territorial exploration is limited only by the cat's physical ability to explore it. In your absence, your young pet can investigate this environment any way he or she chooses and, believe me, the choices may not meet with your approval. Part of the havoc wreaked in your absence is simply due to unsupervised clumsiness. Part of it is due to intentionally pushing items just to investigate them more closely, for example, by gently pushing them closer and closer to the edge of the shelf or tabletop until, ooops! Some kitties will learn to do this to items on your dressing table to wake you up; however, when you are not around, it cannot be considered an attention-seeking behavior.

Another key element in the destruction caused when you are not at home is simply the void left by your absence. A recent study, which I conducted, has finally demonstrated that separation-related anxiety does exist in cats. One of the major symptoms of feline *separation anxiety syndrome* is destructiveness in your absence. Excessive vocalization, inappropriate elimination, and overgrooming are the other three categories of behavior associated with separation anxiety syndrome, although none of these behaviors are exclusive to separation-related distress.

Pet proof your home by placing those fragile collectibles behind glass door cabinets, on unreachable surfaces, or in a box until your kitten turns into a more placid adult. And just in case the misbehavior is due to anxiety because of your absence, spend extra time playing with your kitten before you leave. Ideally, the kitty should be too tired for destructive exploration, accidental or otherwise, while you are away. If necessary, confine the kitty to one room or to a large cage commonly referred to as a kitty "playpen" to prevent any mischief in your absence. It remains essential to get your cat tired before confinement. Rhett was not released to the Norwegian Forest or any other forest for that matter. His owners recognized the simple wisdom in my suggestions and were happy to comply.

HOUSEPLANTS THAT ARE HAZARDOUS
TO YOUR CAT

BartholoMew loved to nibble on plants. The soft leaves of the tabletop fern plant were a favorite, and he soon began to explore new taste sensations. The leaves of the philodendron hung lazily over the sides of the coffee table. Bart could not resist! One day, his dad came home and found his little boy drooling heavily. His mouth was opened slightly, and his tongue protruded oddly. He was restless and seemed to have labored breathing. He scooped Bart up and went through more than one red light on the way to the nearest veterinary clinic. In fact, he was pulled over by a police officer for his failure to stop at a traffic signal. When he explained his emergency to the officer, who was a cat owner himself, he was given a police escort the rest of the way! Bart was one sick boy, but he recovered after several days. By the time he returned home, his favorite plants had been replaced with one very large and prickly cactus and a lovely patch of cat grass that his owner had planted just for him!

Houseplants add color, texture, and a touch of nature to our indoor environments. Unfortunately, some of these are hazardous to our pets. For instance, holiday favorites such as poinsettia (*Euphorbia pulcherrima*) and mistletoe (*Phoradendron flavescens*) are highly irritating. Philodendron and dieffenbachia irritate the mucous membranes as well and, ingested in sufficient quantities, may cause hypersalivation, paralysis of the tongue, and respiratory distress. English ivy (*Hedera helix*) is a gastrointestinal irritant that may cause vomiting and diarrhea, although the grape ivy (*Cissus rhombifolia*) and Swedish ivy (*Plectranthus Australis*) are inoffensive. Spider plants (*Chlorophytum* spp. or *Anthericum* spp.) are not toxic, which is fortunate because these are quite popular with cat owners and cats alike!

It is important to have a sense of which plants are potentially dangerous to your cat and those that should not present a direct threat. Nontoxic ornamental houseplants include: the African violet (*Saintpaulia ionantha*); aluminum plant (*Pilea cadierei*); begonia (*Begonia* sp.); Christmas cactus (*Schlumbergera bridgesii, Zygocactus truncatus*); ficus (*Ficus* sp.); ferns;

jade plant (*Crassula argenta*); mother-in-law tongue (*Sansevieria* sp.); palms; prayer plant (*Maranta leuconeura*); rubber plant (*Crassula arborescens*); Scheffelera (*Brassaia actinophylla*); and wandering Jew (*Zebrina pendula*).

Cats that roam outdoors are exposed to potential poisons from outdoor plants in addition to any their owners may have in their homes. Toxic outdoor ornamental plants include: Black-eyed Susans and coneflowers (*Rudbeckia* spp.); bleeding hearts (*Dicentra* spp.); daffodils (*Narcissus* spp.); euonymus; foxglove (*Digitalis purpurea*); hyacinth (*Hyacinthus orientalis*); iris (*Iris* spp.); lantana (*Lantana camara*); larkspurs and delphiniums (*Delphinium* spp.); lily-of-the-valley (*Convallaria majalis*); lupines (*Lupinus* spp.); poppy (*Papaver* spp.); rhododendron; wisteria (*Wisteria* spp.); and yew (*Taxus* spp.). The yew is particularly dangerous because ingestion of only a small quantity of its needles is lethal. This list of familiar yet toxic plants gives additional impetus to my recommendation that you keep your cherished cat indoors!

It is probably normal for cats to eat a certain amount of plant material. Planting a low container with grass seed will give your cat a place to graze in peace. You may purchase grass for your cat as a kit at a local pet supply store, in pet catalogs, or make and grow your own with simple materials from a garden center. Regardless of the source, your cat will make sure you won't have to mow it!

WOOL AND CLOTH CHEWING

Carlee was a seal-point Siamese who loved to chew holes in her owner's socks and sweaters. By the time she was about eight months old, her list of favorite targets had expanded to include towels, blankets, throw pillows, and many woolen and cloth items. Carlee's hobby was destroying her owner's wardrobe and home decor, not to mention her owner's affections. The final straw came when Carlee was hospitalized for severe vomiting and underwent major surgery to remove a bowel obstruction caused by ingestion of an unidentifiable wad of wool (it later turned out to be a part of a mitten). Things were pretty tense when I was finally asked to investigate Carlee's problem. Within several weeks of our telephone consult, Carlee had stopped chewing most of her favorite objects but occasionally sucked on a fuzzy sock, which was finally discarded.

Wool or cloth sucking and chewing is an undesirable behavior reported in a minority of cats. It is more common in Siamese and Abyssinians and hybrids thereof, but has been described in many breeds. These behaviors are categorized as obsessive-compulsive disorders when they become frequent and habitual. Sucking and chewing may be accompanied by a rhythmic kneading of the front paws typically seen in nursing kittens. The sucking cat may purr loudly and salivate profusely. These behaviors are objectionable if the compulsive cat damages valuable or valued items. However, sucking and chewing becomes a dangerous habit should bulky material be ingested and result in intestinal obstruction.

Part of the treatment of compulsive chewing or sucking is to make target items unavailable as much as possible. If your cat has a preference for socks, put them away like your mother told you to! If your cat is obsessed with your hanging draperies, remove them or lift them out of reach for a time. You may have to close the door to your bedroom or living room or any room that contains items that are irresistible to your obsessive-compulsive kitty. If, however, your cat is only sucking (and not chewing) on a single item, it might make sense to sacrifice that item in the hope that the cat will confine sucking to that item.

The application of a bad-tasting substance to attractive targets is often unsuccessful because the compulsive cat may find an untreated area on the surface. It is also possible for the cat to develop a taste preference for the aversive substance. The aversive taste might not be a sufficiently strong deterent because the satisfaction derived from chewing or sucking the object is so rewarding.

Treatment must involve providing additional alternative activity for your cat. Increased exercise in the form of play or perhaps even leash walks in your yard may help. More time spent interacting with you in general will benefit your cat. Provide a wider variety of toys. Get a fish tank for your cat to watch, making sure, of course, that the fish are safe under a secure lid! My point is that if you intentionally engage your cat's attention and provide more entertainment, your cat will be less interested in looking for other less than desirable outlets.

In some cases it might be helpful to give the compulsively oral cat an alternative item to chew. Small rawhide sticks, which are marketed for dogs, could be attractive to your compulsively chewing cat. Another option would be to offer your cat the tip of a cooked chicken wing once or twice a week, or on a daily basis if necessary, to curb any obsessive search for cloth or wool targets. Chicken wing tips contain only small bones and cooking makes them quite soft. These are unlikely to harm your cat and will satisfy the yen to chew! Most cats outgrow their compulsive sucking and/or chewing by the age of two or three years. In the meantime, it is important to deny your cat the opportunity to practice the behavior by removing her favorite targets or providing equally or more satisfying activities to redirect or override the compulsion to suck or chew.

CHEWING ELECTRIC CORDS

Ziggy was a six-month-old Maine Coon with a taste for adventure. He was always on the prowl, looking for something to stimulate him. Then he discovered the tangled mess of wires behind the TV, video, and stereo that were aligned on milk crates in the den. His owner's makeshift entertainment center was Ziggy's entertainment center, too. Lots of levels to jump on and off, wires and cords to crawl under and nibble on; he was having a helluva time. One evening his mom came back from class and Ziggy was nowhere to be found. With rising panic she searched every place she thought he might be hiding and any closet he might have gotten locked in, but no Ziggy. By then she was frantic and had gone in to the bathroom to wash her tear-stained face when she heard a faint "meow" from behind the shower curtain. And there he was, her pitiful boy. His whiskers were frizzled as if they had been melted down, and indeed, they had. He had burned the hair around his mouth, too. Later, the veterinarian also discovered a large sore on the inside of his mouth and surface of his tongue. Ziggy had serious burns from chomping on the television cable, and he was lucky it was not worse. Ziggy's owner was referred to me so that this accident would not be repeated. One of my suggestions was to replace the milk crates with an entertainment unit to house her equipment and place it so that Ziggy could not get to the wiring. His mom's roommate helped to solve the problem by getting a kitten of her own. Ziggy now had his own entertainment center in the form of three-month-old Zelda, a mischievous seal-point Himalayan, and everyone was happy!

Electrical cords are a common temptation to many young cats. Chewing on wires is more common in kittens who are naturally more active and inquisitive about novel items in their environment. This behavior is not only destructive but could become a fatal attraction. Biting into an electrical cord is a hazardous habit that can result in electric shock, electrocution, burns, respiratory and cardiac arrest, and death. If you suspect that your kitten is investigating electric cords because you (a) catch him in the act, (b) find little teeth marks on a wire or cord, and/or (c) discover a severed electric cord, you must take *immediate* action.

If your cat chews on one particular cord, it should be easy to prevent access to that room by closing the door. It may be helpful to apply a foul-tasting substance along the exposed surface of wire. Periodic application (and reapplication several times each week) of lemon juice, mouthwash, bitter apple, hot pepper sauce, hot mustard, or commercial preparations with a saturated cotton ball along the length of cord may be effective. However, you must remember to reapply the aversive substance on a regular basis, and your cat could acquire a preference for any of these tastes. Or your cat could simply chew on another untreated cord. You may need to experiment with a series of substances to determine which one effectively discourages your cat, and in the meantime, your cat might continue to engage in a dangerous habit. If your cat is intent on chewing on several or more electric cords—or if the first one or two aversive substances do not do the trick—aversive conditioning may not be a practical solution for you.

Your plan must include two elements: first, preventing access to electric cords, and second, providing alternatives that are more interesting. Keep the doors to troublespots closed unless you are in the room to supervise your "wired" cat. It might even be necessary to confine your cat to a single, pet-proofed room when you are busy or away from home. Dangling cords or wires must be secured out of reach by taping them behind appliances or along boards and walls. Cover exposed wires with electrical conduit or other commercial covers. Replace long telephone cords with extendible cords that automatically roll up into a neat enclosed case. Rearrange your furniture so that access to your computer wires, for instance, is blocked by the placement of your desk against the wall. To deter your cat from stepping near exposed wires or cables, place sheets of contact paper, with the sticky side facing up, around the area. No cat likes to step on uncomfortable surfaces! It is essential to minimize your cat's desire to chew on an unsafe object. Additional quality time spent with you, in the form of play or petting, will benefit you both. Provide other appropriate objects for your pet to chew on, for example, rawhide sticks made for dogs could become a popular item for your cat! The occasional tip of a cooked chicken wing is a much safer alternative to chewing on electrical wiring. Your young adventurer is all wired up for now, but will mellow with age. Just make sure your cat lives long enough to prove it!

FOOD-RELATED DESTRUCTIVENESS

Hershey loves to eat; he lives to eat—food is his religion. My cat Hershey is a chowhound. Anything edible (and he has a diverse palate) or left unattended will be found with the wrapping shredded and the contents mutilated or gone. He has even climbed to the top of the pantry shelf, almost seven feet high, to claw and chew his way into a sealed cardboard box of dog biscuits. In his next life Hershey would probably choose to come back as a Sumo wrestler. Eat, eat, sleep, eat, fight, eat, sleep, fight, eat, eat, sleep, eat . . . Or perhaps he might prefer something more creative, returning instead as a gourmet chef. Yup, that would be the good life for him!

Well, it still all comes down to pet proofing your home. And if that means keeping the dog biscuits behind lock and key (or just in storage in the basement) to keep out *your* chowhound cat, so be it! Temptations are all around us compulsive eaters (we can't keep any chocolate in my house), and it is no different for your pet. If your cat is determined to get something, especially food, he or she might knock over, shove off, dig, or chew into anything to reach that goal. There is nothing more rewarding to reinforce a behavior than food. And when food is the goal, the behavior is guaranteed to be repeated. Cats are most attracted to the traditional dairy and meat products. But some cats have eccentric tastes. I once gave my cat Jonathan a choice between raw hamburger meat and fresh cantaloupe. How he loved that melon! My Teddi loves nectarine, tomato, grapes . . .

To keep your cats off kitchen countertops, don't leave food there. Keep surfaces clean of crumbs. Knives that have been used to cut into food will attract your cat and could cause injuries should the blade of the knife be licked. Keep packages that are easily opened in a closed cabinet or transfer their contents to more secure containers that are cat proof. If your cat learns to open kitchen cabinets, which is not uncommon, you may need to place child proof security latches on the doors.

In the process of tracking a tempting treat, your cat might knock over fragile items or worse, he might make it into that box of chocolates. Chocolate is extremely toxic to our pets. Because of their small size, cats need ingest only a small amount to get into real trouble. Bingeing on that gourmet cheese set out for your guest could still make your cat sick. Overeating can lead to gastric distension, diarrhea, and inflammation of the pancreas (pancreatitis) or the sensitive lining of the digestive tract (gastroenteritis), or your cat could just get plain fat. So if your cats are intense about food, protect them from themselves. Divide their daily cat food portion and feed them three or four small meals a day instead of just one or two (*more often* does not mean *more*) so they will not need to resort to their mischievous ways.

DESTRUCTIVE SCRATCHING

Jerry was an orange tabby with a crooked smile due to several missing teeth, the result of a traumatic kittenhood as a stray. He had won the heart of his new owner, who lived in a posh suburb in a posh home, by smiling at her, so she told me, as she tended her rose garden. Jerry had struck it big. He loved his home so much that he wanted to show the world by doing his nails on the arms and backs of the sofa and armchair, as well as the upholstered backs of the expensive dining room chairs. Jerry was on the verge of being returned, unceremoniously, to the streets. I pointed out to his frustrated owner that Jerry was not using the scratching post she had placed next to his litter box in the basement. We discussed how to encourage Jerry's use of scratching posts. My advice must have been helpful because Jerry, I understand, is still smiling his crooked smile.

A cat's claw is a specialized toenail that grows primarily in layers, sort of like the layers of an onion. As older layers are shed, underlying sharper ones are revealed. When a cat scratches a surface, he is not sharpening his nails but helping to shed the outer worn layers to reveal already sharp new ones beneath. Periodic trimming of the sharp tips every few weeks will blunt the claws and minimize damage to property. Tips on training your cat to tolerate pedicures are discussed in chapter 12 ("Grooming"). Your veterinarian will gladly give you a lesson or two to teach you how to do this simple task, or you can bring your cat to the clinic for intermittent pedicures. Jerry's treatment was a three-part plan: first, we had to reduce his ability to damage property by keeping his nails blunted; second, it was necessary to prevent access to his favorite but undesirable scratching targets; third, we needed to retrain his preference for using a cat scratching post.

The use of a scratching post should be encouraged to prevent and to treat destructive scratching. The location, texture, and angle of the post are important because cats can be very particular about their preferences. If your cat has already begun to scratch at an inappropriate location, take a deep breath and understand that this is valuable feedback about what your cat prefers. Place a scratching post directly at this location. Cover the damaged area with some unscratchable wrapping so that he has no choice but to scratch the post instead. Heavy plastic, strips of double-sided sticky tape, or simply a smooth-textured sheet might do the job. In other words, block access to the damage already caused and redirect your cat to the desirable scratching surface. The location may not be convenient for you but it must be conveniently placed in keeping with your kitty's obvious likes and dislikes. Use this information to reinforce scratching post use, and you may be able to relocate the post later on.

If your cat does not seem interested in scratching the post you have presented, try different types to determine your cat's preference. For example, your cat might prefer corrugated cardboard to a sisal-wrapped post. Try inexpensive straw place mats on the floor (my cats love them!). Make your own by wrapping a length of scrap wooden board with carpet remnant or leftovers of the upholstery used to cover your furniture. I made one out of a scrap piece of "one by four," rope, and carpenter's glue. It hangs over the back of my office chair and Teddi loves to scratch it as she climbs up to perch on my shoulder. Your kitty might prefer a scratching board that is placed vertically, at a slight incline, or flat on the floor. Trial and error will provide you with valuable feedback on your cat's preferences. Remember, the only thing that counts is to fulfill your cat's criteria of the ideal scratching post (texture, placement, angle) so that the post will be well used. If all else fails, cats were born to scratch on tree trunks so try a clean log (with or without bark)!

To encourage your cat to scratch, play with your cat using the scratching surface. Hang a small toy from the top of a vertical scratching post or grate the top of the post with your own fingers. Your cat will stretch his front legs to reach the toy or your fingers. Reinforce contact of the front paws with the scratching surface with happy praise. If your cat enjoys catnip, sprinkle this dried herb on the board. Part of the catnip response includes pawing or scratching at the catnip source so this might help training. Cats are not sensitive to catnip until after puberty, however, and a minority of adult cats may not be reactive at all, so this is not a guaranteed trick for every cat.

In Jerry's case, we temporarily covered the chairs with heavy plastic and placed additional scratching posts near the dining room table and other targets. The doors to the living room were closed, and he was allowed in only under supervision. His favorite scratching post was placed directly in front of the sofa arm that he loved so well. Once he was reliably using the posts, they were gradually moved to less conspicuous corners.

Cats prefer to scratch locations that are near their resting areas. They tend to scratch just before or just after taking a nap. They will also scratch at strategic territorial locations, for example, near a favorite window perch in the living room or in your bedroom. Jerry had only one scratching post, and he was not interested in using it in the basement. In my experience, a cat can never have too many scratching posts so *place at least one post on every floor of your home and in your cat's favorite rooms.* There is no point in trying to hide the scratching posts. They will always be less noticeable and more socially acceptable than your ruined furniture!

PROS AND CONS OF DECLAW SURGERY

Sara was declawed at the time of her spay while I was still a veterinary student. I was working eighteen hours a day, longer if I was on call, and living in furnished apartments. I simply could not afford any unforeseen expenses or stress. By the time I got Hershey, then Gracie, and recently Teddi, I had my own furniture, my own home, and had perfected the art of raising a cat with whom I could live happily ever after. For my Sara, and still with a twinge of regret over twenty years later, I felt that I had had no choice. Given the choice I believe that Sara would still have preferred to live a long and happy life with me.

For many cat lovers, this will be the single most sensitive issue of this book. Declaw surgery has become a controversial topic. For some it is an unthinkable mutilation of an innocent animal. Others may not even understand what the fuss is all about. After many years of living with cats and treating misbehaving patients, I have resolved the issues in question and feel comfortable with a moderate viewpoint. Taking an extreme position did not make sense to me. It did not seem reasonable to maintain that a cat should never ever be declawed, nor did it feel right to totally dismiss the voices of objection. I would much prefer that owners try to avoid declawing their cats by (a) directing the natural feline urge to scratch toward a scratching post, and (b) by performing regular pedicures to minimize damage. If this is not possible, I would rather see a cat live happily ever after in a safe and loving home but without his front claws than dead or abandoned with his front claws intact. The short-term discomfort of the declaw surgery must be viewed in perspective of the quality of life the cat can enjoy over a much longer term.

To some, declawing is mutilation, but to many others it is plastic surgery. This is a significant observation. We are all influenced by a unique set of family and cultural biases, modified by our individual life lessons. In some cultures, for example, the circumcision of teenage boys without the benefit of anesthesia is a hallmark of bravery and a proud rite of passage. To others, it is abuse of a minor and sexual mutilation. If you are of the opinion that declawing your cat is unacceptable, you should not have it done. If the surgery would enable you to enjoy your pet for a lifetime, then it may be an option to consider. If you are undecided, try to teach your cat to use scratching posts distributed throughout your home and train the cat to tolerate nail trimming. It is better to declaw a cat when the cat is young. Recovery is more rapid in young cats, but older cats will recover, too.

Destructive scratching is not the only reason to consider declaw surgery. An owner may be injured by a pet cat that is aggressive or simply prone to rough play. This is unfortunate. However, if the owner is diabetic, or is undergoing chemotherapy, or is being treated with anticoagulants for a cardiac problem, or has a compromised immune system because of a chronic and debilitating disease, even a little scratch can have disastrous consequences. I would much rather see such an owner continue to thrive from the psychological and physical health benefits of living with a beloved cat (who happens to have been declawed) so that they may continue to enjoy each other for many years to come. Despite rumors to the contrary, *declawing a cat will not make the cat bite more or increase aggressivity.* Cats who are aggressive prior to surgical declawing will probably still be aggressive postsurgically. However, they will no longer be able to injure anyone with their front paws.

In an ideal world, a pet owner should at least try to train a young kitten or a newly acquired adult cat to use a scratching post before electing to declaw the cat. The decision to declaw a destructive (or aggressive) cat should be based on your personal needs, the values instilled in you by your family, and the philosophies that have come to color your world. Not all kittens or cats are easily trained to use a scratching post. Some cat lovers choose not to risk damage to hard-earned new furniture. Above all, consider your cat's short-term and long-term welfare. One thing is clear. It would be unfair to allow a declawed cat to roam outdoors. Cats will be at a distinct disadvantage in defending themselves against rivals and predators and less able to evade danger. I have known cat owners who have boasted that their declawed cat is still a successful hunter and regularly brings down songbirds and other creatures. Their cruelty is in failing to protect both the cat and the wildlife. My sincere wish is that, whatever you choose, you and your cat will enjoy many long and happy years together.

DECLAWING ADULT CATS

Martina was a longhaired tortoiseshell who hated to be brushed and loved to shred her owner's silk curtains. Martina also had an increasing amount of trouble with hairballs vomited on antique Oriental carpets yet refused grooming. She had inflicted deep scratches on her owner and had injured more than one professional groomer who tried to demat her easily tangled coat. Her owner resented her injuries as well as her husband's complaints about the damage to their prized possessions. Martina's mom was caught between a rock and a hard place. Her beloved cat had strained her affection to the breaking point and now had affected her relationship with her husband. Things were so bad that Martina's owner had decided to either have her put down or declawed. The idea of declawing her cat was giving her nightmares . . . and then she called me.

You, too, may be torn about whether or not to declaw your cat. Things may have gotten far out of hand. You may have fallen out of love with your cat, pushed over the edge by damage to your home or injury to yourself or loved ones. It can be very hard to make a reasonable choice when so many emotions cloud your ability to be objective. If euthanasia has become an option, or if you abhor the idea of declawing your cat, there are alternatives.

Surgical declawing involves removal of the last joint of each toe. The claw grows from this tiny bone. An alternative surgery involves cutting only the ligament that retracts the claw while preserving the claw. This approach is probably less painful and has a shorter recovery time, but the claws will continue to grow and must be kept well trimmed. They can get caught in fabric, for example, but the cat no longer has any control over retracting or extending the claw. In theory, this surgery may be attractive. In reality, it may not give you the results you desire.

A nonsurgical approach has been a happy compromise for some cat owners. It involves the application of plastic tips that are fitted and glued to each claw to form a sheath. The plastic tips (SOFT PAWS) are blunt so that no damage or injury is caused even if the cat scratches. The down side of this option is that you may not have the patience or dexterity to apply the product, and your cat may not allow you to do it. Some cats must be sedated or anesthetized to allow application of the product. Many veterinarians promote this alternative and routinely apply them for their patients in the clinic. The nail tips are not permanent and require periodic replacement. SOFT PAWS may last for weeks, or the cat could learn to remove them the day they are applied. Speak with your veterinarian to investigate this option further. It may be interesting to try.

SCRATCHING BEHAVIOR IN DECLAWED CATS

Sam was a bronze Egyptian Mau who had been declawed as a kitten, yet he still "scratched" the corner of the corduroy-covered sofa and the side of his owner's mattress. He was unable to do any damage, but his owner was concerned that her other cats, who had not been declawed, would begin to scratch where Sam was leaving his mark. We decided to modify the surfaces he was scratching by fastening plastic wrap to the corners of the mattress and a clear acrylic board was secured to the side of the sofa with tape. Sam stopped scratching, his housemates continued to use their own scratching posts, and all was well.

 As I explained to Sam's owner, scratching behavior has more than one function. Scratch marks from clawing at prominent or strategically located surfaces leave a visual territorial claim. Scratching also helps to shed the outer layers of each claw. So why do so many declawed cats still go through the motions of "scratching"? The motion of scratching deposits scent contained in specialized glands of the footpads. As the cat scratches, the paws are wiped against the surface, leaving an individual chemical mark. The act of scratching, with or without claws, is also a visual display to other cats that a territorial claim is being made. Finally, scratching also gives a cat a good upper body workout and stretch.

The need to scratch is still strong even in declawed cats. It is usually not a problem and does not necessarily induce other cats to scratch in the same place. However, because there is a slight possibility that other cats with claws might want to cover another cat's scent with their own scratching, it is usually a good idea to discourage it. Cats are often deterred from returning to an undesirable scratching surface with a firm, "No!" But if this is not successful, altering the surface in some way is usually sufficient. Sam quickly gave up on the sofa and mattress (surprisingly, he was not interested in trying the other corners of this furniture) with the plastic wrap and acrylic cover in place. These were removed after several months. Thereafter, he could occasionally be seen using the more traditional (and acceptable) scratching posts placed around the home for his housemates.

6

Sex-Related Problems

The Owl looked up to the stars above,
And sang to a small guitar,
"O lovely Pussy! O Pussy, my love,
What a beautiful Pussy you are."

—EDWARD LEAR (1812–1888)

SPAY YOUR FEMALE CAT

Sara was spayed at six months of age, the usual time that is recommended for female cats. I was wise enough to know that I could not remain objective and so a colleague was kind enough to do the honors. I stayed with her until she was under the anesthetic, and I was there when she woke up to comfort her the best I could. She came through with flying colors. So did I. It was not until several days later when I noticed the problem. She had begun to pull at the sutures on the neat little incision on her tummy. I trimmed the longer sutures and promised myself to place a light dressing on her incision if she was still bothering it by morning. Morning came along with the horror of discovering what Sara had been busy with all night. She had pulled out her sutures, every one, and the incision had opened up to reveal the underlying muscle wall. Thankfully, the sutures of the muscle were strong and buried in the tissue, but my little girl was in pain from the infection that had set in

and the self-inflicted trauma. Back into surgery she went to repair the incision. This time, she woke up to find herself wearing a most unfashionable plastic collar (called an Elizabethan collar, or "E collar," after the fashionable collars worn by ladies of Elizabethan times). Antibiotics took care of the rest, and she healed quickly and recovered without further incident. It took me a little while longer, however, to get over it.

Surgical sterilization is generally a safe and quick procedure that prevents many problems for the cat over a lifetime. My intent in sharing this story is simply to show that even veterinarians have problems with their own pets once in a while. The risk of infection and other complications associated with the spay surgery are actually quite low, despite the fact that my own cat had problems. The surgery known as "the spay" is the equivalent of hysterovariectomy in women. It involves surgical removal of both ovaries and the uterus. Hormone supplements are not prescribed for spayed pets because they do not have the same emotional or physical symptoms that are so familiar to women who enter postoperative or natural menopause.

In veterinary medicine it does not make sense to remove only the uterus and leave the ovaries or to perform tubal ligation. These options may be appropriate for women but do not apply to your cat. If only the uterus is removed and the ovaries remain (hysterectomy), the female cat will continue to go in and out of estrus as often as every three weeks; to attract males from miles around; to display unpleasant behavior such as urine marking, excessive vocalizing, and agitation; and to be at higher risk for a number of serious medical problems. Because the uterus is not a vital organ and serves no function without the ovaries, both ovaries and the uterus are normally removed.

Female cats should be neutered before the first estrus cycle or "heat" at around six months of age. If the ovaries, which produce estrogen, are removed before estral cycling begins, the incidence of mammary tumors (the equivalent of breast tumors in women) later in the pet's lifetime is significantly reduced. The risk jumps most dramatically after just one "heat." In cats, mammary tumors are aggressively malignant and difficult to control. Because the first "heat" is frequently mild and may go unnoticed, the surgery should be done by six months of age, when the average female cat will reach sexual maturity. Vaccination and general health status must be determined by your veterinarian prior to the procedure.

Despite the problems that can occasionally arise from any surgery, such as the infection and dehiscence that little Sara endured, neutering your cat will prevent many problems that are even more predictable and less responsive to treatment. In addition, it is essential to control the pet population. Neutering (a term that applies to both males and females) your pet will eliminate the dramatic hormonal surges of the sexual cycle and will make for a healthier and happier pet in the long term.

NEUTERING YOUR MALE CAT

Rafferty was a studly cat. He patrolled the house like a tiger in the jungle. When he walked, the ground shook. He was a muscular, beautiful, and well-behaved white cat, but his mom knew that his hormones could push him to do things that she would not appreciate. Her previous male cat had never been neutered and had sprayed in her house because her husband had balked at the idea of neutering his cat. He had stubbornly refused to grant permission for the surgery that might have prevented and reduced the cat's undesirable behavior. The cat sprayed in the house for five years until he finally went out one summer evening and did not return. Rafferty's mom was determined that history would not repeat itself. At eight months of age, Rafferty's urine had the distinct smell of tomcat pheromones. He had made several attempts to escape when the screen door opened, responding to some inaudible yet tantalizing melody that only he could hear. This time, his mom would be successful in rewriting the words to the song.

Sterilization of male cats is called castration or neutering (both terms apply to females as well). The surgical removal of both testicles is effective in preventing the birth of hundreds of kittens that a single male could potentially father in his lifetime. Testosterone, the sexual hormone produced by the testicles, is removed from circulation within hours of the surgery. Roaming and fighting are often eliminated, and most typically, male behaviors such as inappropriate urination and masturbation often decrease in the neutered male.

Vasectomy has little realistic application in veterinary medicine. Simply stopping the passage of sperm cannot resolve or prevent many of the problems that are solved by castration. Cats are not embarrassed by the absence of their testicles nor will they suffer any form of social humiliation. Concerned pet owners must be careful not to confuse what is best for their pet's long-term health and happiness with issues that pertain to human sexuality.

By definition, domesticated animals are selectively bred under human supervision. Whether or not a cat of either gender "enjoys" the sex act does not give him or her the right to reproduce. There is a recognized double standard between neutering males and females, in cats as well as in people. I suspect that pet owners who resist neutering their cats find it difficult to separate their own fears of castration from their responsibility as pet owners. Most men are deeply defensive of their own genitalia, and understandably so. Yet women are unnecessarily castrated, physically or emotionally, all over the world. Such latent and sometimes blatant social attitudes can be projected onto our pets. You yourself might experience a twinge of guilt or panic when it comes to neutering your cat regardless of whether it is male or female. Get over it! Consider the annual destruction of millions of unwanted pets—please, don't contribute to the problem!

MATERNAL REJECTION OF KITTENS

Lady Marmalade was a sassy, orange tabby who had escaped during her first heat and gotten herself in trouble. She belonged to an elderly couple who simply adored her, although they had been a bit forgetful about getting her spayed. She delivered five beautiful kittens under their box spring mattress. Two males looked just like her; one female was a calico with long hair; and the other two females looked like their mother but they had long hair, too. Lady M seemed unaffected by their charms, however, and rejected her litter on the third day. In fact, she was totally uninterested in them and ignored their hungry cries. Her concerned owners immediately brought her and her little family to the veterinary clinic for a checkup. The kittens were pronounced to be in fine health, but Lady M had a fever and an infected mammary gland. The kittens were fostered by one of the clinic's technicians and eventually placed in good homes. Their mother responded to antibiotics and fluids and was spayed several weeks later when her milk dried up.

Kittens are born at intervals of up to one hour but usually are delivered about every fifteen minutes to every half hour or so. Born deaf and blind, kittens rely on their mother for body heat, nourishment, hygiene, and protection from any source of danger. This is a long list of responsibilities for any mother, but it is multiplied by the number of babies in the litter and is magnified by the mother cat's maternal experience and inclination. There is much room for error.

Most animals, and cats are no exception, have an inborn set of directions on how to be successful parents. Male cats generally don't need to know more than how to mate because they rarely become active parents. In fact, males have been known to kill kittens fathered by another male in an effort to bring the mother back into heat more rapidly and to father their own litter with her. Although most reproductive behaviors are governed by inborn behavioral mechanisms, these may not be uniformly inherited in every cat. The maternal instinct seems to be relatively consistent in cats, compared to dogs for instance, but there are always exceptions. A young queen may panic, even try to run away, and appear totally unaware of how to deal with the sudden appearance of her kittens. An anxious or inexperienced queen may kill a kitten by severing the umbilical cord too closely to the kitten's body. Occasionally, kittens may be injured when their mother lies or steps on them. Instinct is fundamental to maternal success but learning plays a part, too. A queen who panics with her first litter might improve with experience. Unfortunately, the high cost of her education is funded by her first kittens. When maternal failure does not improve with experience, or if kittens are intentionally harmed, the individual should not be bred again.

Maternal incompetence can also be the result of illness. Like Lady Marmalade, the mother cat may have an infection of the mammary glands or uterus. Sick or weak babies may be singled out as poor investments of maternal energy and ignored by their mother. She will conserve her energy and concentrate instead on healthy offspring with higher survival potential. This behavior may seem cruel at first, but it is nature's way of ensuring the survival of those who are most likely to benefit. Lady Marmalade's owners acted appropriately by having her and her kittens examined without delay. They had not intended to let Lady M become pregnant to begin with and were eager to ensure her long-term health by having her spayed.

Female cats do not need to experience motherhood to "feel complete"; they just need to belong in a loving home. Cats do not need to have kittens in order to teach your children the facts of life. It is unlikely, for example, that your daughter will need to lick the placenta or sever the cord of her own babies! There are many teaching aids that are more valuable, such as books and videos, at your local library that deal directly with human reproduction. Unless your cat is a star and actively competing on the show cat circuit, the best thing you can do for her is to have her spayed. This will demonstrate to your children the most valuable of all parenting skills—responsibility and love.

ESTRUS AND COURTSHIP BEHAVIOR

Esmerelda was an eleven-month-old tortie point Himalayan who was keeping her owner awake all night. He complained that his cat was acting as if she was intoxicated, rolling around, purring for no particular reason, rubbing against every surface, following him everywhere, and vocalizing incessantly. This had been going on, every few weeks, for months. Recently, a group of cats had begun to congregate at the back porch. Some had begun to spray around the stairs leading to the back door. A few catfights had broken out briefly, but most of these outdoor cats simply passed through or sat quietly, as if they were waiting for something or someone. Esmerelda had tried several times to escape through the back door. Life was beginning to get very complicated for everyone.

To experienced cat people, Esmerelda's sexual behavior is obvious. Once her owner understood what was happening, Esmé was spayed and they both got some much-deserved rest. Heat, or estrus, is the receptive and fertile period of many female mammals. The average female cat reaches puberty around six months of age, although individuals can occasionally begin cycling a bit earlier or much later. Persian cats, for instance, tend to reach sexual maturity later compared to other breeds and may not cycle until they are over one year old. A queen's first estrus, or "silent heat," can be mild and go unnoticed by owners but is quite conspicuous to other cats. Pheromones in the estral queen's urine can cause free-roaming cats to come from miles around, responding to the sexual invitation in her chemical scent. When a female is in heat, she will be attractive to males and interested in mating with them. Males do not go into heat, only females do. Sexually mature male cats are ready and able to mate with any receptive estral female although both male and female cats can show individual preferences in the mates they choose.

Once she begins to cycle, the female cat comes into heat about every two to three weeks. Estrus lasts about one week or so. This means that she will have only one or two weeks of rest between each cycle! The breeding season is determined partly by the climate. In temperate zones, the breeding season is between January and November, with mating peaks in spring and fall. In cats, the egg follicles are not spontaneously released as they are in dogs and people. Instead, "provoked ovulation" requires sexual contact with the male and occurs twenty-four to forty-eight hours after intercourse. Spiny protrusions cover the surface of the tom's penis and irritate the vaginal mucosa during mating. This triggers a neural relay to the queen's brain, which, in turn, produces specific hormones to signal back to the ovaries to release mature eggs (ovulation) for fertilization. Provoked ovulation increases the cat's reproductive success by ensuring that mating always coincides with egg release. The gestation period for most pet cats is about sixty-one days, give or take a few, and *voilà*, kittens! Nursing mothers can and do come back into heat before weaning their litter and can become pregnant right away. Spaying will keep your kitty from the continually stressful cycle of estrus, pregnancy, estrus, pregnancy, estrus, pregnancy, potentially as often as every twelve weeks. Yikes! Please have her spayed; she'll thank you for it!

FALSE PREGNANCY

Chita was a show cat, a slinky Oriental Smoke. At six years old, she had produced several litters and was in heat again. Although she had not been bred, she had begun to act as if she were pregnant. Her mammary glands were enlarged and droplets of milk formed at her nipples. She had collected her owner's socks into a pile in the back of the closet and hovered restlessly over them. Her owner had kept two of Chita's daughters from previous litters and had not intended to breed Chita again. Chita's owner was concerned that the cat was jealous because one of her daughter's was expecting her first litter and the other daughter was in heat, too.

False pregnancy (*pseudopregnancy* or *pseudocyesis*) is associated with a kind of hormonal rut that occurs after the end of true estrus. It is more common in female dogs but is not unknown in cats. The pseudopregnant female develops physical signs of pregnancy, such as lactating mammary glands, an expanding abdomen, and maternal behaviors associated with the delivery and care of surrogate kittens (like Chita's socks). She may be restless and anxious. Although her symptoms will usually resolve without treatment, it can be a stressful time for the pseudopregnant cat and her owners. If she is not a valuable breeder or if she suffers from repeated or severe episodes of false pregnancy, it is best to have her spayed.

False pregnancy has nothing to do with a female's jealousy of another cat or her secret desire to reproduce. Pseudopregnancy may be an adaptation that allows nonpregnant females living in a group to cooperate in rearing each other's young. By acting as surrogate mothers to babies produced by other females, they may benefit by practicing maternal behaviors and by having the favor returned when it is their time to deliver. Females living in a group, like Chita and her daughters, may synchronize their estrus cycles (this phenomenon is noted in women as well), and this may facilitate the cooperative aspect of female reproductive behaviors. Chita was spayed and began to enjoy her retirement. She'd had her career and was tired of traveling from show to show. She kept a watchful eye on her grandkittens as she lounged peacefully nearby. It was her daughters' turns now.

MASTURBATION IN MALE CATS

Lynx was approximately a year old when he was acquired as a stray in the West Indies. He was neutered and brought back to the United States several months later. He soon developed a "romantic interest" in a stuffed toy cat that his owner had given him. He also began to spray urine against the walls inside his new home. His owner was a single woman who admired Lynx for his independent spirit and did not want to see him unhappy. She was at once amused and appalled by his sexual behavior but more appalled than amused by his spraying. Every night when she came home from work, Lynx would mount his stuffed kitty from behind, grasp the nape of its neck with his teeth, and rub rhythmically for about two minutes. His owner had tried, just once, to stop him by hiding the stuffed cat. She told me, however, that he seemed so unhappy and became so agitated in his search for his sex toy that she relented and never removed it again. I ordered some blood tests and determined that Lynx had not been completely castrated. His blood testosterone level confirmed that he still had productive testicular tissue.

Sexual mounting is normally directed by a male toward a receptive estral female. In the absence of a willing mate, a sexually motivated male may masturbate with another available replacement, such as a blanket or soft, fuzzy, stuffed animal. The surrogate object then becomes a habitual trigger for the cat. Early intervention, such as distracting the cat and directing his attention toward an alternative activity, is helpful. If a target object is identified, early removal may be enough to halt the progression of the behavior, although the cat may simply find another object of his desire.

Masturbation is occasionally reported in male cats, although most male cats, intact or neutered, do not masturbate. It is more likely to be seen in individuals who have not been castrated or are neutered later. In sexually experienced individuals, masturbation generally will fade or disappear following castration. It is uncommon to find a case of incomplete castration. Lynx's case was an exception but also very interesting because of the direct link between circulating sexual hormones and his sexual behavior. His owner was entertained, to a degree, by his antics and had become a secondary trigger to his persistent sexual displays. He had become conditioned to masturbate when she returned home from work, perhaps because she paid attention to him when he did so. We placed Lynx on psychoactive medication and added another litter box. Lynx stopped spraying, and surgery to locate and remove the remaining source of testosterone was successful. Once he was neutered, we continued medication for several more weeks. Lynx continued to "date" his stuffed toy on an intermittent basis. Both he and his owner were happy with the arrangement!

MALE SEXUAL BEHAVIOR DIRECTED TOWARD
THE OWNER

Albert was a macho, brown tabby boy who mounted and masturbated on his owner's arm. She was unsure of how to respond and did not want to traumatize him despite the fact that he would bite her and dig his claws into her arm during his nightly "performances." During the visit, we briefly talked about her interesting work. She mentioned that she was frustrated by an overbearing supervisor at work who undermined her self-confidence at every turn and took credit for work that she had done. Albert's mom needed to be reminded that she was in control of setting boundaries at home and at work. She realized that Albert was taking advantage of her, as was her boss, because she allowed them to do so. I made some simple suggestions for her to follow.

Cats masturbate infrequently compared to the frequencies reported in other species. I suspect this is partly because it is underreported. It is unusual for cats to select a person as their love interest. Albert was his mom's only pet, and she indulged him in many ways. It is possible that Albert was imprinted on her and truly related to her as he would to any receptive female cat. His behavior was of concern, however, because his sexual aggressiveness had become increasingly rough on her skin. She called me when she was no longer comfortable with the injuries he inflicted.

Observers may initially find their cat's sexual display entertaining, somewhat comical, and a bit intriguing in a voyeuristic sort of way. The behavior may be unintentionally encouraged when an owner, like Albert's mom, tolerates the behavior by remaining passive. In other cases, such as Lynx's (above), the cat may be encouraged by the owner's attention. Whether the owner contributes to the cat's performance or not, each act of masturbation is so rewarding to the cat that it is a self-reinforcing pattern. In rare instances masturbation in pets can become such an obsession that psychoactive medication, added to a program of behavior modification as prescribed by a veterinary behaviorist, are required to control it. Fortunately, Albert's treatment program was relatively simple. When Albert came for her, his owner assertively pushed him away and said, "No!" Then she invited him to play with his favorite toys. Empowered by this small conquest, she was ready to assert herself at work. Her supervisor was surprised by her unprecedented show of strength, and he eventually was transferred to another department when Albert's mom was promoted to his position!

7

Miscellaneous Cat Tales

Cats and monkeys, monkeys and cats—all human life is there.

—HENRY JAMES (1843–1916)

THE SUPERSTITION OF BLACK CATS

The animal keeper lumbered down the corridor of the small animal clinic at the veterinary school where I was halfway through my veterinary studies. In subdued horror, I saw a tiny black kitten dangling in his grubby hand; his thumb and forefinger encircled her neck. "What are you doing with that kitten?" I half demanded. "She was dropped off to be put to sleep," he responded with a careless shrug. The terrified little thing could not have been older than three weeks. When I asked him to explain, he replied, "It's just a black kitten." His tone was matter of fact, as if I should have known and understood. Her life was inconsequential; she was disposable. All I could think of was to save her from the prejudice and ignorance that would have snuffed out her fragile existence. So I took her home for the weekend, determined to find her a home that would shelter her from a heartless world. And so I did. Her weekend with me has lasted over twenty-two years.

Cats were adored as sacred pets and as gods in ancient Egypt, yet their popularity declined thereafter, although it is not clear why. By the Middle Ages, superstitions of all kinds ruled public thought in Europe. Cats had become symbols of satanic practice and witchcraft.

In particular, black cats were associated with demons and evil spirits. Anyone seen befriending a cat could be persecuted. Many of these people, predominantly women, were accused of practicing "the black arts" because of any association with cats. Ironically, cats were tortured and sacrificed at a time when their talents could have saved millions of people killed by plague, which was disseminated by rodents.

Medieval superstition is alive and well. Amazingly, many people still believe that black cats are unlucky. Some folks still cringe when a black cat crosses their path. Black kittens may be culled from the litter just as Sara was. Fortune or misfortune, luck is a force that seems to affect every aspect of our lives. I believe that luck is also, in part, what you make it. The day Sara crossed my path was one of my luckiest days. And if you have welcomed a black cat into your life, you are, indeed, lucky.

A CAT'S WHISKERS

A cat's whiskers are a marvel of nature. Each one feels like a thin plastic strand, but it is flexible and strong. Thickened at the base where the hair follicle anchors it to the skin, each whisker tapers to a point. Hershey's whiskers are white. Just before he yawns, he moves them forward. When I scratch him in just the right place, he squishes his nose a bit, and his whiskers stand straight out. Sara's whiskers blend with her glossy blackness. Gracie's whiskers are very long and white on both the white and the gray sides of her face. Teddi's delicate white whiskers curve slightly to frame her pretty porcelain face. Some cats have almost curly whiskers and others have wavy ones. Have you admired your cat's whiskers lately?

Whiskers *(vibrissae)* are a wonderful invention. Long, specialized facial hairs on either side of the upper lip are called the *mystacial vibrissae.* These are unique tactile hairs that are sensitive to displacement and help the cat during hunting. Feline vision is actually not very clear at close range (less than a foot or so), and the facial whiskers help cats to sense what is in front of their noses! There is a myth that cutting a cat's whiskers will make a cat blind. This is not true; however, it will limit an important accessory organ and could present a handicap of sorts. The facial whiskers are somewhat mobile and can be moved slightly forward or flattened against the face. They are part of what makes a cat's facial expressions more appealing to us and probably are used in social communication between cats as well.

The mystacials are not the only tactile hairs on a cat's body, although they are certainly the largest. Vibrissae are also located above the eyes *(superciliary vibrissae),* under the chin (the *interrampal tuft*), and on the cheeks *(genal vibrissae).* The *carpal hairs* are located on the foreleg just above the paws and are specifically adapted to detect movement and objects near the forelegs, which undoubtedly aids in predatory behavior and movement in dim light.

Whiskers are periodically shed and replaced with a new shaft, just like other hairs. Each whisker is associated with hair follicle receptors that send information about the cat's intimate space directly to the brain. The cat can then use this information during a catfight for self-defense or to pounce on a mouse or to blink the eyes when that little ball you threw bounces by! Regardless of their length, color, or texture, whiskers on kittens are certainly one of my favorite things.

THE CATNIP RESPONSE

Three of my four cats are catnip afficionados. Sara is the exception. She sniffed it, walked away, and has not shown any further interest since then. In fact, she seems to actively avoid it. Catnip is not lost on Hershey, Gracie, or Teddi. Once a week or so, I sprinkle a pinch of the dried leaves at three separate sites and stand back. They eagerly trot in and proceed to sniff, lick and roll, chew and roll, roll and stretch, and seem altogether very pleased. I wonder whether cats enjoy catnip more than their owners enjoy watching their cats react to it!

Contact with the catnip plant *(Nepeta cataria),* a plant native to North America, causes a peculiar reaction called the catnip response in most members of the cat family. Dried catnip leaves smell like alfalfa and fresh catnip leaves have a mintlike scent, but both can trigger the response in sensitive cats. A minority of pet cats is not affected by catnip, which suggests a genetic component. Interestingly, some cats (like Sara) appear to avoid it, even though the catnip reaction seems pleasurable to most reactive cats.

Nepetalactone is the primary active compound in catnip. Although catnip is not toxic to pets, nepetalactone is chemically similar to the hallucinogenic compound found in marijuana. The catnip response lasts an average of about six minutes but is at its peak for just two to three minutes. The sequence begins with initial investigation and oral contact. This is followed by grasping and kicking, rolling, and abandonment. Adult and young adult cats are more sensitive to catnip than very young or old cats. The catnip reaction is similar in some regards to the sexual response of female cats but also contains some predatory and playful elements. For example, pawing, clasping, kicking, and rolling are hunting and play behaviors that are also common to the catnip response. It is unclear how nepetalactone exerts its effect on the feline nervous system.

Dried catnip is commonly sold as a cat treat, but it is by no means a necessity for feline physical or mental health. Catnip has become an important marketing tool and is commonly incorporated into cat toys and applied to the surface of scratching posts. Fresh catnip can also be grown indoors to provide an attractive alternative to the undesirable destruction of ornamental houseplants. Because it is not clear how catnip exerts its action, and whether or not there is any adverse effect associated with frequent and long-term use, I reserve it as a special treat for my own pets. Somehow depriving my cats of catnip altogether would be like depriving myself of chocolate. I could live without it if I had to, but . . . life is short!

PURRING

According to her owners, Marcella was a spoiled little kitty. She was a three-month-old Scottish Fold kitten and had been living with them for more than a month. Marcella ate well, played often, cuddled frequently, and slept soundly. But she did not purr. Did this mean Marcella was not happy, her owners worried. Was something wrong?

Purring must surely be one of the most splendid sounds of life. I wonder if angels purr, too. The purr is a true vocalization because the sound is generated by the vocal apparatus. In fact, we know that purring is made by the alternating contractions of the glottis and laryngeal muscles, and the diaphragm. Every cat has his or her own style and volume of purring. . . . Our littlest cat Teddi is the one with the loudest purr. Big boy Hershey's purr is a low, inconspicuous rumble, but little Teddi's purr vibrates every cell in her being. If someone made a recording of my cats while they purred, I am certain I could identify them by the distinctive sound made by each one.

A purring cat is signaling contentment. For example, relaxed and comfortable cats purr when they feel drowsy or just plain cozy. Purring is associated with positive social contact with people and with other cats. I have also heard my Teddi purring when she cuddles with her pal Georgyanna, our Boston Terrier (when they take a moment to rest between bouts of playfully chomping on each other). But purring does not always mean that all is well. Purring may also be linked with anxiety and pain. An injured or sick cat may purr as an anxiety-releasing mechanism and will, of course, exhibit other physical and behavioral symptoms associated with illness. It may be similar to whistling when you are nervous or giggling when you are afraid.

So why did Marcella not purr? Upper respiratory infections in kittens can affect the vocal apparatus and cause a sort of laryngitis. Sneezing, sinus congestion, and other symptoms may be obvious, but they can be subclinical, too. In most cases inflammation subsequent to an upper respiratory infection is temporary, and the ability to purr returns. I suspected this was why Marcella was silent and suggested that her owners be patient awhile longer. Several weeks later Marcella's owners confirmed their kitten's purr had become their favorite lullaby. Now that's a happy way to end the day, don't you agree?

KNEADING

Leo was a three-month-old Maine Coon who was driving his owner crazy. Every night he nuzzled into her neck and began to knead. He extended and retracted his sharp kitten claws rhythmically into her skin, again and again. He purred and kneaded, purred and kneaded. She felt like a pin cushion but was afraid to do or say anything for fear of traumatizing her little boy. She needed to stop being so kneaded. Could I make him stop?

Leo's mom had always had the ability to shape her cat's behaviors. All she had to do was to say, "No!" or, "Ow!" and gently push him away. Some kittens can be quite persistent about this, but if you insist and remain steadfast, they will eventually learn not to knead or at least to redirect toward another surface. Kneading is a normal kitten behavior. Nursing kittens knead to massage the queen's mammary gland and provoke milk letdown. Kneading persists in many older kittens and into adulthood and becomes associated with contentment and relaxation. It is accompanied by enthusiastic purring and, sometimes, drooling.

It is completely acceptable to set limits to your cat's behavior. Your car needs to know what makes you happy or not, but how will he know if you don't tell him? Discouraging kneading does not traumatize a kitten if you do it kindly. Leo eventually stopped kneading into his owner's neck, but she didn't mind when he did it to the pillow next to her. As he grew, he gave up kneading but not needing her. Apparently, it was a mutual thing. She soon found she couldn't fall asleep without Leo purring his pussycat lullaby.

CATS AND WATER

As soon as she hears the shower water running, Teddi appears. She loves the water. She sits in the stream and splashes around, seemingly unconcerned by the tradition that, as a cat, she is not supposed to like water. I haven't shattered her obvious pleasure by reminding her that she is a kitten and not a puppy. She is happy, but my rubber ducky is miffed. I have not needed my little yellow duck for bathing companionship since Teddi arrived!

I don't really know where the myth about cats and water arose. Well, it certainly is true that most cats don't seek water the way a Golden Retriever would, but many cats have a sort of fascination with water. Take your cat, for instance. Does she hop up on the counter next to the sink to play with the water streaming from the faucet, or does she prefer catching droplets from a dripping faucet? Does she stick a paw in the stream and lick the water from her toes, or does she stick her face under the drip drip drip and try to catch the droplets as they fall? Does your cat sit on the edge of the tub and watch as your bubble bath fizzes around you? Does he watch the water swirl around and around in the toilet bowl after you flush? Teddi has actually fallen in, and we have to keep the lids carefully closed, which is yet another example of pet proofing your home! I've known cats that would only drink fresh water running from the tap. Is this because it mimics a natural source of water or perhaps these cats just find running water more entertaining?

Cats have not evolved to pursue aquatic prey and would never be considered amphibious, but they can swim if they have to. Cats can hunt in water if they need to; just watch your cat staring at your goldfish (and please keep the lid securely over the tank top!). Teddi goes out of her way to drink from a little tabletop fountain with cherubs on it (she can't reach the one laden with gargoyles in my husband's office). But we don't let Teddi in the shower anymore. She developed a bladder infection from sitting in the water for so long every day. Now she sits outside the shower door and tries to catch the water as it trickles down the glass. I guess it's still me and my rubber ducky in the shower after all.

DEAFNESS IN KITTENS AND YOUNG ADULT CATS

Alba was a seven-month-old domestic shorthair. She was a pretty white kitten with bright blue eyes. Her owners had contacted me with the complaint that she seemed to ignore them and was easily startled. Things had worsened since they moved to a new home. When we met during a house call, I noticed that Alba meowed unusually loudly for such a little bit of a thing. She did not react when I clapped my hands behind her head, and her ears did not perk up when I softly called her name. Alba's owners were accurate in their observations. She did indeed live in her own little world; but she was not behaving maliciously, and the barriers were not self-imposed. . . .

Deafness is not common in cats, but it is not unusual either. Certain forms of deafness are inherited. In people with Wartenburg's syndrome, for example, a streak of white hair near or around the face is a recognized marker for inherited deafness. Similarly, white cats with one or both blue eyes are more likely to inherit partial or total deafness. Kittens with congenitally impaired hearing tend to vocalize more loudly, compared to hearing kittens, by the time they are three or four months old. Their voices may also be lower in pitch. These kittens may seem more skittish when someone enters the room and may be more easily startled. Hearing-impaired kittens eventually learn to rely on other senses, such as smell and vibration, to detect their owner's approach, but this takes time.

Partial deafness in cats is probably more common than a total inability to hear. Some white kittens may be deaf only along a certain range of sound. However, partial deafness may progress, and some kittens lose whatever hearing they have, as they grow older. Not all deafness is genetic in origin. Some cats are born deaf because their mothers were infected with certain viruses in a critical stage of their development. Deafness can also result from ear infections in kittens or even in adults. And in some individuals, a reduction in acoustic sensitivity is part of aging (see chapter 13, "Golden-Age Cats"). The ability to hear is difficult to assess in animals without referral to a veterinary neurologist who will have special equipment to evaluate your cat's hearing if an accurate diagnosis is required.

When Alba's owners understood her problem, her behavior became less objectionable. They learned to get her attention by tapping on the floor or lightly scratching on the pillow where she slept. Alba got better at compensating for her inability to hear and became less nervous as she acclimated to her new surroundings. I reminded her owners that it is even more important to keep handicapped pets indoors, and they heartily agreed!

VOCAL COMMUNICATION IN CATS

Gracie always says "hello" to me when she senses that I am nearby. She says, "rrrrrrrppp!" and raises her tail as if she were waving her hand. This chirr (or chirrup) is a lovely sound made by cats in greeting. Next to purring, it is one of the loveliest sounds I know. Gracie's vision is severely limited, and I suspect her open greeting is exaggerated defensively to clearly signal her friendly approach. My other cats do not chirr to greet me, although Teddi occasionally does, perhaps because they are less vocal overall or because they can rely on an exchange of clearly visible signals. Or maybe they just have less to say?

Cats have been accredited with more than a dozen types of vocalizations, which are considerably more than the six vocal patterns identified in dogs. The fact that their repertoire is so varied is another indication of just how social cats are. The relatively complex vocal repertoire of cats implies that communication is paramount. Acoustic communication is associated with animals who are more active in dim light, are social as adults, and have extended maternal care. Sound is an effective means of communication because it travels over long distances and can be projected in many directions without betraying the caller's precise location, which is vital if you are vulnerable. Acoustic signals can be sent rapidly, compared to odor markers, for example, and are effective any time of day or night.

Feline vocalizations are categorized into two main groups: sounds made with an open mouth, and those made with a closed mouth. Closed-mouth sounds include the purr and the chirr or chirrup, which is made in greeting. Open-mouth sounds are further divided into two groups: Sounds that are made with an open mouth throughout, and sounds that begin with an open mouth and end with a closed mouth. Exclusively open-mouth sounds include the growl, snarl, hiss, spit, yowl (or caterwaul), and the shriek that is related to pain or fear. Open-mouth signals that end with a closed mouth include the ever-popular meow, which is used in greeting. The meow has three versions. A cat can emit a short or long meow, but there is also a silent version where the mouth is opened but no sound is made. This soundless call may be a visual display, but the functions of the meow call are unclear overall. It is often given as a greeting, but it may be heard as an attention-seeking display or as a contact-seeking or distress call. Another subgroup of open/closed-mouth vocalization includes the distinctive sexual calls made by males and females during courtship and sexual signaling.

Some cats seem more vocal than others. A physical handicap such as blindness or deafness, for example, may impact the cat's ability to detect and convey important social signals. The feline voice identifies the individual. Owners of multiple cats often learn, as I have, to identify the calls and distinctive vocal traits associated with each pet. Interestingly, kittens learn to recognize their own mother's voice from that of another female as early as twenty-one days of age. Voice recognition must indeed be a valuable asset in feline social communication. The feline voice also identifies the breed, particularly true for Siamese cats. Although not all Siamese grow up to be as chatty as their reputation would lead you to believe, and many non-Siamese cats can be very vocal, Siamese do indeed have a distinctive quality to their voices that is unmatched in the cat world.

MOVING TO A NEW HOME WITH YOUR CAT

Tigger was upset. The big, orange tabby paced restlessly up and down the alleys made by several growing stacks of boxes. He watched anxiously as his owners packed up their belongings. Their home, his home, no longer looked or felt like his comfortable castle. Tigger began to urinate on the bath mat more and more frequently as home seemed less and less his own. His owners knew that it was best to resolve the problem before they moved into their new home and called me for help. It was clear that Tigger was responding to the physical transformation of his domain, but he was also mirroring the stress that was plain to see on the faces of his owners. Moving is a nightmare for every member of the family, and that certainly includes the pets.

Moving to a new home is an emotional and physical upheaval for you and for your cat. Your pet senses your increasing anxiety as moving day approaches. Your home is your cat's core territory, and any changes will impact your cat's sense of security. Packing, stacking boxes, and re-arranging furniture are as disturbing to your cat as they are to you. Misbehavior is a common symptom of anxiety in cats. Not surprisingly, moving is often associated with a variety of behavior problems. In the period preceding and following a move, anxious cats may mark their territories with deposits of urine or stool. An outdoor cat will likely be challenged by an entire set of new rivals when released in the new territory. It is not uncommon for your cat's sleeping patterns to be disrupted until he relaxes in his new home.

Moving day is a major event in everyone's existence. Your cat may be confined in a cage during travel by car, rail, air, or sea. He has been plucked from a familiar place he called his own and launched into motion toward an unknown destination. Moving day may be less stressful for both you and your cat if he is shielded from the immediate chaos of the move. Ask a friend to care for your cat for the day or board your pet at the veterinary clinic or at a boarding facility. At the very least, confine your cat to a comfortable carrier in a quiet corner of the house before you begin to load up the car or moving van.

When you arrive at your destination, keep your cat in one room or a pet carrier to avoid injury and to prevent escape while you are distracted with the arrival of heavy boxes and furniture. Confine the cat to a comfortable room, such as your bedroom, for the first few days before he or she is allowed to explore the rest of your home for brief periods. This way your cat will not be overwhelmed by his new territory and can adjust more gradually. Set up your kitty's favorite toys and bed and visit often while you unpack. Place the litter box in a quiet corner of this room. You can move it to a more ideal location later on if you like or add a second box elsewhere. Eventually, it will be important to place the box in a spot that most resembles its location in your previous home. Do not discard the old litter box when you move. Your cat has enough change to deal with right now. Make sure your cat knows where to find food and water and avoid placing the cat's bowls near the litter box. Keep the same feeding schedule. Familiarity and continuity are stabilizing factors that comfort us all during periods of transition.

You can minimize the trauma of relocation. Continuity in routine, food, and familiar objects will help your cat feel more secure. Take frequent breaks during packing and unpacking to spend time with your cat. Just a few moments here and there to play with or pet your cat will provide much needed contact. Besides, it will be a good stress release for you both! A little extra praise and attention will go a long way to encourage your cat's adjustment. The mayhem is temporary, and good times will return. As long as your kitty is eating well and using the box, you know things are all right. And when normal playing, grooming, and purring return, you will know that your cat is feeling right at home.

CAR TRAVEL TIPS FOR CATS

Sara hyperventilates and Gracie just cuddles on my lap. Hershey tries to disappear, and Teddi will sit on the dashboard to help navigate if we let her. Cats in cars can make wonderful travel companions, or they can make the miles stretch on endlessly in your own private hell on wheels. Countless cat owners have described to me how their placid pets turn into frothing, demented whirlwinds during road trips. Some cats yowl and drool for hours even when confined to a comfortable carrier. Do you suppose that some cats are simply reacting to the way we drive? Hmmm . . .

Every cat has individual coping mechanisms in a frightening and unfamiliar context and car travel is no exception. Some are happy just to be near you. Others panic the moment that carrier comes out of storage. Feeling helpless and out of control is a sensation with which none of us is comfortable. Your cat's fear of car travel can be broken down into several component fears. First, there is the fear of leaving the security of your home. Then there is the fear related to the car itself. The scent of exhaust, the vibration of the motor and the vehicle in motion, and confinement in a restricted space are all part of the negative experience. Your cat may also develop a fear of the cat carrier if it only comes out of storage just before she is unceremoniously shoved into it. The anticipation of an unknown destination is bad enough; however, the terror of an anticipated destination may be worse. If your cat only goes for car rides when she travels to the veterinary clinic, for instance, it is easy to understand that car travel can become a powerful negative in her life. It is normal for young animals to instinctively fear unfamiliar situations. However, gradual exposure to a car ride for frequent short trips will help your cat associate car travel with a less horrific outcome. Here are some tips to help your cat feel more comfortable "on the road again . . .":

- Leave the cat carrier out rather than storing it away or bring it out weeks before a planned trip and leave the door open; your pet will grow accustomed to seeing it, perhaps playing or sleeping in it, too, and it will no longer signal impending doom;
- Feed your cat in the crate but do not close the door; when the cat feels relaxed entering the crate, close the door briefly and open it after a few moments; release your cat *before* any anxious meows or other worried behaviors begin;
- Next, bring the cat in the carrier to the car and spend a few minutes a day (for at least a week) with your cat just sitting in your parked car in your driveway with the ignition off; when the cat seems calm and relatively unaffected, offer a special food treat that the cat only gets when you are in the car;

- Turn on the ignition but go nowhere; it may take another few days for your cat to get used to the sound of the engine; then, when your fraidy cat remains unruffled by the motor, take a short trip around the block and go home!
- Go on gradually longer trips as often as you can (the more frequently the better), and your cat will be a fine travel companion in no time!

LONG-DISTANCE TRAVEL WITH YOUR CAT

Fiona, a beautiful Chartreuse with copper eyes, was not a good traveler despite the fact that she had made many trips with her folks to their weekend cottage in the mountains of Vermont. She thrashed around in the little crate and meowed as she frantically clawed at anything she could reach through the bars of her carrier. Fiona's owners were preparing to move to another state and wondered whether it would be appropriate to sedate her during the trip. In the past her veterinarian had prescribed tranquilizers, but Fiona seemed unaffected at a lower dose, and the higher dose turned her into a zombie for two days. Fiona's hysteria was distracting to her owners and had nearly caused several car accidents. They had already abandoned bringing her to the cottage she enjoyed so much and left her alone on the weekend instead. Fiona's troubles were impacting the quality of everyone's life.

Fiona's story is pretty typical of cats who are phobic to travel. Their fearful response is clearly out of proportion to the actual danger presented by car travel. It is this excessive response that characterizes the phobia to travel. Traditionally, most veterinarians have prescribed sedatives (the phenothiazine tranquilizer acetylpromazine has been most popular), but this is not the ideal solution. Indeed, many cats are not helped by medication or are difficult to pill. Most cat owners would prefer not to medicate their pets if an alternative solution could resolve the problem for the long term.

The American Veterinary Medical Association no longer recommends routine sedation of pets for travel. Some cats can be quite sensitive to medication, and the margin of safety for the prescribed dose of tranquilizers can be slim. Underlying medical problems can be exacerbated by the stress of travel, and tranquilizers are not advised for pets with many preexisting (or undiagnosed) ailments. In most cases frightened animals are best left to their own devices. Sedation numbs the senses and dulls important coping mechanisms that have evolved to support cats through stressful events. Your cat is almost certainly better off without medication unless the benefit of medication clearly outweighs the risk.

The step-by-step description of how to desensitize your cat to the carrier and to car travel outlined above is relevant here as well. You will all benefit from methodically working with your cat in advance of an upcoming trip or cross-country move. If absolutely necessary, your veterinarian can prescribe a sedative or tranquilizer to calm your pet for car travel. I prefer to use specific antianxiety medication in such cases. However, it would be wise to have your veterinarian thoroughly examine your cat and draw a blood sample to test for any latent disease before any psychoactive drug is prescribed. If you have made the decision to sedate your cat for travel, I often recommend doing a trial of the medication in advance of your departure day. This will allow you to verify the dose that your cat will need and to screen for any adverse effects that might appear. If you are planning to travel by air, check with the airlines for their specific requirements for carrier dimension and special documents. This information may help to direct your choice of airline. It would be ideal if your cat could travel in the cabin under the seat in front of you (which some airlines allow), but airlines may require pets to travel in the baggage compartment. Make certain that this compartment is climate controlled, that personnel are trained to handle pets in carriers, and that the airline's safety record is good. Air travel is a risk even for the healthiest pet.

Fiona's parents knew in advance that they would be driving cross-country to their new home and worked diligently with her to reduce her phobic response. She improved significantly within several weeks. In the process they discovered that a part of Fiona's panic was eliminated if she was removed from the carrier. Most cats feel more secure in a carrier because it resembles a sheltered nook they might seek on their own. However, every cat is an individual. I suggested that they place her in a soft-sided gym bag made comfy with a soft blanket and her owner's old flannel shirt. The bag was left slightly unzipped for good ventilation and Fiona felt sheltered rather than suffocated. Several months later her owners reported that Fiona had breezed through the trip without sedatives and was adapting well to life on the West Coast.

8

Secrets of Pet Selection

When all candles be out, all cats be gray.

—JOHN HEYWOOD (1497–1580)

HOW I FOUND MY CATS

Like many cat owners, I suspect that my cats were somehow destined to live with me. Jonathan was a barn cat who was discovered during my days as a veterinary student. Sara came shortly after, when I rescued her at only a few weeks of age from being unnecessarily destroyed. After Jonathan died, it took some time to recover, and so Sara and I enjoyed each other's company for a while. One spring day I learned about a stray's litter. A friend of mine had asked me to find a new kitten, so I went to check them out. I came home with two kittens and kept one of them, Hershey, who grew into the manliest man cat I have ever known. Hershey, however, began tormenting Sara, who is fifteen years his senior, and I realized that he needed a playmate closer to his own age. A patient of mine had brought in her female cat for examination prior to being spayed, and her recent litter of kittens came along for the ride. I fell in love with Gracie, and although she had been promised to someone else, her owner told me that she could not have a better home than with me. Teddi was the teeniest, tiniest runt of a litter that had been brought in by a pet store owner for vaccinations. I convinced him that she needed a bit of extra attention, which, of course, I would gladly provide! So far, all my kitties have found me when I was open to finding them. If you are open to the opportunities that are placed before you, your destiny will unfold as it should. You will know your cat when you see him, unless he sees you first!

A lthough I freely admit that selecting a pet is a very emotional experience, it must always be tempered with an underlying sense of practicality and sense of self. As cat lovers, we will be tempted by many beautiful kittens (aren't they all?) and charming adult cats in need of a loving home. But before you act on your emotions, you must know your limitations. Recognize that a pet's appearance is just like gift wrap—it may be pretty but what really counts is what's inside the box!

Consider these two fundamental guidelines before claiming your new companion:

1. Are you (a) *willing* and (b) *able* to provide love, quality attention, shelter, food, and regular veterinary care for this new kitty? Are you too busy at work or too distracted at home to invest the necessary time, energy, and finances in raising a new pet? What about the long-term care for this creature? Consider your emotional and practical limitations now and in ten or twenty years from now.

2. What is the *general health and basic temperament* of the cat that has caught your eye? It is understandable that the cat's appearance is what will attract you at first. We each have preferences for a particular coat color, eye color, or hair length. However, these should be preliminary criteria that are overridden by problems related to health or temperament.

Before adopting a cat or kitten, consider:

MOTIVATION. Is this a whim or a choice? Have you been thinking of getting a cat for a while? Never adopt a pet as a frivolous or spontaneous gesture . . . you will both suffer for it.

FINANCIAL INVESTMENT. Consider the short-term cost of neutering and the vaccination series for kittens; in the long-term, adult cats will require annual vaccines and veterinary care for any problems that may arise.

HOUSEHOLD MODIFICATIONS. The addition of a new cat might require you to secure fragile objects, place screens on windows to prevent escape, tolerate occasional breaks in litter box use, rearrange your house plants, hide electric cords, keep some rooms closed.

ADULT SIZE. Although variation in size is not as marked as between dog breeds, cats do range in size from small (less than ten pounds), medium (ten to fifteen pounds), and large (over sixteen pounds); size is a function of gender (females are generally smaller), breed, health, and luck of the draw. It may be difficult to predict the exact adult size of individual cats, although you can safely assume that large cat breeds, such as the Maine Coon and the newly introduced Siberian, will produce big kitties.

BREED CHARACTERISTICS. Most of the sweeping generalities concerning the behavior and temperament of cat breeds should be taken with a grain of salt; many of these reports have yet to be proven and there are more similarities than differences between breeds. Some breed traits are obvious: physical attributes such as hair length, average adult size, and overall activity level are breed related. There are many breeds that closely resemble each other (e.g., Chartreuse and blue British Shorthair).

GENDER. Males tend to be larger and rowdier than females of any given breed; of course, there are many large and rowdy girls out there, but boys will be boys. Male kittens often play more roughly, so be prepared to invest in some serious playtime to satisfy him. Inappropriate elimination is more common among males than in females, but most cats of either sex happily use their box.

AGE. There are advantages and disadvantages to adopting an adult pet rather than a kitten. Kittens are easily adopted so you will be doing a good deed by taking home an adult. An adult cat is generally not as active as a young kitten and should make a calmer companion; kittens demand more time and attention, but you get to watch them grow up and enjoy their silly antics. You may not know if an adult cat has any bad habits, but a kitten can develop these along the way, too. Even if a cat misbehaved in his or her last home, the cat may be perfect in yours.

SIZE OF YOUR HOME. This is a factor that is most important for indoor cats, of course; the square footage of your home is important because it determines the density of your feline population. Some cats can be very territorial and do not tolerate crowding. As a general rule of thumb (and this depends on the size of the rooms and the temperament of individual cats in the mix), you can have as many as two cats for every floor in your home. Another guideline is not to exceed one cat for every bedroom plus one (e.g., a one-room apartment should hold two cats comfortably if they get along and if it is roomy; a three-bedroom home should not have more than four cats).

DAILY MAINTENANCE. Consider the time and energy that must be devoted to your cat; interaction in the form of play, grooming, more play, and cuddling will detract from other responsibilities, but your pet must have consistent quality attention.

MUNICIPAL AND STATE REGULATIONS. Speak with local officials and your veterinarian regarding any special licenses, the maximum number of pets allowed in a household, required vaccines, additionally recommended vaccines, wildlife that might affect your outdoor cat, and current epidemics in the outdoor feline population. Life will be simpler if you keep your new cat inside.

YOUR PREVIOUS EXPERIENCE WITH CATS. Every new cat is a new experience. Your last cat might have required little attention, but this one may be more social or simply more assertive; of course, the reverse could be true!

A SECONDARY CARETAKER. Think about who will take care of your cat(s) if you go on vacation or become ill; this might influence the number of kitties you collect or how long you feel comfortable being away from home. Speak with friends, family, veterinary staff, or professional pet sitters for preliminary impressions on who would be available if necessary.

HEALTH STATUS. Make an *immediate* appointment with your veterinarian to have your new cat examined; it is wise to do this before you even bring your cat home, especially if you have other cats. Protect your resident cats from problems harbored by the new kitty, such as external and internal parasites (worms, fleas, ear mites) and transmissible feline diseases (e.g., upper respiratory infections, the feline leukemias). Some dormant problems may not be immediately evident, but at least you can identify anything obvious. If a serious problem is identified, you may be able to return your new pet before you become too attached.

CONSIDER THE SOURCE. Are the breeders or store owners concerned about the cat's welfare in a caring, new home? Are the kittens or cats kept in a clean and comfortable environment? Ask questions about the cat's history, breed, lineage, and behavior or health problems. Much of the details may remain a mystery for shelter kitties or strays, but gather as many details as you can. You might hear something that makes you change your mind, or that will become useful later on.

Cats of all kinds are available through breeders, shelters, pet stores, neighbors, and newspaper advertisements. Veterinarians often help to find homes for abandoned pets or patients in need of a new home. Adopting a cat from animal shelters can save a healthy animal from destruction. Try to spend time with the cat or kitten before making your final selection. If possible, make more than one visit on successive days or at least twice on the same day. Your first impression of a calm kitty might change on your next visit if the kitten was sleepy or sick.

CHOOSING YOUR BREED

Ming was a Siamese. His blue-violet crossed eyes gazed at the two of me with friendly interest. I was there to meet him because his owner could not understand why he "talked" so much and was increasingly irritated by his plaintive calls. Needless to say, Ming was her first Siamese cat.

Although the similarities between cat breeds vastly outweigh their differences, some breeds are more unique than others in both behavior and appearance. The Siamese is one of them. It has yet to be proven whether Siamese truly do vocalize *more* than other cats or whether their undeniably distinctive voice is simply impossible to ignore. Ming's owner had purchased him on impulse from a local pet store because she thought he was cute. She had not researched the breed and had not had a cat since she was a child. We talked about the Siamese cat. Ming's mom learned that her boy was naturally friskier compared to some other more placid breeds, such as the Persian, and that his voice was indeed unique. We also discussed the importance of increased interactive play to get him tired so he would not pace and meow, looking for something to do.

Learn about cat breeds before you acquire a pet cat. Your local public library and pet store may have books about specific breeds. There are hundreds of sites on the Internet devoted to cats. Many cat breeders now have their own web sites, as do feline organizations. Bear in mind that generalizations regarding breed-specific traits are often exaggerated and possibly unfounded. Remember, too, that there may be remarkable variation between individuals of a breed despite your expectations. For instance, a claim that particular breeds are better with children than others is probably not reliable. It depends on the individual cat, the individual children, and how they are raised together. Avoid choosing a cat breed because it is in fashion or because it is a novelty. Inbred diseases or poor temperaments are often more common in popular breeds because breeders are under pressure to supply an increased demand for their kittens. Hybrids (mixed purebred cats) or domestic cats may be less prone to inherited health problems. Do some basic research. Your selection should not be based on whim or purely on the physical appeal of a pet. Living happily ever after requires some planning.

WELL-MATCHED CATS AND OWNERS

Malika was a Somali cat who had become quite a princess. She lived with a retired police officer whose wife of thirty-five years had recently died. Despite the severe arthritis in his hands, he would often tell me how much Malika enjoyed being brushed every day. He had been a dog owner for many years, but arthritis in his knees prevented him from taking the long walks that he knew a healthy dog would need. Malika had become the light of his life. He played with her whenever she dropped the ball at his feet. She cuddled next to him wherever he was and woke him gently each morning with a soft paw on his cheek. He took great pride in caring for her every need, and she was totally smitten with him. It was easy to see how good they were for each other. Taking care of Malika forced him to exercise despite his inflamed joints and to remain active during a difficult period in his life. Malika's affectionate and playful style gave him focus and pulled him out of his depression. Her daily schedule required him to stick to a routine rather than retreating further into his solitude. When he was ready to participate in community social events the following year, talking about his cat gave him an easy way to start a conversation. His obvious pleasure in his pet gave everyone a good impression of him and helped him make new friends, including a special lady who loved cats.

A pet that satisfies your needs on an esthetic, practical, emotional, and spiritual level is a true gift. There is nothing that compares to the simplicity and clarity of living with a cat that is well suited to you. Unfortunately, I have witnessed some pet-owner relationships that were less than ideal. By this I do not necessarily mean cat owners who must deal with misbehaving cats. Most behavior problems are solvable if help is appropriate and timely. I refer to a special minority of cat owners who somehow end up with a cat whose temperament or level of activity conflicts with their concept of the ideal pet. Earlier in this book I recounted the story of an elderly lady whose young male cat resorted to biting her legs when she walked by. He was a high-energy kitten who had no other playmates and no outlets for his physical or intellectual needs. Her son took in this cat, and I found her a lovely Persian hybrid to keep her company.

It is important to consider not just what a cat looks like but how the cat will mesh with your lifestyle and your limitations. You may like the look of a longhaired cat, but do you have the patience and ability to brush this cat at least several times each week? If you are an elderly person, you may do well with a kitten as long as you provide that kitten with adequate playtime and attention. If you feel this may be more of a challenge than you would like, an adult cat with a more passive temperament would be a better match. Adopting two cats that are bonded to each other, or two kittens that can grow up together, may be an alternative for someone who has limited time or energy to focus on a young and active cat. If you have a limited income, your veterinary bill will certainly be lower if you do not let your cat roam outdoors. Before you bring your next cat home, take a few moments to make a list of the criteria that describe your ideal pet. Be realistic about your schedule, health status, patience, and finances. You will have a better chance of making an objective choice and finding the cat that was meant to be yours.

GROOMING REQUIREMENTS AS A CRITERIA FOR
BREED CHOICE

Bertha was a two-year-old tortoiseshell Persian who hated to be brushed. Consequently, the long, silky hair on her belly and much of her legs and back had become a thick and painful mat. Bertha was a mess, and her new owner was increasingly discouraged by the time and trouble necessary to keep Bertha looking beautiful.

Certain cat breeds, such as the Himalayan, domestic longhair, and Persian, require frequent grooming. In fact, these cats may require brushing or combing on a daily basis to prevent their coats from tangling. Static electricity, dust, and debris all contribute to grooming problems in longhaired cats. Some pet owners prefer to have their longhaired cats professionally groomed. This is often a simple solution and, indeed, it may be the only solution for those cats who resist being groomed at home. Before you acquire a longhaired cat, consult pet groomers and other cat owners to gage the frequency and cost to groom the cat breed in question. Ask about the amount of shedding that can be expected normally and seasonally. Cats with hair will shed. They will shed more when they are nervous, recently bathed, or ill. Products marketed to prevent shedding may not be proven reliable.

Cat breeds with reduced surface hair, such as the Sphynx and Cornish Rex, require minimal grooming. Shorthaired cats still shed but usually require less frequent grooming compared to longhaired varieties. Regardless of the breed you choose, grooming should be introduced as a pleasurable interaction from a young age. Grooming is discussed in greater detail in chapter 12 ("Grooming").

CATS ARE NOT JUST "WOMEN'S PETS"

It was clear from the moment his owner laid eyes on him at the shelter, Deuteronomy was the one. A big, burly boy who had been found as a stray, his age had been estimated at around five years. Despite his appearance, Deuteronomy was a lover not a fighter. He was a marshmallow who happened to be built like a piano. He happily lounged with his new dad, an avid viewer of televised sports events. Saturday baseball, Sunday golf, Monday football, and any sports broadcast any day of the week, Deuteronomy and his dad could be found on their favorite sofa. Napping in the sun, snacking often, quick trips to the litter box during commercials . . . who said that cats aren't perfect pets for men?

Well, I admit, the stereotype of the couch potato male is a negative male stereotype. That is my point. My sense is that the notion that cats are "women's pets" is perpetuated largely by men who have never truly appreciated either cats or women. I believe that this view is a misogynist myth. It slanders both women and felines. According to some men, cats are characterized as aloof, emotionally cool, self-indulgent, fickle, and moody. By labeling cats as "women's pets," women are stereotyped as feline by association. Men who are cat lovers may be tagged as effeminate by their peers, yet many professional male athletes and other masculine men know better.

Cats have become the most popular pet in the United States and outnumber pet dogs by a significant margin. Men constitute half the adult population; therefore many cat owners must be men! The myth that suggests that "real men" don't keep feline company is simply untrue. Cats are the perfect pet for any man. Cats will be there when their owners want companionship and can manage on their own when their owners are temporarily preoccupied. A cat's self-sufficiency matches well with the independent nature boasted by many men. A cat can be taught to fetch balls, retrieve objects, jump through hoops, climb an obstacle course, and many things that a dog can learn. My boy Hershel Walker is the manliest man cat I know and would gladly toss a football around if his chunky paws could hold onto one. A cat just needs more motivation to perform certain tasks compared to the average dog. Sort of like getting your husband off the couch to paint that spare bedroom!

EVALUATING A LITTER OF KITTENS

Jeepers was eight weeks old when his owners contacted me. Would it be a good idea, they wondered, to adopt his sister, too? They had chosen him from a litter of kittens that had been found in the woods near a fire station and turned in to a local animal shelter. Only two kittens remained when they selected Jeepers, and they regretted leaving his solitary littermate behind. I suggested that two kittens are usually good company for each other, and that if she was still available it might be nice to take her. If not, odds were that an unrelated kitten would still work out fine. They went back to the shelter and were very pleased to find Jeepers's little sister. Apparently, so was he.

It is not always possible to evaluate an entire litter of kittens. Kittens are snatched up fast, and you may meet only a remainder of the original group. If you are lucky, you will get to meet the mother. You will have a better chance at seeing both parents if you are selecting a purebred kitten from a breeder, or perhaps a litter born to an unexpected mating of unneutered housemates whose owners were delinquent in having them neutered.

It can be helpful to learn what you can about a kitten's parents. If the mother (queen) and father (tom) are both friendly, chances are that the kittens will be social toward people as well. Paternal care is negligible in cats, however, and a tom's contribution toward his kittens' temperaments is limited. In most cases the father is unknown anyway. Most kittens can learn to be friendly if they are appropriately socialized, and many negative inborn tendencies can be modified. Kittens born to an unfriendly queen or fathered by an unsociable tom may still become good pets, although this is less likely if both parents are extremely wild. This, too, can be misleading. For instance, the queen could give you a negative first impression; she might just be frightened, protective of her litter, or poorly socialized to people yet have the genetic potential to be a wonderful pet. When adopting kittens at a young age, the inborn "tameness" of one or both parents is important yet may be difficult to gauge.

So with or without details of a kitten's parentage, how do you select your kitten from a litter of kittens? In most cases you will have a predilection for coat color, but try to remain somewhat flexible in your selection. Observe the kittens as they interact. Which is biggest, most active, smallest, or most shy? In nearly every case, you will be better off with the average kitten. A kitten that resents handling, seems excessively shy, and hisses at you may not be the ideal choice for a house pet. This kitten could learn to tolerate human handling, but an early peak at this genetic inclination puts in doubt whether the tiny terror will make a tame pet. Of course, an assertive and calmly confident kitten could turn out to be more of a challenge than you are looking for. In general, avoid temperamental extremes. There is a lot to be said for the average kitten.

If possible, make more than one visit to get a realistic impression of your kitten. A quiet and shy kitten could just be slow to wake up from a long nap. Observe your kitten's interaction with littermates, but keep in mind that kittens go through developmental phases and that his or her "personality" will certainly be influenced by the environment you provide. My Teddi, for example, was the runt of her litter. She was barely half the size of her littermates, and they gleefully used her as a Ping-Pong ball. Removed from their influence and introduced into a loving home, her confidence has blossomed. She has become an affectionate and self-assured kitten who respects her older housemates and interacts actively with everyone, dogs and people included.

Gender is also an important consideration. In general, males tend to be larger and more active. Female kittens are as playful as males but usually do not play as roughly. Taking Jeepers's sister home (or another female kitten) was a good choice because she would be a contemporary playmate but not a rival. On the other hand, I have known adult males who became preferred alliances (what we call "friends") without ever exchanging a hiss or a spit. Cats are always full of surprises.

Although your new kitten may appear to be healthy and may not be due for vaccination just yet, arrange a veterinary examination right away before you permit any direct contact with any resident pets (see chapter 10, regarding "Feline Health" and chapter 2's discussion of how to introduce new cats). It all comes down to a simple recommendation.

Choose a healthy kitten with a friendly temperament. What happens with these good basic ingredients is up to you.

AGE AT ADOPTION

Pumpkin was not fond of visitors. Actually, he barely tolerated his owner. Basically, Pumpkin was not a people cat. His owner liked him that way because, he said, he admired the wild cat in him. Pumpkin was happiest when he had the apartment to himself. Unfortunately, his owner was a bit of a party animal. Pumpkin's response was to lunge at visitors as they passed by his favorite chair. Because his early history was unknown, it was unclear whether this cat's behavior was due to a bad experience with people. More than likely, however, his problem was deeper than that.

To develop healthy social attitudes toward people, kittens should be exposed to people at a very young age. A kitten's earliest experiences will leave their marks and can be as important as the genetic makeup. A kitten is most sensitive to interaction with people between three and seven weeks. Cats who are acquired over the age of three months without prior human contact are unlikely to become lap cats. Of course, there are always exceptions. Feral cats (cats that were born wild or returned to live wild) are not necessarily untamable. Feral kittens can make marvelous pets if they are introduced to people before their attitudes are formed. Feral adult cats may require patience and an experienced hand if they are to become civilized company. Some adapt quickly; others never do. It should also be noted that some kittens, born to perfectly tame parents and hand raised by cat people, grow into unpleasant and unfriendly cats. These kittens usually show their colors early on in life.

Excessive handling in newborn kittens younger than two weeks should be limited because it can have a negative impact on them. When their eyes begin to open, however, they should be handled for short periods every day. This will increase their tolerance of close human contact and facilitate the development of desirable social skills. The advantage of acquiring a kitten is that you can influence your pet's sociability during a critical stage of development. This does not mean that you should not adopt adult cats. On the contrary, an adult cat may be the ideal pet for someone who does not relish the thought of a kitten bouncing off the walls or hanging from the draperies.

Pumpkin's history was unclear because he had been acquired as a young adult. He may have had limited social exposure to people as a youngster; he may have had negative experiences that he never forgot; or, he may have been a territorially possessive cat. His owner recognized his cat's limitations and did not have a problem with them, except when he had parties. Your cat's behavior is a problem only if *you* think it is a problem. *Your cat has to be perfect for you, not for anyone else.* In Pumpkin's case, we simply opted to keep him in a large crate in a back room when social events were planned. Sometimes, avoiding the problem context is an elegant solution.

THE ADVANTAGES OF PET CATS

Macavity was an Egyptian Mau. His owners were both busy professionals whose childhood pets had been dogs. They had little time or energy to walk a dog and yet longed to find a pet who would make their home come alive at the end of a hard day. They'd considered pet rabbits, snakes, hamsters, and tropical fish until they realized that the solution was an obvious one. A cat would provide entertainment and companionship without the complications of dog ownership. And Macavity more than fit the bill. He greeted them at the door with his tail held high, sat on their newspapers when they tried to read, untied their shoelaces on the way out the door, and kept the pillows warm for them each night. Macavity was better than a puppy—he was their cat!

It's not that dogs don't make wonderful pets. They do, in a different way than do cats. And depending on the circumstances, cats may be a more attractive option to animal lovers looking for a new friend. Cats do not need to be walked outside despite all kinds of inclement weather like dogs do (although teaching your cat to walk on a leash could be an interesting diversion for you both). Cats easily adapt to smaller homes or apartments, in part because they use horizontal as well as vertical space.

Cats thrive on human attention and contact but do not necessarily rely on it if it is briefly unavailable. They can entertain themselves better than most dogs. Cats can be as demonstrative and responsive as any dog, yet are often more subtle and discreet in their displays. Although some cats are as boisterous and mischievous as many dogs, cats make generally less demanding pets. Small size and autonomy make the domestic cat an attractive candidate for a modern world. It is no wonder that they have become the most popular pet in the United States, and their attractions are becoming increasingly appreciated worldwide.

"HYPOALLERGENIC" CATS

Shaka was a slender Sphynx who had been selected because of the hairlessness that characterizes his breed. Shaka's owner had been allergic to cats and a cat lover all her life. The pet store owner had convinced her that Sphynx were nonallergenic because they had no hair. Unfortunately, Shaka's owner soon found this to be inaccurate. She had increasing respiratory difficulties and was unable to fully appreciate her cat's company. Heartbroken, she gave Shaka to a friend who had fallen in love with him and took an interest in aquarium fish instead.

There is no such thing as a nonallergenic cat (or dog). Interestingly, it is not the quality of the cat's coat that is key, as it might be with an allergy to particular dog breeds. A protein in cat saliva has been identified as the culprit. It is distributed over the cat's body surface, with or without hair, during normal self-grooming. As the hair is shed, the protein allergen travels inside the home. Even cats with no hair groom themselves by licking, although there may be less environmental contamination by hairless cats because there is little or no shedding of hairs that are covered with the triggering protein. Cat lovers with an allergy to cats are discussed in greater detail in chapter 1 ("General Stuff About Living Happily Ever After with Your Cat").

If you have an allergy to cats, it can be very helpful to restrict a pet from access to your bedroom or confine your cat to a limited area of your home. You may find it easier to live with a shorthaired cat or a hairless cat because housecleaning may be simplified. Remember, however, that it is still possible to develop an allergy to a pet long after you have acquired the animal. Frequent bathing of cats should be avoided because this can cause skin problems and might lead to increased self-grooming after the bath. Alternatively, wipe your pet with a dampened cloth or even an antistatic dryer sheet. Dry shampoos may be effective in absorbing oils and odors but fine powder particles may exacerbate your allergy. You might even develop sensitivities to the products you use on your pet.

Keep your home well vacuumed and well ventilated. Use special air purifiers and change air filters on heating ducts regularly. Should an allergy to your cat cause serious medical problems that impact your ability to enjoy your pet, your cat cannot enjoy being with you. You must not jeopardize your health, however, it may be worth consulting an allergist to investigate short-term control of your symptoms and de-sensitizing injections to increase your long-term tolerance of your pet. If this is not an option for you, placing your pet in another loving home may benefit everyone in the long run.

9

Cats and Kids

High diddle diddle
The cat and the fiddle,
The cow jumped over the moon;
The little dog laughed
To see such craft
And the dish ran away with the spoon.

—ANONYMOUS

A CAT AS THE FAMILY PET

Annie was an eleven-year-old Ragdoll who lived with a family of four young children under the age of ten. Although Ragdolls have the reputation for being tolerant, passive, and patient pets, Annie had been pushed way past her limits. She had become a nervous and easily frazzled cat. She hid under the beds when the children approached her and was more and more irritable. Her owner reminisced about how lovely and docile her cat used to be—but that was before the children began to arrive.

Most families with children will come to discuss the addition of some kind of pet sooner or later. In many homes the pet predates the arrival of kids and may not have been exposed to young children. Prior experience with people of all ages during a sensitive phase in a young kitten's early life can have long-lasting effects on how they perceive and interact with kids later in life. Whether or not a cat has ex-

perience with kids, the basic nature of the individual cat, the personalities of the children, and parental instruction (or lack thereof) will determine how they get along. If your previously perfect little cat is becoming a frazzled feline because of your youngsters, it is high time to intervene. Instruct them on how to gently interact with the cat. Demonstrate how to calmly approach the cat and, gently pet, hold, pick up, and put down the family pet. Explain that the kitty must not be forced to do anything. If the cat tries to get away, they must not restrain or pursue the kitten or cat.

The Ragdoll is a striking American breed named for its characteristic passiveness when picked up. Ragdolls are reputed to have a higher threshold to pain although this has not been proven. These traits are seen in individuals of other breeds, however, and not all Ragdolls are equally limp or tolerant. Many of the behavioral traits associated with a particular breed are inconsistent and have not been proven in clinical studies. *The bottom line is that any cat, regardless of the breed's reputation as a family pet or the cat's early positive exposure to children, has limits of endurance.* Children can be overwhelming and overly attentive to a cat. It may be that docile cats tolerate greater persecution, compared to less patient pets who express their displeasure much sooner. Be realistic about your kids; be fair to your kitty!

If you have young children and are considering acquiring a pet cat, think it over carefully. Consider the demands of a new cat and the strain it might put on your other priorities. You know your children better than anyone. Are they ready to help care for this cat? Can they be trusted to be gentle and not to use a defenseless kitten as a bouncing ball? Traumatic and sometimes fatal injury of young kittens by children is not unheard of, although most of these interactions are mischievous rather than malicious. How long can we expect any cat to stand being dressed in doll's clothing? It might be best to delay welcoming a pet into your family until you and your cat can expect some peace of mind.

As for Annie, she was confined to the privacy of her favorite room to regain her emotional balance. After several weeks of tranquility, the children were allowed to visit her for brief periods, one at a time and with parental supervision. They spent quiet time with her and gave Annie a special food tidbit, such as a dab of cream cheese. Eventually, Annie relaxed, and the children learned new respect for her. They all lived happily ever after.

PREPARING FOR YOUR BABY'S ARRIVAL

Reba was a quiet, little brown tabby who was a bit out of sorts since the baby came home. On the positive side, she discovered that the baby's crib was a terrific place to nap. In a nice sunny corner, the crib had plush blankets and a window view. She did not understand when her mom shooed her away. She just wanted to snuggle next to the nice warm baby. Later, when the crib was empty, she went back and defecated in it. That way everyone would know it was her special place. Marking her territory had always made her feel much better. Her owner had intended to deal with Reba's occasional lapse in litter box use but had never quite found the time.

Reba had already begun to defecate out of the box before the baby was born. She was totally surprised by this new addition and had no previous experience with children. Reba was unprepared and bewildered. She could not know that defecating in the baby's crib was beyond unacceptable. (Please refer to detailed discussions about inappropriate elimination in chapter 4, "Your Cat and the Litter Box"). Reba also could not understand her owner's concern when she curled up next to the baby's head. It is a popular misconception that a cat will suffocate a sleeping infant. Nevertheless, a baby should not be left unattended with anyone, even your cat. Until babies can adjust their own position, they should be monitored when any pet is near. Your baby does not need to live in a sterile bubble, but should not be exposed to unnecessary health risks.

Dr. Cookie®'s Tips on How to Prepare Your Cat for Your Baby's Arrival

- Behavior problems are usually simpler to resolve as soon as they appear because they often worsen over time. Solve any preexisting behavior problems, however small, before the baby comes with the help of a veterinary behaviorist. Even minor issues are amplified in the eyes of sleep-deprived and easily annoyed new parents!

- Let your cat investigate a blanket that was used to wrap your baby in the hospital; give your pet a special treat and gentle praise so that a positive association with the baby can be formed before they ever meet.

- Carry a doll as an imaginary baby and pretend to do diaper changes or feed the doll with a bottle; rehearse the activities that will be part of your lives so they will not seem so unfamiliar when the real baby arrives.

- Record a crying infant at the hospital and play this at gradually increased volume while you play with or pet your cat over two or three days.

- Train your cat to stay out of the baby's room. Consider setting up a motion detector across the threshold at floor level. This will sound an alarm that you can hear, and it might also startle your cat and discourage her entry.

- Replace the door to the baby's room with a screen door. You will be able to see and hear the baby and prevent the cat from entering unless you are there.

- You can also make a tent out of netting to cover the crib and keep your kitty out. Ready-made crib covers can be purchased from baby supply stores as well.

• If you are a new parent who is considering adding a cat to keep you company during 3 A.M. feedings, think again. Your new pet will be an additional responsibility and deserves time and energy that you might not have to give just now.

When the Baby Comes Home from the Hospital

• Confine your pet to his or her favorite room for the first few days until you get more comfortable with your infant. Your cat needs time to adjust to this new addition to the family. Come to think of it, so do you!

• Although you will be tired and understandably preoccupied, make an extra effort to spend "quality" time with your cat. After all, your cat was there first. Your pet's needs have not changed, although yours certainly have. Keep to your cat's familiar routines as closely as possible. This will minimize the emotional stress and give much needed comfort.

• A curious and affectionate pet can unintentionally harm a baby. Trim your cat's nails every few weeks so that your child will not be accidentally scratched.

• Brush your cat more regularly to minimize the quantity of hair shed in your home; this will help you to keep up with housework as well as keep your baby's environment neater and cleaner.

• Do not leave your infant alone when your cat is nearby. Chances are your cat will do little more than briefly approach the baby and run away! Still, accidents happen. Your cat could accidentally trip a toddler or push over an infant; you will never regret being a bit overly cautious with your child's (or your cat's) safety!

TEACH YOUR CHILD PET ETIQUETTE

Stuart was a stately black Persian with long, flowing hair who loved everyone, except the three-year-old boy who relentlessly pursued him. From the moment the child became mobile, first crawling and then running, Stuart

could find no peace. He had even started urinating in an upstairs closet af-
ter the little boy pounced on him while he was in his litter box. Stuart was
losing weight and avoiding his owners. He was depressed. The little boy,
however, was ecstatic. His favorite toy was soft, interactive, and required no
batteries!

Do your pet a favor. Teach your child pet etiquette as soon as the child shows interest in any kind of interaction. It is normal for children to investigate the world around them from the moment they begin to crawl. Their discovery will also include your cat's food, water bowl, and litter box. These are not the most hygienic objects, and your child should learn to leave them alone. This will also prevent conflicts near your cat's cherished resources. In Stuart's case, a covered litter box was placed in his chosen closet and a baby gate was placed across the room where the other box was kept. This kept the toddler out, but Stuart could easily scale the gate and find safe haven behind the barrier.

Teach your child from a young age that pets are not toys. Your child needs to learn the difference between inanimate objects and living beings who feel pain. Telling your child what *not* to do is only part of the lesson. Show the child how to gently caress your pet and which body parts should not be touched. Praise your child for his or her gentleness. Teach your child not to disturb your cat when the cat is resting or sleeping, enjoying a meal, or anywhere near the litter box. As difficult as it may be, your child must come to understand the consequences of his or her behavior. Role-playing can be a help-ful way to teach your child to appreciate his or her own physical strength. Pretend that you are the child and ask your child to pretend to be your cat. Show your child what it feels like to be poked and prodded or touched against his or her will. This might be uncomfort-able for your child, but it is far kinder than allowing the child to be bitten or scratched by a cat that has been pushed beyond patience. It is also more humane compared to failing to prevent serious injury to a beautiful and sensitive creature.

Stuart's "little brother" did not cooperate with his parents' efforts to tame his relationship with their cat. He continued to playfully harass the poor cat at every opportunity. I suggested that they at least keep Stuart confined to a separate area of their home until the child was more mature and had better self-control. In the end Stuart was returned to his breeder who knew of a good home. This was the kindest solution for everyone concerned.

TODDLERS AND CATS

Sara stared in wonder at the three-year-old child. Although she had not been exposed to many children, she was tolerant and patient with my nephew Alec, who loved her from the moment they met. She allowed him to pet her and nuzzle her soft fur. He stretched out on the floor next to her or knelt beside the chair she had selected for her nap. She looked at him with an expression of infinite wisdom and what can only be described as kindness. I wonder if he will remember her when he is older. I know he will be fond of cats for having met Sara. She is my special girl.

Not every child is as responsive and sweet as little Alec. He is fascinated with my menagerie and looks forward to his visits (so do I). Still, I keep a watchful eye over what he is doing and what is being done to him when my critters are nearby. The cats have not been a problem so far; however, our puppy Georgyanna did steal Alec's socks right off his feet! He was only two years old at the time and still recalls the event with indignation!

At first, many cats probably are afraid of small children. They are more likely to run away from than to approach your child. Most problems between a pet and a child begin at the toddler stage. When the baby learns to crawl and then to walk, it enters a new phase, and your pet's view of the child may change. It is unlikely that your kitty will intentionally injure your child unless the cat is forced to behave defensively. Unlike some dogs with a strong predatory instinct who might be a threat to a small child, a domestic cat's hunting instincts are triggered by even smaller prey. Your cat will not be tempted to stalk your baby like the cat would a mouse. Although some cats prefer larger prey such as rabbits, your baby is still not an attractive target for your pet cat.

However, toddlers and young children can provoke even the most patient of cats.

Young children are often unaware that they can hurt your pet. Cats and kittens are lightweights compared to dogs, and children can easily pick up a trusting cat. Geriatric cats or those debilitated by illness may not be fast enough to avoid a mischievous child in hot pursuit. Or they may be taken off guard in a vulnerable moment, like when they are in the litter box. Some kids enjoy waking a sleeping pet by screaming at or jumping on the unsuspecting creature. Kids have been known to bite, kick, stomp, squeeze, hit, pinch, twist, and pull at the ears, tail, and other body parts of the family pet. Most of this is playful and innocent. However, in extreme cases of repeated or escalating pet abuse, experts urge parents to seek professional counseling for their child. Serious abuse of pets by children implies emotional problems that deserve immediate attention. I have treated pets injured by children who dropped or tossed them around like a ball, throwing them down the stairs and worse. Even if your child is pet friendly, your child's friends and those of your own acquaintances must be monitored around your cat. Remember this, it is more probable by far that you will need to protect your cat from your child.

YOUR CAT AND YOUR BABY'S FOOD

Fargo was a big white cat who liked to eat. At first, he didn't like the new baby. She fussed, cried, smelled funny, and stole attention away from him, too! Then he discovered something wonderful. This baby gave him food! Sometimes she dropped it on the floor. Other times it was stuck to the high chair or even the baby's face (although Mom was quick to wipe these off unless Fargo arrived first)! At mealtime Fargo enjoyed sharing the baby's food. All he had to do was reach up with his hefty paw and pull the food right out of the baby's pudgy little fist. Fargo was beginning to look like Moby Dick. But, boy oh boy, he really liked that baby now!

Babies and pets can be a good combination, but even the most trusted pet needs close supervision near your baby. *Regardless of their age, no one should be left alone with an animal they cannot control.* Infants, in particular, can be unintentionally injured by any pet. The baby can be knocked over and fall against a coffee table's edge or down the stairs. A cat who is eager to share that cookie could scratch the baby who holds the treat.

Pets learn quickly that a baby's feeding time means easy pickings. There are always falling crumbs or mouthfuls spit out or flung onto the floor. Your cat might become an obstacle for you at feedings, too. You are concentrating on attending to your child, but your cat could trip you when he races for a fallen treasure! You may have to confine your cat to another room with his or her own meal while you feed the baby. Sometimes, cats just need to be protected from themselves. Overeating results in obesity, which is the most common and most important health problem in pet cats. A more complete discussion on obesity in cats can be found elsewhere in this book (see chapter 10, "Feline Health"; chapter 11, "Nutrition").

TERRITORIAL MARKING OF BABY ITEMS

Paolo had decided that the baby's playpen was a jumbo litter box that had been provided especially for him. He had always used his litter box religiously, but here was a new one that was nice and roomy. It felt good to layer his scent over the baby's odors. It made him feel closer to the baby. He was puzzled when he noticed that his mom seemed irritated with him. This made Paolo anxious, so he urinated in the playpen again! Mom was even angrier now, and she finally called me. . . .

It is not uncommon for pets to urinate or defecate on baby blankets or baby clothes. A newborn's crib is another attractive location that visually resembles a rectangular litter box. Your cat is not acting out of malice or jealousy. Territorial marking with urine and stool serves to reduce your cat's level of anxiety, although it may well send your anxiety level through the roof! Your cat feels immediate relief by layering identifying smells over your baby's scent (or yours). It is understandable that this will make you feel frustrated and angry, but scolding or rejecting your pet for this misbehavior will only aggravate the problem. The best remedy is to prevent your cat's access to these undesirable targets:

- Place a cover made of netting over the playpen when it is not in use; monitor the cat's whereabouts while your baby is in the playpen.
- Make certain that the litter box is kept clean. Add another one or two boxes in a corner near these new albeit undesirable targets to retrain your cat, who will likely return to refresh the desposit scent.
- Keep soiled diapers in a "pet-proof" hamper or an enclosed diaper pail.
- Prevent access to the baby's room by closing the door and using baby monitors, putting up a screen door, or using motion detectors.
- Finally, spend more and not less time with your pet.

Additional ideas are shared elsewhere in this chapter and in chapter 4 ("Your Cat and the Litter Box"). Change is stressful and we all need time to adjust. You will all regain your emotional equilibrium and live happily ever after.

CATS AND CHILDREN'S TOYS

Simon was a Birman who loved the holidays. The tinsel, the ornaments suspended from the tree, the food . . . he was a happy boy. He especially enjoyed the ribbons and bows, and the new and endless variety of children's toys. In the middle of the holiday activities, Simon threw up. And threw up again and again. He did not look too well at all. He was rushed to the veterinary emergency clinic and immediately admitted for surgery. His anxious owner still wore his red suit and white beard as he paced nervously in the waiting area. Simon recovered from his ordeal but not before a fifteen-inch piece of tinsel and a miniature toy giraffe were recovered from his intestines. Ho, ho, ho!

Don't forget your pets despite the holiday preparations and festivities. These are the times that your pets are most susceptible to ingesting foreign objects and overindulgence in rich foods. Young cats in particular are very inquisitive. Your home must be pet proofed on an ongoing basis, especially when new items are introduced. Cats are continually exploring their territory and its contents. Christmas tree decorations are a *major* attraction to curious cats. Dangling objects of all shapes and sizes, many of them shiny, some of them edible, beckon to your kitty! Tinsel, ribbons, and elastics can cause the intestines to twist and tangle into knots that can be fatal if not surgically repaired in time. Don't forget that mistletoe and poinsettias, traditional ornamental plants, are toxic to your cat. Toys manufactured for children are not necessarily proven safe for pets. Button eyes, small parts, miniature components are attractive to your cat and, if swallowed, can obstruct the digestive tract and put a serious damper on your celebrations. Training your children to put away their toys will help to safeguard your cat and to keep a tidy home.

It is not just at holiday time that your cat is vulnerable to over-indulgence and less supervision. Other celebrations, such as your child's bris, christening, or baptism, may be accompanied by similar pet hazards. Later on, children's birthday parties will also introduce gift-wrapping accessories, toys, and a new selection of ingestible parts (not to mention other children who might not have acquired pet etiquette). If a special occasion is planned, it might be wise to restrict your cat's activities until the party is over. Confine your cat (with food, water, and litter, of course) to a large crate in your bedroom while you entertain your guests. Find a nice quiet place where your cat will not be disturbed. If you prefer, have your cat boarded at your veterinary clinic or a kennel that they recommend until life is back to normal. Enjoy!

CATS AS CHILDREN

Peaches was a cream domestic longhair. Her newlywed owners doted on her. She was their baby. When Peaches was five years old, her owners had a baby of their own. They had gone through many years of infertility problems and several miscarriages until finally their dreams of starting a family came true. Peaches was practically forgotten overnight. She tried to cuddle while her mom fed the infant, but she was pushed away. She tried to play with her dad, but he was too preoccupied with the baby to notice her. After several months of being ignored, Peaches was brought in for euthanasia. Her owners did not have the time to find her another home, and they told the shelter attendant that they were worried she would be abused in another home. They could not see that Peaches had already been abused. "No one could love her as much as we do," they said. Real love does not fade overnight.

It is common for new life partners to acquire a pet. This nesting behavior is the first focus of shared responsibility for a couple. It also allows the pair to experiment with their parenting skills and to learn about each other's parental styles. *We project many deep emotions onto our pets; but more than anything, they symbolize children.* They depend on us for nurturing, love, and attention. We naturally channel our maternal and paternal energies into them and feel a sense of fulfillment until the real children arrive. When you hold your child for the first time, you may suddenly be reminded that your pets are animals, after all. Your cat might become an unnecessary distraction, a nuisance, and a needless complication to your suddenly very complicated existence. All of a sudden, this once loved and still loving creature has become dispensable. Luckily for Peaches, the shelter staff was able to convince her owners to place her up for adoption. She found a new home the same day with a veterinary technician who worked at the shelter part time. They were completely thrilled to find each other.

We live in a society where relationships are easily severed. Families are dispersed, lives are fragmented, and individuals are isolated. Our pets help us to remember what is important and what really matters. We are here to love each other. You chose your cat, or your cat chose you, out of a need to connect. This emotional and spiritual bond, along with your love for your human family and friends, is unique and indispensable. We are born with an infinite capacity to love. The arrival of a new child, the start of a new job, or any other of life's challenges need not transform your cat into overweight baggage. You have enough love to go around if you open your heart. Stop. Take a deep breath. Look into those pussycat eyes that gaze up at you with so much trust and devotion and remember how it all began. Hold on to that memory, to those emotions, and hold on as tight as you can to your pet, regardless of what is going on around you. Your cat is a gift that cannot be replaced.

TEACHING YOUR KIDS THE FACTS OF LIFE

Kendra was having kittens. Her owners had decided to let her have a litter to teach their children, aged six, nine, and thirteen, the facts of life. Kendra was eight months old when she had her first litter, too great a stress for her young body. The kittens were delivered by caesarean section, and the children were not permitted in the operating room. The two surviving kittens were given to a local pet store. Kendra's owners never did get around to having her spayed, and she continued to go outside. One of her litters was born outside. The hawks enjoyed the kittens. Kendra died from complications of feline leukemia, which she contracted during her outdoor escapades. She was two years old. So much for the facts of life.

A cat is not an educational tool. Your pet is a living creature who should be cherished and protected from harm. Parents who want their child to learn about sexual reproduction can find resources that are more appropriate. Feline mating, pregnancy, and delivery of kittens will teach your child about reproduction in cats, not people. There are some excellent books and videos available for children at different stages of development regarding human sexuality. Most schools now teach sex education at appropriate levels. If you really want to teach your children to be responsible, have your pet neutered before he or she reaches sexual maturity. This will teach your children everything they need to know about responsibility, compassion, and consideration. Sex means nothing without an understanding of these.

If you have children who are pleading with you for a pet, make sure your expectations are realistic. In most cases, no matter how much your kids promise to help, pet care will likely be *your* responsibility. This won't teach your children to be responsible. It will only teach them that *you* will bear the consequences of *their* actions, or lack of them. Unless your kids have reliably demonstrated their maturity, wait until you ac-quire any pet. Even if cats are somewhat self-sufficient, they still need your attention and devotion. Unless you have time to spare from your own parental and professional duties, wait before getting a cat. Your cat will suffer the consequences more than anyone.

10

Feline Health

There was a crooked man, and he went a crooked mile,
He found a crooked sixpence against a crooked stile;
He bought a crooked cat, which caught a crooked mouse,
And they all lived together in a little crooked house.

—ANONYMOUS

VISUALLY IMPAIRED CATS

Gracie was a shy and quiet kitten when she came home with me. She was
an irresistible fuzzy baby with a sweet disposition. She didn't flinch when
Hershey hissed at her. She didn't back away when Sara sniffed her up and
down. She wasn't a wildly playful girl nor was she very adventurous. Gracie
didn't bounce around the furniture or jump onto the window ledge or walk
through the plants. She was an angel. Too angelic for a kitten. I didn't
become overly concerned until she was about four months old. It was around
that time that I saw her walk into a wall for the first time. Soon after, a
veterinary ophthalmologist confirmed my suspicion; Gracie was losing what
little eyesight she'd been born with and could see very little at all. She had
congenital retinal atrophy, a progressive and irreversible degeneration of the
retina, a rare condition in cats. I was so sad for her until I realized that
Gracie couldn't miss what she had never had. She is still my Gracie. She
doesn't know she's blind and we don't intend to tell her.

Visual deficits in cats from birth are uncommon. Kittens with poor
eyesight simply would not survive in the wild. Cats are primarily

visual creatures and rely on their eyes for detection of prey, evasion from predators, and social interaction. Of course, their other senses are very evolved and contribute to their survival, but their eyesight is vital. Feline vision is the most highly developed among all mammals.

Cats lose their eyesight for a multitude of reasons. Some, like Gracie, are born with congenital problems. More commonly, normal kittens lose their vision to viral or bacterial infections. Trauma, in cats of any age, can cause corneal laceration, infection, or eye rupture. Glaucoma and high blood pressure also affect the sensitive ocular tissue and lead to retinal detachment and blindness. If your cat has any sign of an eye problem, do not delay veterinary attention. You may notice a change in pigment of the iris (the colored part of the eye) to brown or black; persistent redness, tearing, blinking, yellow or green discharge; or swelling around the eye or even swelling of the eyeball itself. Your cat will keep an injured eye squeezed tightly shut or hide in a dark place to avoid bright light. You might notice that your cat hesitates to move freely around your home, or walks into or along the walls. Timely diagnosis and treatment are critical.

In Siamese cats, and some Siamese-derived breeds, eye problems are famous. Many Siamese are cross-eyed *(convergent strabismus)*, but that is just the tip of the iceberg. Their visual systems are abnormal from the eyeballs and all along the neural pathways leading up to the brain. The optic fibers emanating from the retina frequently transmit visual signals to the wrong cerebral hemisphere. You may also notice a slight tremor in the movement of the eyeball *(nystagmus)* due to anomalies of motor control. These cats probably do not have normal depth perception, and their visual acuity may be seriously affected in general.

Visually impaired cats should not be allowed to roam outdoors. They are vulnerable and unable to foresee or forestall danger. Confined to a safe and constant environment, blind cats will study the placement of furniture and the floor plan. In a familiar environment, these cats become so adept at maneuvering that you may not even notice their deficits. If you rearrange the furniture, your cat might bump into things at first until he or she learns the new position of obstacles. If you are moving to a new home, your cat might need some extra time to figure things out. Keep your handicapped kitty confined to one room at first to establish a comfortable base from which to explore. Let your blind cat learn a small area at a time so that the cat is not overwhelmed. Just make sure that doorways to the basement stairs, for example, are kept closed at first so that your cat does not fall.

Avoid startling a cat with visual deficits by announcing yourself as you enter the room or if the cat wanders into the room where you are. A friendly, "Hi, Gracie!" goes a long way if my kitty seems a bit worried or confused. Visually impaired cats sometimes conflict with others in the household because they fail to detect them or their social signals. For example, Gracie occasionally walks into Hershey and he gets upset; although if she collides with the other girls, they graciously nuzzle her and step out of her way. Gracie might have a few fragile moments now and again, but her blindness has not kept her from becoming the dominant cat in my household. No one, not even the dogs, messes with her. Gracie rules my home and my heart. She doesn't need eyesight to see how much she is loved.

EAR MITES

Mitzi was miserable. The three-month-old white shorthaired kitten with orange eyes scratched and cried and shook her head and cried some more. When her owner noticed that Mitzi had bloody sores in her ears, she brought her to the clinic. Mitzi's doctor found dry clumps of dark brown debris in her ears. He took a cotton swab and removed a sample. Under the microscope, he could easily see the tiny insects that had colonized Mitzi's ears. The microscopic mites were crawling around inside her ear canals and driving her "buggy."

Ear mites are an external parasite of cats. These insects look like six-legged spiders staring back at you under the microscope (I know, spiders have eight legs and are not considered insects, but you know what I mean). Just believe me when I tell you that ear mites are not pretty! Ear mites are contagious between cats. They are not contagious to people, but dogs can become infested from carrier cats. Fortunately, ear mites are easily treated with a number of medications. Over-the-counter remedies are available at pet stores, but the most reliable treatment options are prescribed by your veterinarian. Your veterinarian should see your cat to make certain the problem is ear mites rather than an ear infection, which would require a different treatment. Eardrops, injections, and even new liquid medication absorbed through the skin of your cat's back are among the possible treatments for ear mite infestation.

There is no immunity to ear mites. Contact with another carrier will lead to reinfestation. This parasite is common among outdoor cats and newly acquired stray cats and kittens. If you are introducing a new cat to your household, schedule a veterinary appointment *before* the new pet comes in contact with your resident cats.

FELINE LOWER URINARY TRACT DISEASE (FLUTD)

Ramone was restless. He paced, made frequent trips to his box, cried while he urinated, and repeatedly licked his penis. Something was very wrong. By the second day he had become lethargic and stopped eating. His concerned owner described his symptoms to the receptionist at the animal clinic. She urged Ramone's mom to bring him in right away. He was diagnosed with urinary blockage and immediately admitted to the hospital for treatment. A urinary catheter was inserted to allow his distended bladder to empty. He was given intravenous fluids and treated with antibiotics and anti-inflammatory medication. After three days, he was released with a recommendation for a new diet. Ramone was a lucky boy.

Feline lower urinary tract disease (FLUTD) is a generic name for a group of problems that primarily affect the feline bladder and urethra (the tube that carries urine out of the body). It was previously known as feline urethral syndrome (FUS), but the term has been revised. Common symptoms of FLUTD include blood in the urine, urination out of the box, frequent urination, pain associated with urination, inability to urinate, excessive grooming of the genitalia, restlessness, lethargy, decreased or loss of appetite, vomiting, and diarrhea. The symptoms of FLUTD are nonspecific and may be caused by a long list of problems affecting the lower urinary tract of cats. These include several types of urinary crystals, a multitude of bacterial infections, viral infections, inflammatory disease, and tumors.

FLUTD becomes an acutely life-threatening illness should it result in a blockage of the urinary bladder. Urinary blockage is more common in males than in female cats. A blocked cat is in extreme pain as the urine fills the bladder without emptying. In addition, toxic by-products of metabolism that would ordinarily be eliminated with the urine instead build up in the bloodstream. The blocked cat may experience vomiting, diarrhea, and seizures. The bladder may rupture and spill urine into the abdominal cavity. Urinary blockages are considered extreme emergencies. If your cat shows any of the early symptoms of FLUTD, he or she should be seen at once. FLUTD may not progress to an actual blockage, but you cannot take the risk of waiting to find out.

In rare cases surgery may be necessary to open the bladder to remove large crystals. Some males with recurring blockages, or blockages that are difficult to relieve, may require a life-saving plastic surgery to reconstruct the urinary opening *(urethroplasty)*. Because the majority of blockages occur at the level of a male's penis, the penis may have to be amputated and the opening carefully reconstructed and widened. Antibiotics will treat any underlying infection or prevent bacteria from compounding your cat's problem. Anti-inflammatory medication helps to relieve the discomfort of irritated tissue. Diet changes are recommended if crystals in the urine cause the problem. Some cat foods have been associated with crystal formation in predisposed cats, and prescription diets are invaluable in preventing recurrences. Your veterinarian will explain what is necessary to diagnose (urine and blood samples, X-ray, biopsy, or ultrasound) and treat your pet.

EXCESSIVE LICKING IN CATS

Six-year-old Francesca was adorable. She was a brown tabby Cymric (a longhaired Manx) and resembled a mini bobcat. Francesca lived exclusively indoors and had recently developed a somewhat peculiar habit: she licked plastic bags, she licked her lips, she licked the air. Francesca was eating a bit less than usual but seemed fine otherwise, according to her worried owner. Could I determine her problem and resolve this odd behavior?

Excessive licking can be a sign of a variety of things. Among the behavioral causes, excessive licking and/or self-grooming can be symptoms of an obsessive-compulsive disorder. This would be treated with behavior modification and the potential use of psychoactive drugs. Peculiar facial and head movements can sometimes be a type of abbreviated seizure, which would be treated with anticonvulsant medication.

Before considering these more unusual ailments, however, it was important not to overlook a more obvious and common explanation for

Francesca's recent eccentricity. The most frequent source of bizarre tongue and jaw movement is in the mouth. Oral disease includes problems of the teeth, gums, throat, tongue, jaw, and the mucosal surface on the inside of the cheeks. When I looked inside Francesca's mouth, I immediately saw the problem. She had broken her upper left canine tooth, and her gums were infected as well.

Veterinary dentistry is one of the fastest-growing areas in the field. Veterinarians offer general teeth cleaning and other basic dental care; however, your cat may be referred to veterinary dentists for techniques and procedures that are more specialized. Some cats never have problems with their teeth, and others have recurring difficulties. Dry food may help, although I have seen many cats that never eat canned food with significant dental disease. Additional factors such as genetics, viral infections, and inflammatory disorders certainly influence the predisposition toward *dental calculus* (tartar) and *gingivitis*. Francesca's fractured tooth was extracted by her regular veterinarian. Her teeth were scaled with an ultrasonic dental apparatus to remove the build-up of tartar, and the infection healed with antibiotics. Francesca's excessive licking disappeared, although she did continue to give her mom little kisses at bedtime. That, however, was a good thing!

QUARANTINE OF NEW CATS

Clarissa was a little "tuxedo cat," black and white, who had been living in the back shed for about six months. She worked her confidence up gradually and finally allowed herself to be petted by the cat lover who lived in the big house. Clarissa was invited in to meet the rest of the cats. Surprisingly, no one minded her much after the first few days. Clarissa's new owner decided she could stay. Within several weeks, however, all the cats were itchy, and their owner noticed little red bites on her lower legs. It was time for a visit to the veterinarian.

Well it turns out that the visit was overdue. The veterinarian gave the good news first. Clarissa had already been spayed, given the telltale scar on her tummy, and was estimated to be about one year old. She must have been abandoned or lost and was lucky to find such a good home. Then came the bad news. Clarissa had fleas, ear mites, and tested positive for feline leukemia (FeLV). All the cats had to be treated for fleas and ear mites. Luckily, they had all been vaccinated against FeLV just in case any of them escaped through the screen door that occasionally bounced open as the children raced through. All the cats received a booster of the FeLV vaccine as an extra measure of precaution. As for Clarissa, she was isolated to a spare room and retested several weeks later. This time, she tested negative. The veterinarian explained that she might have been exposed to the virus but had been able to fight it off. It was also possible that she might become symptomatic months or even years later. Feline leukemia is transmitted by direct contact with the body fluids of infected cats or to kittens of infected mothers. Clarissa's new owner had to make a difficult decision. Should she continue to allow Clarissa to live with her? It was possible that Clarissa would never become ill and never become a carrier of the FeLV virus. It was probable that the vaccine gave the other cats almost complete protection; but was "almost" good enough? Should Clarissa be euthanized to prevent her from possible suffering?

Clarissa was placed with the lady's aunt, whose own cat had died peacefully at nineteen years of age several months earlier. Clarissa adored her, and the older lady adored Clarissa. The little cat lived happily until she was around nine years old. She developed chronic diarrhea and, this time, tested positive for feline leukemia. The diarrhea was controlled with treatment. Over the next two years, Clarissa developed recurring upper respiratory infections, gum infections, and intermittent diarrhea, which were treated in turn. Before the quality of her life was seriously impacted, euthanasia provided her with a peaceful and dignified end. Her elderly owner took comfort in knowing that Clarissa's life would have ended in misery far sooner. She wanted to do some traveling and decided to postpone adopting another pet. As for the cats in Clarissa's first home, none developed feline leukemia.

Gradual introduction of new cats to a resident population is so very important. Every cat should first be examined by your veterinarian before ever bringing her home. Fleas and ear mites are easily treated, and the new cat should be quarantined in your home until these problems are resolved so your other cats aren't exposed. Gradual introduction of new pets is also important from an emotional perspective in order to lessen the impact on resident cats. You will never regret taking these reasonable precautions given the somber consequences of failing to do so.

THE DANGERS OF OBESITY IN CATS

Maxwell was a moose, a happy moose, but a moose nonetheless. The gray, longhaired tabby did not seem to eat very much, according to his owner, but he obviously ate enough to reach twenty-three pounds and maintain his weight. Whatever he was being fed, it was too much. His veterinarian tried to explain to Maxwell's dad that the four-year-old cat was at high risk to develop inflammatory joint disease, diabetes, heart disease, lower urinary tract disease, high blood pressure, glaucoma . . . but Maxwell's guardian seemed to be in some sort of denial. He continued to fill Maxwell's bowl to the rim and to feed him table scraps. At six years of age, Maxwell tore a ligament in his knee while jumping onto the bed. It would require surgical repair, but the twenty-five-pound Maxwell was no candidate for surgery. He had developed a serious heart murmur, a result of years of strain on the heart muscle and valves, and knee surgery was out of the question. Cardiac drugs helped to improve his cardiac function, but Maxwell developed arthritis in both knees. He had periodic bladder infections, probably the result of infrequent trips to the box. Obese cats are less active in general and tend to pool their urine, which predisposes them to urinary tract problems. Eventually, a routine urine analysis following yet another bladder infection revealed a high concentration of glucose in his urine. Maxwell had indeed developed diabetes. It was very difficult to control Maxwell's diabetes. His owner was becoming increasingly frustrated with rising veterinary bills and the need to medicate Maxwell for a growing list of ailments. By the time he was eight years old, Maxwell showed increasing difficulty using the litter box. His barely controlled diabetes made him urinate more frequently, but he was too fat and too slow because of cardiac disease to get to the box in time to urinate. So he began to urinate indiscriminately around the house. Even when he made it to the box in time, he had trouble getting into it because of his arthritis. His owner became increas-

ingly disenchanted with Maxwell. At nine years of age, Maxwell went into cardiac failure, and his owner elected to forego further treatment and had him put down. Poor Maxwell. He was a moose, but inside him, there was a slim cat dying to get out.

Speak to your veterinarian today about how to maintain your cat's normal weight and how to shed any excess pounds in a carefully supervised feeding program. Tips are also given elsewhere in this book (see chapter 11, "Nutrition").

CAT SCRATCHES AND CAT FIGHTS

Clancy was the neighborhood bully. He was a burly orange cat with a somewhat scruffy coat, tattered ears, and a limp, the only sign of surviving impact with a car one year earlier when Clancy was five years old. He was a regular at the clinic. Seems like he had a scratch or an abscess somewhere on his battered self at least every other month. When he was about six years old, his owner noticed he seemed to be losing weight and had a cold that was just not going away. He was almost due for his annual vaccines anyway, so an appointment was scheduled the following week.

Cats fight when tempers flare over territorial conflicts between rivals and newcomers. Social tension also runs high during mating season. Even neutered cats can get involved in sexual competitions, and mating season in cats is virtually all year, although it declines for a month or two in the dead of winter. In other words, there may be many excuses for fighting in cats who roam outdoors. Superficial scratches or microscopic nicks can turn into seriously smelly, very painful, and definitely dangerous infections. Catfight abscesses require veterinary care, which may include antibiotics, rabies vaccine boosters, quarantine, hospitalization, and surgical drainage and repair. As if this isn't bad enough, there is an even more insidious consequence. Cat bites are one of the major modes of transmission of the feline immunodeficiency virus (FIV).

FIV is a fatal viral infection of cats for which there is no vaccine and no cure. It is caused by a different virus than the feline leukemia virus

(FeLV). FIV is thought to be transmitted to cats by bites during catfights and, like FeLV, direct contact with infected cats. *Neither virus is contagious to people.* FIV is a member of the same family of viruses that includes the human immunodeficiency virus (HIV), which causes acquired immunodeficiency syndrome (AIDS) in people. Like HIV, it can lie dormant in the infected cat for months or years before it begins to weaken the immune system and cause a complex of symptoms that eventually take the cat's life. In the meantime, the infected cat may continue to roam and spread the virus along the way.

Some people, including some veterinarians, have acquired the unfortunate habit of referring to FIV as "feline AIDS." Although there are some parallels, this term is inaccurate and should be avoided. For one thing, unlike FIV in cats, HIV is primarily a sexually transmitted disease in people. My primary objection, however, to the reference of this deadly disease as "feline AIDS" is that it sends fear into many people that cats are carriers of HIV and responsible for the transmission of AIDS. FIV (and FeLV) are exclusively feline problems. Research into these feline disorders is ongoing and may benefit the fight against AIDS.

Fortunately, Clancy was tested and cleared for both FIV and FeLV. His chronic upper respiratory infection responded to antibiotics and vitamins. Please consult your own veterinarian for further details about FeLV, FIV, and other serious feline diseases.

CAR ACCIDENTS

Asa was missing. She had gone out three days earlier and had not returned. Her mom was frantic. She had called every clinic in the area and every shelter within fifteen miles in case someone had brought her in. She had posted flyers on every street corner and telephone pole for blocks around, but still no Asa. On the morning of the fourth day, she heard a plaintive and very weak "meow" outside the back door. Her heart leapt and then crashed hard. She opened the door to find her little gray cat covered in blood. She had a four-inch laceration across her chest, abrasions almost everywhere, and she was dragging her tail and left rear leg. Asa collapsed when she saw her mom and was rushed to the hospital.

Motor vehicles are among the many dangers to which cats are exposed outside the safety of their homes. Cats are hit and killed by cars every day, even in quiet suburban or rural neighborhoods. I will never quite understand the practice of letting a cherished pet roam outdoors. It is like allowing your two-year-old child to play in traffic.

Cats do not always die when they are hit by cars. Sometimes they survive the initial impact and manage to find shelter. If they have minor injuries, they may hide and nurse their wounds and return home with no one the wiser. If their wounds are more serious, they may manage to crawl a short distance before collapsing from shock. Many cats die from shock before they succumb to the actual injuries sustained during the accident. Many more cats are dead before they even hit the pavement. Those who survive may be euthanized because of the cost of veterinary care that would be required to save their lives. Those who are treated and survive will have one less life to count down from nine. Cats who are hit by cars break bones and sustain internal injuries that require emergency surgery and blood transfusion. Head trauma can cause neurological problems, including the risk of seizures later in life. And every day, owners around the country tell their veterinarians that their cats would be so unhappy if they could not go outside.

Asa's tail was amputated because the nerves had been severed and she could no longer feel it or move it voluntarily. Her superficial wounds were repaired. She had a fractured pelvis and left rear leg. Her owner could not afford to see a veterinary orthopedic surgeon, and so her primary care veterinarian suggested that they try confining Asa to a cage for six weeks in the hope that the bones would mend on their own. They did, just barely. Asa walked with a limp, but she was alive. She stayed inside after that. Her owner said that Asa actually seemed to cringe when cars drove by. If you really love your cats and are concerned for their physical and emotional welfare, keep them indoors where they can safely roam.

MAMMARY TUMORS IN CATS

Zoe was a calico cat who won her home by sitting in the geraniums and looking beautiful. She was just a kitten when they took her in; and somehow, after her initial vaccinations, her parents forgot to have her spayed. She was three years old before the surgery was done, but at least she was an indoor cat and had not produced any kittens to add to the cat population explosion. After the spay, her owners noted that she was finally calm and no longer so thin and nervous. Zoe was nine years old when the first lump was found by her mom. She had been petting her tummy when her fingers slid over a hard and irregular lump near one of Zoe's nipples. Her veterinarian found several more lumps along that row of nipples and another small one on the opposite row of nipples.

Mammary tumors in cats can be benign or malignant. Benign tumors may be associated with the use of a synthetic progesterone medication that is no longer popular. The use of this hormone has fallen out of favor in part because it was linked to a list of reversible side effects, including the development of benign mammary hyperplasia. Malignant mammary tumors in cats, however, spell real trouble. They are rapidly invasive locally and often spread by metastases throughout the body before they are discovered at the primary site.

Cats that are not spayed before their first heat are at higher risk to develop malignant mammary tumors later in life. This is why veterinarians urge their clients to schedule a kitten's spay before six months of age when she is increasingly likely to begin cycling. The longer the cat is allowed to cycle, the greater her risk will be. The first heat alone, however, more than doubles her risk to develop mammary cancer. Zoe's tumors had already seeded along both mammary chains. She underwent a double mastectomy and chemotherapy in an effort to save her life. She lived another sixteen months before the tumors were detected in her lungs. By then, Zoe was losing weight and the spring had left her step. Her owners elected to have her euthanized so that she would not suffer. I tried to console them in their grief and reminded them that Zoe had had a better life for having found them. Sadly, they knew it could have been a longer one had they understood the consequences of delaying her spay. Each spring her owner faithfully grows geraniums over Zoe's sunlit grave. Zoe would have loved them. And who knows, perhaps she is nearby.

FLEAS, TICKS, AND WORMS

Jasmine was an orange-and-white, domestic longhaired cat who enjoyed the outdoor life. She took great care of her fluffy coat and flirted shamelessly with her owner. One summer day he noticed that his Jasmine looked a bit more raggedy than usual. She kept scratching at her back, and the hair near her tail was looking a bit thin. On closer inspection, he noticed what looked like dried white rice sticking to the hairs around her anus. The thought of anything hurting his Jasmine sent him into a panic, and he made an appointment for her to be seen that same day.

Jasmine had fleas. A diagnosis of these external parasites is based on the symptoms of itchiness, patchy hair thinning or loss, adult fleas on the cat's skin, and flea "dirt" (black specks on the cat's skin that are, in fact, flea feces). In some cases, a cat may be so sensitive to the bite of a single flea that the only noticeable signs are intense itchiness and a patchy coat. The treatment of fleas has come a long way in the last five years or so. The days of flea powder, flea spray, flea baths, and environmental insecticides are behind us thanks to new products that kill any fleas on your cat within hours. Other products help by sterilizing the insects, but these do not kill the adults and are usually not enough to manage a severe infestation. Your veterinarian can guide your decision toward appropriate treatment options.

Jasmine also had tapeworm. This is an intestinal worm that is transmitted by fleas and by other carriers such as field mice. This worm grows in length by the addition of segments, which each carry hundreds of eggs. The segments break away from the worm's tail end and are voided. Segments may adhere to the cat's behind and resemble rice when they dry. Tapeworm is treated by an injection or pill and by eliminating the source of the infestation. If your cat goes outside, your veterinarian may recommend treating your cat for tapeworm as a precaution even when dried segments are not visible on the coat. Tapeworm can be a silent problem that goes undetected for extended periods. The only sign might be a dull coat or an increasingly thin cat. It is often difficult to detect from microscopic analysis of stool samples.

Cats can get many other types of parasites, too. Among the most common are roundworms and coccidia. These are most serious in very young animals but can affect cats at any age and cause diarrhea, vomiting, and weight loss. They are more easily detected in stool samples. *Intestinal parasites may be contagious to people.* Young children are especially susceptible because they are notorious for putting unwashed fingers in their mouths. If you suspect that your cat has an intestinal parasite, or if your cat goes outdoors, bring a fecal sample for analysis at least once or twice every year.

Poor Jasmine. Her doctor found a surprise, a tick on her ear. It had not been there for very long, but it was in a place that was difficult for Jasmine to reach. Cats are not as severely affected by ticks as dogs. This may be because they are more flexible and more fastidious self-groomers. In many parts of the country, ticks carry serious diseases such as Lyme disease, Rocky Mountain spotted fever (RMSF), and ehrlichiosis. Ticks are easily removed by firmly grasping them as close to the cat's skin as possible with a tweezer. They should be killed before they are discarded by separating the head from the body or drowning them in rubbing alcohol or mineral oil. Some people hold them into the fire of a burning matchstick. Examine your outdoor cat daily to check for the presence of ticks. Your veterinarian can also recommend products to control ticks.

Jasmine quickly recovered from the problems she collected that summer. Her owner, however, did not. As a result of this experience, he became determined that his cat would never again be exposed to these nasty critters. Jasmine was kept inside, and after a transition period during which she loudly protested, she became a much happier and healthier pet.

HEARTWORM DISEASE IN CATS

Ernie had a cough. He was a big, brawny, brown tabby with yellow eyes who loved to sit out on the back patio and watch the sunset. He did not stray far from his yard and came back in long before bedtime. During his annual checkup Ernie's owner reported that Ernie had been coughing for about a month. His veterinarian listened to Ernie's heart and did not hear anything unusual, but he suggested they run some tests, just in case. Much to everyone's surprise, Ernie tested positive for heartworm.

Heartworms live in the heart chambers and in the major vessels of the heart. They are transmitted by the bites of carrier mosquitoes. Heartworm disease is insidious in cats. It may take months and years to develop any clinical signs, if indeed any do develop. Sudden death may be the solitary and unprecedented sign of illness in some infected cats. A cat who contracts heartworm can become quite ill with only a few adult worms in his heart. This is in contrast to adult dogs, who may harbor hundreds of worms, although a load this large is often discovered only at autopsy.

Heartworm in dogs can be treated successfully but always with great caution. The toxicity of the therapeutic drugs, coupled with the disease's side effects, make for a somewhat precarious period for dogs during treatment and recovery. In cats, however, the only treatment currently available is the prevention of further accumulation of adult worms. In severe cases where cardiac function is impaired, it may be necessary to physically remove the adult worms from the heart during delicate surgical procedures. In most cases heartworm-positive cats are treated with drugs, which kill immature heartworm, and with cardiac medication, as needed. A heartworm preventative drug for cats has recently become available and should be considered for cats who roam outdoors in heartworm-prevalent areas. It is a disease that is much easier to prevent than to treat. Ernie's owner declined treatment and decided to let nature take its course. Ernie's cough got worse, and he stayed closer to home. He got tired more easily but continued to eat well. One day, about a year after his diagnosis, Ernie went out on the back porch and watched his last sunset.

VACCINE-RELATED PROBLEMS

Buddy was vaccinated annually against the feline viral and bacterial infections included in the "feline distemper" vaccine. Despite this common reference, this combination vaccine has no effect on a cat's temperament. Buddy's owner also made sure that his rabies vaccine was given on schedule. At his third annual checkup, his distemper vaccine was boosted by his veterinarian. About forty-five minutes after returning home, Buddy seemed distressed. He started to drool profusely and then he vomited. A few minutes later he passed watery diarrhea and seemed to collapse in the middle of the floor. He was unusually quiet and sluggish. Maintaining her calm, Buddy's mom called the clinic to report his condition. She was told to give him 50 mg of diphenhydramine, an antihistamine she kept in her own medicine cabinet for her allergy to bee stings. She was instructed to bring him back to the clinic right away. Buddy was treated for his vaccine reaction; and by the time he was released a short time later, he felt just fine. Buddy had had enough needles for one day.

Vaccines are good things. I firmly believe in vaccinating my pets against everything I can if they are at risk. Any protection I can offer them from illness is all right with me. However, vaccine reactions do occur. A more common vaccine reaction is swelling at the injection site that can take days or weeks to disappear. Less common is the systemic reaction that Buddy experienced. Hypersensitivity to any component of a vaccine can develop following repeated vaccination or after a single injection. In some cases your veterinarian might advise you to forego that vaccine in the future. Alternately, it might be recommended to pretreat your cat with medication to curb any vaccine reaction. For example, your state law might require your cat to be inoculated against rabies. If your cat has had a reaction to the rabies vaccine, your veterinarian must decide whether your cat can be safely vaccinated.

In recent years more serious vaccine-related problems have emerged in a very small percentage of cats. Sporadic reports of cats around the country suggested the development of tumors at vaccine sites years later. Vaccine-related sarcomas are exceedingly rare, and their precise cause remains a mystery. New, reformulated vaccines seem promising and should reduce the incidence of many side effects. The incidence of these tumors is extremely low and should not dissuade any cat owner from having their pet vaccinated against a variety of more common and grave illnesses. Speak with your veterinarian about the availability and advisability of these new-generation cat vaccines for your cat.

FELINE ASTHMA

When Sara was sixteen years old, she developed an overactive thyroid gland. Because she was unable to tolerate the oral medication recommended to treat this disease, I elected to have her undergo radiation therapy. She would have to be hospitalized for two weeks but would not need any medication after treatment. At the time, Hershey and Sara were my only pets. Hershey was barely one year old when Sara became ill and had never been separated from her. The day she was admitted for her treatment, Hershey was beside himself. When I returned from the hospital, he was anxious and agitated. He paced restlessly, looking everywhere for Sara. He began to "meow" in a panicky voice, and his respiration rate increased. Soon he was panting and coughing. In obvious distress, I tried to calm him; but the more labored his breathing became, the more he panicked. I recognized that Hershey was having an acute asthma attack and immediately began the appropriate medication. He was better within the hour and slept through the night, even though I didn't. He was fine the next day and has never had an attack since then.

The next time I spoke with the veterinarian who was treating Sara, I asked her what she thought of Hershey's episode. I explained my suspicion that feline asthma might be triggered by an intense emotional state such as separation anxiety. A board-certified specialist in internal medicine, she confirmed that, yes, it was entirely possible, although it had never been documented in cats.

Feline asthma is easily confused with a hairball cough, cardiac cough, or upper respiratory infection. It is important to rule out these other possibilities before concluding that your cat has feline asthma. You may notice that your cat's breathing seems labored. He or she may appear breathless, pant, be easily tired, or cough. These symptoms may be signs of other conditions and are not unique to any single ailment; nevertheless, feline asthma should be considered among the list of possibilities. Your veterinarian will advise blood tests and X-rays to make the diagnosis. Once feline asthma is determined, it is generally simple to treat. Some cats need treatment for several days or weeks, and others require a lifetime of medication. Feline asthma is most frequently an allergy-related condition. As a board-certified veterinary behaviorist, however, I suspect that emotional factors might be involved more often than is currently recognized. Although many asthmatic cats probably have allergies, I expect that more cats will be identified with anxiety-related asthma in the future. At the very least it is probable that some cats with allergy-induced asthma are more ill during times of stress. This phenomenon is recognized in human medicine and will probably be demonstrated in cats someday.

Feline hyperthyroidism is a disease of middle-aged and geriatric cats. It is reviewed in more detail in chapter 13 ("Golden-Age Cats"). It is caused by thyroid tumors that are usually benign and slow growing, and is generally controlled with oral medication, radiation therapy, or surgery. The thyroid gland sets the level of a cat's metabolism, and when it is set too high (hyperthyroid) it is associated with a number of serious consequences. Most cats do very well if treatment is begun before the disease irreversibly affects other organs. Sara breezed through the radiation treatment and her two weeks away from us. When Sara came home, cured of her hyperthyroidism, Hershey was ecstatic. So was I! We all breathed easier after that.

HEART DISEASE IN CATS

Dominic was a fat boy. His dad was a baker, and Dominic was treated regularly to Bavarian cream and pastry crumbs. Dominic was fat, but he sure was happy! At twenty pounds, Dominic didn't move around too much;

however, when he failed to come for his Bavarian cream nightcap, his dad became concerned. The next day his veterinarian confirmed that Dominic was ill. He had a marked heart murmur, and his lungs were filling with fluid. His failing heart could not keep up with the demand to pump blood. Dominic's obesity was on the verge of becoming a fatal illness. His dad had been killing him with kindness for years and had ignored his veterinarian's words of warning. Dominic's condition was stabilized with cardiac medication. He was discharged with a strict new diet to provide optimum nutrition for cardiac patients and to reduce his body weight in a careful regimen. Within six months he had lost five pounds and the murmur was not as severe. Within nine months, he was down to a trim twelve pounds and was removed from all medication. No more Bavarian cream for Dominic, although his dad does admit to giving him an occasional bowl of skim milk.

Cats can suffer from many of the same heart diseases that people do. Feline *cardiomyopathy* is divided into two main categories. *Dilatative* cardiomyopathy refers to conditions that dilate the heart chambers. *Hypertrophic* cardiomyopathy implies conditions that make the heart muscle abnormally thick. Cats can have faulty heart valves, congenital malformations, heartworm, bacterial and viral cardiac infections, electrical conduction disturbances, cardiac infarct, and many more problems that impact heart function.

A precise diagnosis of cardiac disease in cats requires X-rays, an electrocardiogram (ECG or EKG), ultrasound (echocardiagram), a Doppler study, vascular catheterization, blood tests, and, of course, physical examination. Your primary-care veterinarian may have all these available at his or her facility, or you may be referred to a veterinary cardiologist for ongoing care. Treatment may include a variety of medications, prescription diet, and periodic reevaluation to monitor your cat and regulate treatment as necessary.

Obesity is a major trigger for many illnesses. It puts undue pressure on latent problems and weakens healthy organs in the long run. If a cat is too heavy, the heart has to work harder than it should and will eventually become diseased. A fat cat cannot really be considered healthy. Speak with your veterinarian about how to control your cat's weight in view of preventing or minimizing cardiac disease.

11

Nutrition

"I will eat first and wash my face afterwards."
Which all cats do, even to this day.

—CHARLES H. ROSS (1868)

NORMAL FEEDING BEHAVIOR IN CATS

*Emmett was a finicky eater. He was certainly not starving. He weighed in
at a hefty fourteen pounds, which was more than plenty for his medium-sized
frame. When Emmett turned his nose up at canned turkey-and-giblets cat
food, his mom offered liver-and-bacon flavor. The blue point Siamese cross
looked at her as if to say, "Is that all you've got to eat?" When he snubbed
the beef in gravy, she tried seafood supreme. He picked at the dry food, and
she swore she heard him say, "You've got to be kidding!" Emmett finally
settled for canned chicken, which is what he had started with. Despite pulling so much of it out because of Emmett, his mom's hair eventually did
grow back.*

In cats, feeding patterns normally fluctuate in cycles. They may lose
and gain weight at intervals of a few months. Cats will eat more in
colder weather, especially if they go outside where extra calories are
needed to stay warm. And, like us, cats may reduce food intake during
very warm weather. Cats eat less of a food they don't like and consequently may lose weight. However, adding water to food may increase
their consumption. Cats who have continual access to their food eat

about a dozen small meals a day. It has been shown that the calories in each meal are equivalent to one small mouse! A cat does not normally have such an easy time catching and eating so many mice in a day, which could be why house cats are prone to weight gain when they are free fed!

Cats have taste preferences, too. Given the choice, a cat would choose fish over meat. Fish-based diets have been associated with feline urinary tract disease and so should probably be offered infrequently; or if your cat has a history of urinary tract problems, perhaps not at all. Canned food may be more palatable, but it is also more expensive, higher in sugar (which may promote obesity), and there is some evidence that it contributes more to dental tartar than dry food. Although I have seen cats who eat only dry food develop tartar on their teeth, dental tartar does seem to be more common, and worse, in cats who eat canned food.

Cats do not require a varied diet, but they may have a preference for novelty. If your cat seems a bit disinterested in the food currently offered, the cat may be going through a normal feeding cycle. (If your cat is not eating at all, your veterinarian should be consulted, of course.) If you respond to your cat's normal fussiness by offering a new food, the cat may be more interested, at first. The novelty will wear off quickly, and the cat may again nibble or refuse it. You may get worried and offer your fickle friend some other new flavor or brand. The cat will love it at first but then become finicky. You get the picture. The point is, *you have created a finicky eater.* An occasional change is fine, but be aware that your cat's appetite will naturally wax and wane. If the new food you offer isn't quite as tasty as the cat's familiar diet, your cat will soon prefer the usual food. Don't play "musical cat food" with your cat!

HAND-RAISING ORPHANED KITTENS

Sara was just over two weeks old when I took the abandoned kitten home with me. Her little ears were rounded, and her little tail looked like it had just been glued on. She was a downy black ball who had been separated too soon from her mama. She was not ready for solid food and too young to eat anything from a bowl. So I became Mama. She did not like the kitten-nursing nipple, so I fed her with an oral syringe. I sat cross-legged on the floor feeding this fragile creature whose tiny paws wrapped around my fingers, the little foot pads so shiny and new. Within three weeks, she could eat on her own. She thrived. Twenty-two years later, she is still thriving. I must have done something right.

When the mother cat is not available, her kittens will require your assistance if they are to survive. Newborn kittens would normally nurse every few hours, and so you need to feed them about six to eight times every day. Newborns need to drink milk replacement made specifically for kittens, which is available through your veterinary clinic or pet supply store. By the time they are two or three weeks old, they can be fed a minimum of four meals a day (every six hours). You should feed kittens as much as they want at each feeding. Use a kitten nursing bottle (from your veterinarian or pet store) or even an eyedropper. If the kitten is not gaining weight (you can use a kitchen food scale for very young kittens) or is crying constantly, the kitty should be seen by a veterinarian right away. By about three or four weeks of age, your kitten will be ready for a gradual introduction of solid food. A teaspoon of finely ground canned kitten food can be mixed with some warm water to the consistency of soup at first. After a few days, you can add less water so that it is more of a paste. By the time your little orphan is six weeks old, regular kitten food should be just fine. You can mix dry and canned food, or make dry food moist with some warm water, until your kitten is a bit older and can easily eat dry food.

Until they are three or four weeks old, young kittens do not void urine or stools voluntarily. To help your baby kitty, you can use a cotton ball moistened with warm tap water. Gently stroke the genitals and anus, located just under the tail, and hold the kitten over the sink or a paper towel. It may take a few minutes, but they will feel much better when you are done!

Keep your kitten in a warm room (about 85°F for newborns, 80°F for weeks two to five, 70–75°F by six weeks) that is free of drafts. Keep young kittens in a cardboard box, lined with soft towels or old sheets, to prevent them from wandering away from the nest when you are not there. If you like, you can also place a small basket or even a baseball cap in the box as a little bed for your kitten. Be very careful not to burn your kitten in the first week or two with an external heat source. Some recommend a heat lamp or heating pad, but these can generate too much heat and a young kitten cannot move away and could get burned. It would be better to use a hot-water bottle covered with a towel. An excellent alternative is to fill an empty plastic container from milk or juice with hot water and cover it with a towel. Place it in the box but not too close to the kitten. This will generate enough heat within the box to keep your baby warm. Refill it every few hours or before it feels cool to the touch.

If you have other cats, keep your kitten isolated until at least eight weeks of age. This is to protect the kitty from any hostility from resident cats but also to protect them from her. Your kitten might have fleas, ear mites, intestinal parasites, and could even harbor one of the fatal feline viruses (FeLV, FIV, etc.). Arrange a veterinary appointment for your newcomer before introducing the cats. Speak to your veterinarian about any risks posed by your new kitten to the other cats in your home. There are few things more satisfying than rescuing abandoned or orphaned kittens. Take the basic precautions until the kitten can be safely incorporated into your household.

AGGRESSION AT MEALTIMES IN MULTICAT HOUSEHOLDS

The boys were at odds, and that was an understatement. Mealtime was a traumatic event for Jamison, Jefferson, and Jeremiah. The three orange tabby littermates had always been fed together. As kittens, they came trotting along to chow down from a single large bowl when it was filled once each day. At almost a year old, however, that bowl did not seem as large as it once had. They were big boys now with big heads and big appetites. Instead of trotting happily to the kitchen, Jamison lunged at both of his brothers; Jefferson shrank away until the other two had eaten their fill, only to vomit what he finally could eat; and Jeremiah was gaining weight at an alarming rate.

Mealtime can become an anxious time for cats in a multicat household. Competition for food can make enemies out of cats who otherwise get along. Feeding is an activity, a major event. Particularly for indoor cats with more limited entertainment, mealtime is a highlight of their day. Outdoor cats or stray cats probably eat about a dozen small meals throughout the day. Indoor cats, however, rely on the feeding schedule we impose.

How was I to help these guys? I generally do not support free feeding for cats because it is the best way to produce an obese cat. Feeding should be an activity to look forward to, whether the cat goes out or stays inside. My suggestion for Jamison, Jefferson, and Jeremiah was to feed them at least twice daily from separate bowls and confined to separate rooms. They were trained in no time to trot off to their respective feeding areas. Jamison relaxed and enjoyed every mouthful. Jefferson ate slowly and savored his food. Jeremiah shed four pounds, and his compulsive overeating disappeared. The boys eventually learned to eat from separate bowls in different corners of the kitchen. And their first feeding bowl made a very nice water dish.

In my own household, Hershey eats alone in the dining room because he tends to get very cantankerous and would steal food from the other bowls if he had the chance. Gracie and Teddi eat together in the pantry and enjoy each other's company. Sara eats in the bathroom, where she does not have to compete and can enjoy the prescription diet formulated for her aging kidneys. They all know where to wait by their own colored bowls, although Hershey still tries to cheat!

STRANGE THINGS THAT CATS EAT

I discovered my cat Jonathan's peculiar preference quite by accident when he pleaded with me to give him a little taste. He ate the cantaloupe with such enthusiasm you could practically taste it yourself. From that day onward, my boy got to feast on his own little piece whenever I had a slice. When he saw cantaloupe, his bright green eyes lit up, and he pranced around until he got his share. He liked watermelon, honeydew so-so, but that cantaloupe was his all-time favorite! I once offered Jonathan a choice between raw hamburger meat and cantaloupe just to see what he'd do. He never even hesitated and went straight for the melon! He was my Jonathan, the cantaloupe cat.

Every cat person knows that cats appear from nowhere when a can of tuna fish is opened. Cats quickly learn to come running when they hear a can opener (electric or manual) in case it is their tuna treat or a can of cat food. Even opening the refrigerator door is cause for feline celebration! Dairy products in any shape and form are traditional cat favorites. Cheese, cream, butter, margarine, yogurt, milk, of course, are definitely part of their wish list. But what about those weird things that cats seem to love . . . cantaloupe, for example? Some cats indulge in raisins, apples, and many kinds of fruit. Cats do not like citrus—oranges, lemons, limes, or grapefruit generally make their toes curl. Coconut is another of their natural aversions. Apparently, it tastes quite bitter to them. On the other hand, I have known cats, my Teddi for one, who would kill for olives and pickles. Pasta of any kind is a great treat, though spaghetti is a particular favorite. Cats love to eat the long, skinny noodle from the bottom up to your fingers! Bread, cookies, cake . . . cats are not really known for their sweet tooth but given the opportunity they'd eat it all!

And that, I think, is the secret to weird cat cravings. Opportunity. Any normal cat is definitely interested in trying unfamiliar foods. Novelty is the thing. Unless the odor is enough to put them off, the cats will try new taste sensations should the opportunity be presented. Cats are carnivores. They evolved to eat a meat-and-bones diet, along with a bit of fresh grass on the side, and a few crickets and flies, of course. Dogs are more like people in their range of diet choices. We are omnivores, eating a wide range of foods that include meat, dairy, carbohydrates, fruits, and vegetables. In many other parts of the world, additional protein is derived from insects and a variety of other sources that we do not generally exploit. I suspect that cats are dietary opportunists, but they remain true carnivores at heart. They do not require carbohydrates in their diet, but they learn by trial and error to try it and like it. We really do need to protect them from themselves.

Yes, it is true. I give my cats an occasional table scrap as a special treat. The operative word is *occasional*. It has been traditional for veterinarians to forbid their clients to feed "people food" to pets. However, giving pets a taste of leftovers now and then is so widespread (even among veterinarians) that I think it makes more sense to advise moderation rather than abstinence! So a special treat is fine, as long as it does not become the mainstay of your cat's diet. Indulge, yes; overindulge, no. Cats can have sensitive digestive systems, and it is better to stay away from anything too exotic or spicy that might upset their tummies. A tiny taste is better than a big piece of anything unfamiliar to their systems.

Cats can also have inborn food allergies or can acquire dietary sensitivities over time. Food allergies can develop suddenly in cats who have always eaten the same food, or they can be discovered accidentally after feeding a cat a special treat. If your cat is itchy, vomiting, or has diarrhea, food allergy should be included in a long list of possible diagnoses for these common symptoms. *Never ever feed your kitty chocolate or onions.* The former can be toxic in small quantities to even a ten-pound cat. The darker the chocolate, the more dangerous it may be.

Onions, cooked or raw, can cause a particular kind of anemia in cats if consumed often or in large quantities.

PRESCRIPTION DIETS FOR HEALTH

Jonathan was a sick cat for many years. He had chronic inflammatory bowel disease, which hit him hard when he was just four years old. I tried every medication known to try to control his symptoms and his discomfort. Nothing really worked. He ate a prescription diet that is formulated for cats with intestinal problems. It contains a quantity of plain rice, which is wonderful for absorbing intestinal fluids and helps to minimize diarrhea. He was not particularly thrilled with the bland food, but I know the prescription diet helped. Eventually, he developed kidney failure. Another prescription diet is formulated for kidney patients. I mixed the intestinal and kidney diets, knowing that he would enjoy more flavor from the kidney diet. With so many counts against him, his failing health would take him from me too soon. He was a brave boy, and I miss him still.

Commercial cat foods are formulated to provide your cat with a balanced and complete diet. There are product lines for healthy kittens, adults, and less active adults. Should your cat become ill, however, his nutritional needs will change. For example, a bland diet (no spices, boiled chicken, or hamburger meat, and boiled white rice) is the first thing your veterinarian will recommend when your cat has diarrhea. If the illness becomes protracted and this diet is required for more than just a few days, prescription diets are available to satisfy your cat's nutritional requirements.

Your veterinarian is the best person to recommend which diet is right for your cat's specific condition. There are prescription diets for cats with kidney and liver disease, heart disease, and urinary bladder disease. There are other diets that will help your cat to lose weight if you have been unsuccessful on your own. There is a diet for intestinal problems, and a high-protein diet for cats recovering from serious illness. Recently, a new diet has been introduced to prevent the buildup of dental tartar, and another prevents problems related to hairball formation. There are even a number of special diets for cats with food allergies. The convenience and quality of these prescription diets are wonderful. We are all so busy that it is nice to know that there are alternatives to help our cats maintain healthy lives for as long as they have to live. Enjoy every moment. Living happily ever after is never long enough.

THE DIFFICULTY OF TREATING DIABETES IN CATS

Sara first became diabetic when she was eighteen years old. I noticed that she was drinking a lot of water and urinating even more. A blood test revealed that she had an elevated glucose level. I began insulin treatment immediately. She seemed to require more and more insulin over the next few weeks. I tested her blood sugar daily, twice a day at first, and then monitored her overall appearance and water consumption. After a few weeks on her maintenance dose, she seemed to become quieter than usual. I retested her blood glucose, and sure enough, it was too low. This meant she was getting too much insulin. For the next several weeks, I kept reducing her insulin and her glucose continued to drop. She required less and less insulin until I finally stopped it all together. She was fine for the next three years. Recently, she did it again. She was on insulin for a total of six weeks, and has been weaned off it again. So why am I telling you about Sara's diabetes in a chapter about nutrition?

Well, because diabetes is often intimately related to food. The relationship is as much causative as it is curative, or at least part of the treatment. Obese cats are particularly prone to developing diabetes, among other major problems. Cats who have recurring gastrointestinal upset are also prone to it. For example, feeding your cat spicy table scraps might create inflammation in the digestive tract. Cats who get into the garbage, inside or outside, consume less than wholesome contents. Recurring problems with hairballs might even be enough to inflame the intestinal lining. Feline diabetes is a complicated disorder that is different in every cat and demands close cooperation with your veterinarian.

Diabetes is caused by malfunction of the pancreas, which is connected to the intestine. If the intestine becomes inflamed near the pancreatic duct, the pancreas could become affected *(pancreatitis)*. The signs of pancreatitis can include diarrhea and vomiting, or the inflammation can be mild and go unnoticed. There are primary diseases of the pancreas, too, such as benign or malignant tumors. In Sara's case her body weight has always been normal. She has occasional bouts of hairball regurgitation; but other than that, she is healthy. I suspect that her bouts with diabetes were due to a mild pancreatitis that resolved after several weeks of supportive insulin treatment.

Diabetes, even when it is a permanent condition in cats, is notoriously difficult to treat. The dose may need frequent adjustments. It is important to be patient and to work with your veterinarian, who will be just as frustrated as you are! One of the things that your veterinarian will certainly discuss with you is your cat's diet. If you are able to reduce your obese cat's body weight, the insulin dose will be reduced. It is possible that your cat might not even need insulin after a while! Canned cat food should be avoided in diabetic cats because it is higher in sugar than dry food. You might be advised to feed your cat a high-fiber prescription food or to add fiber to her regular food, because fiber helps to capture sugars in the digestive tract before they are absorbed into the system. It is also important to make sure that your diabetic cat eats at regular intervals so that the insulin does not act to lower the blood sugar on an empty stomach and make the glucose levels plummet.

So now you see that diabetes has a lot to do with food! Food can cause diabetes (too much, too spicy, too rotten) and it can help to control it (prescription diets, high-fiber diet, weight reduction, and regular meals).

WHAT CATS DRINK

Butch was a burly boy who swaggered when he walked. A neutered, brown patched tabby of five or so years, he was a husky lad who probably would have been a Marine had he been human. He liked to get into scraps with other neighborhood toms, had a girlfriend or three, and drank water only from the tap. The water bowl was just not his thing. Every day, several times a day, he hopped up on the kitchen counter for his mom to turn on the faucet.

He liked to have a long, cool drink when she was washing her hands anywhere in the house. Sometimes he played with the stream and shook the droplets off his paw, sprinkling everything around him. If he was thirsty, he stood up by a sink and meowed. His mom knew that this was part entertainment and part attention-seeking behavior, but she also knew it was good for Butchie to drink. When she went away for a few days, she would leave a little tabletop water fountain so that her boy would have the running water he craved. Butchie had high standards. Yup, he would have made a great Marine if he weren't such a big pussy!

Some pet owners think that cats do not require much liquid, but they do. Our pet cats are descendants of the African wild cat (*Felis lybica*). The feline ability to produce highly concentrated urine, necessary when water is scarce, probably originates from their adaptation to the African climate. Your cat needs to drink a minimum of 30 ml (six teaspoons) of water for every pound of body weight every day. If your cat weighs ten pounds, he should have a minimum of 300 ml of water, the equivalent of sixty teaspoons, or twenty tablespoons, or ten ounces of water daily! This requirement increases if your cat is stressed, has a fever, or is ill. Even healthy pet cats must be encouraged to drink adequate water, or they will be predisposed to urinary tract disease. Kittens may drink twice the amount of adult cats. Normal cats drink twice as much water by weight than they eat in food. Cats who are fed canned food obtain much of their water in the food and don't need to drink as much water from their water bowl. Cats who eat dry or semi-moist food need to drink water.

Because they are mammals, cats have a natural preference for milk. After they are weaned, however, kittens and cats no longer require milk as part of their basic diet. An occasional treat is fine, but you do not *have* to give cats milk for them to be healthy. Milk contains water, and calcium, and a bit of protein. Your cat can get all of these elements in a good cat food and a water bowl. If your cat has not had any milk for some time, the ability to digest it, will likely be lost, and milk might cause diarrhea. The enzyme necessary to digest lactose, the sugar in milk, is called *lactase*. Lactase is not produced unless milk is ingested on a regular basis. In fact, some cats actually develop a permanent inability to digest milk or acquire a dietary hypersensitivity to milk. This is similar to lactose intolerance in people. If you want to give your cat milk as a special treat, offer a small bowl of low-fat or skim milk diluted with water. This way, you will encourage the cat to drink and still spoil your kitty just a bit! On a daily basis, however, encourage your cat to drink by keeping the water bowl clean and filled with fresh water. You can even add a bit of salt (to make them thirstier) or water to your cat's food. And if your cat prefers running water, have fun choosing a tabletop fountain. These will add to your decor as well as reduce your stress level with the same sound of running water that delights your cat!

RAW FISH AND THIAMINE DEFICIENCY

Clyde loved raw fish. His dad owned a seafood restaurant, and he frequently spoiled his big black cat with meals of the best and freshest fish. One day he noticed that Clyde was looking a bit ragged and walking in a hunched position. He seemed to be less interested in food, too. Clyde's dad decided to wait a few days to see how his condition improved. He brought home an extra special treat of fresh trout to boost Clyde's spirits. The next morning Clyde seemed worse. His dad vowed to take him to the veterinary clinic later that day; but before he left for work, Clyde had a seizure. His dad drove like a madman to the veterinary hospital and burst in just as they were opening the doors for clinic hours. After a few questions, the veterinarian swept Clyde off to the treatment area to place an intravenous catheter and to administer medication to control the seizure. He soon came out and chatted with Clyde's owner. He asked him if Clyde had eaten anything unusual in the last few days. Clyde's dad replied that he had eaten his usual favorite raw fish. This information was the key to saving Clyde's life. Following treatment, Clyde recovered so quickly that he was home by the end of the day! From then on, he learned to love his cat food and still enjoyed an occasional snack of fried haddock, too.

Fresh, uncooked fish may contain high amounts of an enzyme called thiaminase. Thiaminase, as the name implies, destroys the B vitamin thiamine. Cooked fish does not cause the same rapid destruction of thiamine because the enzyme is easily neutralized with heat. Thiamine deficiency is responsible for neurological and cardiac irregularities, but the most common symptoms of a thiamine-deficient cat include poor appetite, a hunched body position, and an unkempt coat. These symptoms are, of course, common to many other ailments. A history of eating raw fish is significant to your veterinarian and will help to pinpoint the diagnosis. Treatment includes the administration of thiamine, which improves the cat's status within minutes or hours, followed, of course, with a balanced diet that contains adequate supplies of thiamine.

An occasional taste of tuna fish or the liquid in a can of tuna fish will not cause a thiamine deficiency. Canned tuna is cooked during its preparation. Too much consumption of a fish-based diet has been linked with the development of urinary tract disease and should only be given on an occasional basis.

VITAMIN SUPPLEMENTS AND YOUR CAT

Katrina was a Birman under strain. She was four months old and had a persistent upper respiratory infection. Her nose was very congested, and she lost her appetite until the antibiotics prescribed by her veterinarian finally helped her to turn the corner toward healthy kittenhood. Still, she had lost her zip, and her coat and expression seemed a bit dull. Her owner was advised to add warm water to her high-protein canned food to make certain she was drinking enough. A vitamin powder was also sprinkled onto her food. Her veterinarian explained that she needed short-term supplementation because she had stopped eating for almost a week. Katrina's blue-violet eyes soon regained their sparkle, and her dainty white feet slid across the tile floors once more.

Most commercial cat foods are already nutritionally complete and balanced. They are fortified with the vitamins, minerals, and essential amino acids (such as taurine, which is necessary for normal vision), to meet the daily requirements of a healthy cat. Vitamin supplements may be recommended, however, for cats and kittens who are ill or recovering from a condition that depletes their energies. Postpartum queens, for example, may benefit from a high-calorie vitamin paste. Cats who are anemic, anorectic, and suffering from stress from any number of physical ailments may benefit from nutritional supplements. Sick kitties lose some vitamins, in particular the B vitamins, at a more rapid rate during illness or stress.

There are two types of vitamins. The *fat-soluble* vitamins are A, D, E, and K; these are not eliminated as readily as other vitamins, and it is important not to overdose them. For example, feeding your cat too much liver will result in hypervitaminosis A. Cats are unusual in that they cannot convert beta-carotene to vitamin A, and commercial cat foods contain preformed quantities. Vitamin D deficiency is rare but is occasionally seen in kittens born in winter when sunlight is low. Sunshine is required to create vitamin D from its precursor in the skin. Vitamin E overdose can occur from excessive consumption of marine fish oils (e.g., cod liver oil). The actual requirement of vitamin K has yet to be determined in cats, but it is essential for normal clotting of blood.

The second type of vitamins is the *water-soluble* vitamin, which include the B and C vitamins. Problems associated with water-soluble vitamins are likely to be deficiencies since these are easily eliminated from the body when consumed in excess. Thiamine deficiency is seen in cats who are fed a diet high in uncooked fish, primarily freshwater fish, and is easily avoided by feeding a good quality commercial diet. Speak with your veterinarian for specific nutritional recommendations that may benefit your pet cat.

EXCLUSIVE MEAT DIETS AND YOUR CAT

Minnie was a very chubby two-year-old Russian Blue. She lived quietly with her devoted mom, who fed her only the best that money could buy. Liver, filet mignon, pork chops, steak tips . . . only choice cuts of meat would do for her Minnie. She went to the butcher shop every day to bring home Minnie's morsels. When she noticed that Minnie was limping, she took her to be examined; but the veterinarian's initial exam did not reveal anything significant. He thought that Minnie had overexerted her chubby self and would be fine with a few days' rest. Well, a few days later, Minnie hopped

*off the sofa and screamed in pain. She lifted her paw up and would not walk
on it at all. An X ray revealed that she had broken her leg! It also showed
something more insidious. Minnie's bones were thin and pale. In addition,
she had a hairline fracture on another leg and several of her ribs. What was
happening to Minnie?*

A diet of meat only is inadequate nutrition for cats. Yes, cats are carnivores, but they cannot survive on meat alone. In the wild, cats hunt
for small prey and insects and supplement these with some grasses. They
consume small mammals from the head downward, generally in the
direction of hair growth. Bones and other organs are eaten in addition
to muscle. Insects usually are eaten whole. If your cats eat only meat,
even the best cuts of meat or liver, they will not be getting adequate
minerals or vitamins. A deficiency in calcium will result and lead to
bone resorption as the body tries to deliver calcium to vital organs such
as the heart. In other words, calcium will be stolen from bone deposits
and redistributed to satisfy the need. Eventually, the bones will become
thin and brittle, resulting in pathological fractures and abnormal movement, among other problems. This condition is reversible in most cases,
but it is even easier to avoid.

The fat content is also important. Cats need higher levels of fat compared to dogs or people, for instance, and this too will be lacking in an
exclusive meat diet. Cats require as much as 60 percent of their caloric
intake in fat. This is twice the amount that dogs require! Food intake
must be limited, particularly with very tasty diets, because cats will not
limit the amount they consume and will become obese.

Most commercial diets are already formulated to satisfy your cat's
nutritional needs. Choose the better-known brands that have stood the
test of time. Some pet foods are marketed as "natural" but this does not
mean that they are any more, or less, natural than a product without
this label. There is no regulated definition for just what "natural" means.
A label of "natural" does not carry any real meaning except that it is a
useful marketing tool. Your objection to the use of preservatives and
color additives to your pet's food is understandable; however, there is
no evidence of any health problems associated with their use. If you
choose to feed your pet a preservative-free food, the food may have a

shorter shelf life, and it might be better to purchase it in smaller quantities. Read the labels carefully and consider the quality of the ingredients. For example, a food may contain 29 percent protein, but it could be a poor quality food compared to another higher quality brand that offers 28 percent protein instead.

Cats need more protein than many other animals. Growing kittens, for instance, need at least 28 percent protein and reach their adult size by the time they are nine or ten months old. The most rapid growth phase occurs up to three or four months of age. Adult cats need a minimum of 21 percent protein, but pregnant and nursing females require as much protein as growing kittens. For this reason it is recommended that breeding and lactating females be fed kitten food until the kittens are weaned. In fact, it is advised to allow pregnant and nursing females to free feed to make certain that their intake is adequate. Nursing females may require as much as two to three times the amount of food normally consumed to meet the demand of her litter. The size of the litter will, of course, impact the mother's caloric intake.

Minnie's skeletal injuries mended with cage rest (to promote healing and to prevent additional trauma to her brittle bones), calcium supplement, and a balanced diet. Her owner felt strongly about preparing her cat's food and reported that Minnie refused store-bought cat food (no wonder, she was offered filet mignon instead). Her veterinarian helped her to devise a home-cooked, balanced meal for Minnie to enjoy. Minnie, however, would not help her wash the dishes despite her extra efforts!

PERILS OF FREE-FEEDING

Johnny Carson, Ed McMahon, and Doc Severinson had some issues over food. Johnny was thin, Ed was plump and gaining more, and Doc maintained a relatively healthy weight. At two years of age, they were no longer young kittens and didn't burn off the calories the way they once had. Doc ate well but didn't overdo it. He was a busy guy, chasing the other two away from the food bowl when he was nearby, even when he had no interest in a snack. Johnny was the shy boy. He was easily intimidated and seemed anxious when he ate, almost looking over his shoulder as if on the lookout for his two bully brothers. He ate quickly and gorged himself, then scurried away in a nervous tizzy. He often vomited half of what he'd eaten, and the other two hovered nearby to enjoy the surprise meal. Ed was a recreational eater. He just nibbled every time he walked by his food (and Doc wasn't there). He nibbled before and after a snooze. He nibbled when his owners had their breakfast and dinner. He nibbled at bedtime. Any excuse to eat was a good excuse.

It can be difficult to control your cat's weight, especially in a multicat household. Cats, like people, may have emotional attitudes about food. And like us, every cat metabolizes their food differently. Cats who have been food-deprived do not necessarily eat more, but they may eat more quickly. Social stress, which is common in homes with more than one cat, can also impact a cat's appetite. For example, a dominant cat (like Doc) might ambush a subordinate cat near the feeding area. This might discourage a submissive cat (like Johnny) from eating, and he might lose weight or he could learn to feed at odd hours (like Ed) and consume as much as possible in a short period in case his tormentor appeared!

Neutering your cats will alter their metabolism, and they may be more prone to weight gain. This means that it is important to control food intake in neutered pets. Although many commercial food labels recommend that you feed your cat kitten food for the first year, this may be far more protein than your young cat requires. Cats are generally grown by the age of nine or ten months, and most pet cats are neutered long before this. Feeding your cat a high-protein kitten food will result in a conversion of the unused protein into fat deposits. And the battle of the bulge will begin at an early age. For most cats, begin gradual introduction of a commercial adult-formula food by approximately six months of age, or about one month prior to neutering. After neutering, decrease the quantity of kitten food over several weeks until he or she is eating exclusively adult food. If your cat has been neutered younger than six months, begin a mixture of kitten and adult food until about six months of age before feeding adult food only.

Left to their own devices, most cats would probably eat at least a dozen or more small meals a day. Obesity is just a few mouthfuls away for indoor or outdoor cats if food is always available. Free feeding, or *ad lib* feeding, is a common practice among many cat owners. It may also be the single most important reason that so many pets become obese. Cats do not limit their intake when food is available. They seem to eat to maintain their weight; but if that weight is already excessive, they will remain obese. Add to this the fact that some cats eat just to have something to do, and obesity is almost unavoidable. In addition, some cats learn to vocalize or resort to some other mischief in order to be fed. Their owner may mistake the cat's need for attention with hunger and give him or her food, which reinforces mischievous attention-seeking behavior. The cat then learns to misbehave in order to get extra helpings of food. This cat will be chubby in no time!

Owners will often report how little their obese cat eats. The cat is obviously still eating more than a healthy serving! Weight is a function of intake (food) and output (exercise!). Therefore, *weight loss is a matter of reducing intake and increasing output!* Play with your cat more to burn off those extra calories! It is far easier to monitor your cat's intake by keeping to a feeding schedule and removing the uneaten portion immediately after the cat has eaten enough and leaves the food bowl. If you are not sure how much your cat is eating, give about three or four tablespoons of food, the amount that will fill a cat's stomach in one meal. Whatever is left over, give that much less at the next meal. Two daily feedings, about twelve hours apart, is fine for most cats. Some cats can be very preoccupied with food, however; so if your cat is one of these, offer food three times a day. This does not mean that you feed your cat more! Distribute the newly reduced food ration over each daily meal.

If your cat is not losing weight after a few weeks, reduce this quantity by about 25 percent. Remember, in order to lose weight your cat must burn up the fat reserves, and this can only happen if you feed a bit less than what the cat needs to maintain the current weight. Your cat may become a bit irritable at first and demand more food, but don't give in. This is for the cat's own good! Your cat will get used to eating less and will feel better, too! On the other hand, you don't want your cat to lose too much weight too rapidly. A weight loss of about one-quarter to one-half pound a week is acceptable. If your cat is losing weight more rapidly than this, increase food intake a bit more to slow down the pace! If your cat is still not losing weight by simply reducing the usual food, your veterinarian can offer you prescription diets to help your cat regain that svelte physique.

12

Grooming

I like little pussy, her coat is so warm;
And if I don't hurt her she'll do me no harm.

—JANE TAYLOR (1783–1824)

HOW AND WHY TO BATHE A CAT

As part of my veterinary training, I spent a good deal of time with farm animals. This included visiting outlying farms and treating injured or sick cows, sheep, pigs, goats, and horses on site. Barns were a whole new scene to this city girl. With the exception of calvings at 3 A.M. during frigid Canadian winters, I enjoyed it immensely. Part of the farm menagerie always included colonies of feral cats. They were not quite pets, not quite wild. They lived in an easy truce with the farmers who poured milk, straight from the udder, into huge pans set on bails of hay. The rest of their diet consisted of mice and other pests. Most of these cats were cautious with strangers, but occasionally they were very sweet and friendly. It was from just such a place that my first cat, Jonathan, was found. He had fleas, ear mites, and smelled, well, like a barn. The scent of manure clung to his skinny four-month-old frame. He was one stinky boy. I gave him a flea bath before his feet ever touched the ground in my apartment. However, the bath was not enough to erase the perfume of "eau de moo" and a second shampoo with dishwashing liquid soon followed. Finally, the luster returned to his long, black hair, and his emerald green eyes sparkled. It was the start of something big for us both.

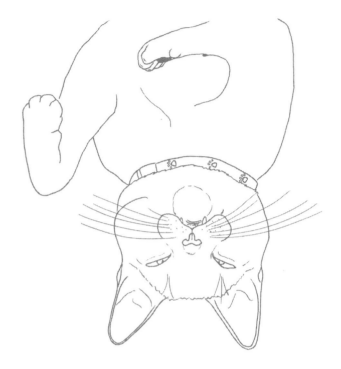

Cats are not usually keen on getting wet. They can swim, as instinct would dictate their feline version of the "dog paddle," but most cats would not elect it as a favorite recreation. Adapted to the arid climate of the African continent where their wild ancestor *(Felis lybica)* still roams the underbrush of the plains and forests, cats much prefer to be warm and dry. Most cats probably are insulted by being immersed in water, although some (like my Teddi) seem to relish the experience. The shampoo part can't be much appreciated either, especially if soap gets in their eyes. Detergent shampoos, such as dishwashing liquid, baby shampoos, or pet shampoos, do not sting a kitty's beautiful eyes as much as other shampoos might.

Ultimately, cats are not meant to be bathed frequently. In fact, they should be bathed only if absolutely necessary. A slightly soiled coat is usually something that a cat can take care of by himself. A bit of mud is quick to dry and is easily brushed away. Indoor cats usually stay very clean, and even cats who are permitted to roam outdoors do a nice job of maintaining their appearance. Longhaired cats are more prone to tangles and mats and often require consistent grooming. Persians, for example, have a very fine yet dense coat that must be groomed daily to keep it silky and neat.

Bathing a cat with a normal, healthy coat simply isn't necessary. It is traumatic for some cats, and it is a waste of your valuable time! There are other reasons to avoid bathing your pet unnecessarily. Shampoos strip away the natural oils that protect your cat's skin from infection. Frequent baths will promote dry, flaky skin and predispose your pussycat to bacterial and fungal infections. Ear infections, eye infections, even urinary tract infections can also be associated with excessive bathing.

Medicinal baths, as directed by your veterinarian for the treatment of fleas or other skin ailments, are a good reason to bathe your cat. If you really must bathe your cat, here are some tips to help make it easier for you both:

- Trim the cat's nails a day or two before the bath to minimize any injury to you if your cat tries to bolt or has a hissy fit. Yes, you could trim your cat's nails the same day, but if your cat resents being handled it is usually better to avoid doing too much in a single day!
- If possible, brush the cat's coat the day of the bath to eliminate tangles and remove at least some of the dead hair before the coat is wet.
- A deep sink or basin is usually best. A bathtub with a glass door (to prevent escapes!) is even handier.
- I recommend that you prepare the bathwater before you bring your cat into the room. Your cat may panic at the sound of running water, particularly if this is not the first bathing experience.
- It might be helpful to confine your cat to another room while you prepare the bathwater so that the cat is available when the bath is drawn (and not hiding under the basement stairs!).
- Fill the basin of the sink or tub to the cat's midchest level. Water

temperature should be lukewarm. Test with your elbow or the inside of your wrist to make sure the water is not hot but not cold either.

- Gently collect the cat with a towel or light blanket; carry the cat with his or her head covered to keep the bath a surprise. Place the cat in the water immediately. Scruff your cat's neck or use a harness and leash (tied to the faucet) to keep the cat in the tub. Don't forget to close the door behind you. Keep the bathroom or kitchen door closed to prevent drafts and an easy getaway.

- A handheld shower is a wonderful tool (test the water temperature first!), but if you don't have one, a plastic container is just as good to ladle water over the cat's back. Use your hand to wet down the head and face so that you won't get too much water in the kitty's ears or nose.

- Lather and rinse with the plastic bowl or cup (although if this is a medicated bath it might be necessary to delay rinsing). A second lather is unlikely to be necessary, but a thorough rinse is important.

- The most important tip is to *plan ahead*. The water, the ladle, the harness, and several plush towels should be on hand. Consider taking the phone off the hook. Make sure that nothing on the stove or in the oven needs your attention. Clear your agenda and you will be more relaxed. If you approach the experience in a calm and relaxed way, your cat is more likely to take it in stride.

- Never leave your cat unattended in the water!

- Let the water drain without letting go of your cat. Keep the cat on the floor or in the empty tub so that you are less likely to be scratched.

- Keep the towels within easy reach so that you don't have to leave the cat before the job is done. Reach for the towel and bundle the cat up as soon as you can. Your job is to blot the excess, not to buff him dry. Change to a dry towel as soon as the first one is saturated.

- Some cats will tolerate a blow dryer if you let the motor run for a few minutes before taking it anywhere near your cat. Keep it at a distance, on a low or medium setting. If your cat does not take to this, put it away. Keep the cat in an easy-to-clean room (bathing will loosen up any remaining dead hair that wasn't brushed away prior to bathing) until the cat is almost dry. Offer your pet a special treat during the drying phase for some much-needed reassurance and to signal that the worst is over.

. . . or make an appointment with a pet groomer! Your veterinarian can recommend groomers who are comfortable grooming cats. In fact, many veterinary clinics offer grooming services as well. Save yourself some time and energy! Relax, be happy! Either way, your cat will forgive you in no time! .

HOW TO GROOM YOUR CAT/KITTEN

My Sara has never really enjoyed being held, but she loves to be brushed. Well, not exactly brushed, combed really. She hated the wire brush that is most often recommended for cats. So I tried a simple plastic comb with short, rounded teeth made for people. And, lo and behold, she loved it! I gave her a special little food treat (a dab of a kitty vitamin paste of which she is very fond) during her initial grooming sessions to make sure she associated the new experience with something appealing. Eventually, no treats were necessary. She arches her back into each stroke as I gently run the little comb through her plush coat. Her faint purr is my reward. I have often found that the best solutions to life's problems are the simple ones.

Have you ever touched the bristles on some of the brushes manufactured for use on cats? They are sharp and prickly, and judging from the reactions of many cats, they must tug at the hair and irritate a cat's sensitive skin. There are metal combs as alternatives, but these, too, feel cold and hard. A soft, pliable comb with rounded teeth is much more comfortable and far less expensive than most cat-grooming devices. Another nice option is a grooming mitt that is sold in pet stores. Whatever tool you choose, it should be gentle, effective, and as close to the sensation of petting your cat as possible. Try a variety of grooming tools to see which one your cat prefers.

Brush or comb your pet along the direction of hair growth. This is infinitely more comfortable than going against the coat. Some cats will become irritated if you brush their hair the wrong way, and this will put a damper on future grooming sessions. It can be helpful to remove additional hairs by combing "backwards," but if you notice any sign of resentment when you do, be considerate of your cat's preferences.

The normal hair-growth cycle is about four months. Each hair follicle will produce a new hair and drop the old one in that time. But there are seasonal peaks, as you may already know. Spring and fall seem to be the most active times for the old coat to be shed. Heavier winter coats are shed in the spring, and in the fall, hormonal changes promote the growth of a new winter coat.

It is amazing how much hair a healthy cat can shed. It's better to help it along with regular grooming to prevent hairballs and cat hair blanketing every surface in your home. There is nothing that will prevent your cat from shedding. It is a normal and healthy phenomenon. There are many products sold that claim to stop this natural process, but they are generally ineffective. Brushing your cat will help to remove hairs that would otherwise come out in clumps or adhere to your upholstery and clothing. A healthy diet and a clean environment will promote a healthy coat. A healthy cat will have a healthy coat. If your cat's coat looks dull, patchy, flaky, or if your cat is itchy and scratches or licks excessively, your veterinarian should be consulted.

If you would like to have your cat groomed by a professional, introduce them to each other early. Provide the groomer with your pet's favorite treat to help their relationship get off on the right foot, or paw. Ask for feedback about your cat's behavior after each appointment. Don't be afraid to make suggestions regarding choice of comb or brush. Supply one that you have already tested and your cat seems to enjoy. You could also stay periodically to watch your pet being groomed. Your discussions and observations will help to identify problems so that you can work with the groomer to prevent them from getting worse along the way. A caring professional will always be happy to comply with your suggestions when they are intended to keep your cat comfortable and to keep your business!

HOW TO INTRODUCE GROOMING TO YOUR KITTEN OR CAT

Rumplepuss hated to be brushed. He was a scraggly cat with missing teeth and a crumpled ear, but he was, oh, so grateful to be out of the cold and off the streets. He would tolerate only a stroke or two before regressing to his alley cat ways, hissing and spitting and running off in a huff. His owner was exasperated, and Rumplepuss had begun to avoid her when she approached. I advised her to stop trying to groom him altogether for a month or so. I also recommended that she play more with him and feed him by hand for a while so that she could casually and briefly pet him with her free hand. Eventually, she was able to get in a few brush strokes several times a week while he ate his dinner. Soon he was neat and polished and a lap cat, much to his owner's delight. Rumplepuss wasn't a rumpled puss after all!

Introduce your kitten or cat to a gentle grooming mitt or comb as soon as you can. Keep the introductory sessions very brief. Do one or two strokes on a daily basis rather than trying to do the whole coat in one sitting every once in a while. As you stroke your cat's coat, give your cat a little bit of cream cheese or something else equally yummy. Use a treat that is reserved for grooming only so that it acquires special significance and appreciation. This will also keep your kitty from biting at the comb or playing with your hand. The treat should be a tiny tidbit— just a little taste, not an entire meal. You won't need to use bribes forever, only at first, when you are training your cat to tolerate grooming. Another way to distract your cat and to make grooming an enjoyable activity is to play with the cat as you brush or comb the coat. Dangle a toy on a string with one hand while you gently groom with the other. The idea is that grooming should be fun and not an uncomfortable or forced event that leaves you both frazzled and disenchanted with each other. Keep initial sessions brief and reward your cat's patience. Build on a positive experience over many weeks, and your cat's trust will grow. Eventually, you should be able to extend grooming sessions and successfully comb the entire coat.

Stroke your cat from front to back in the direction of hair growth. Going against the pattern of hair growth can be uncomfortable, and few cats will tolerate it for very long. Many cats are naturally defensive of vulnerable body parts, such as the belly, and resent being petted or groomed there. My advice is simple: Avoid tender areas, particularly if the cat can easily reach these. Emphasize the positive, avoid the negative. If your cat tries to get away, let the kitty go! Forcing a cat to be groomed is generally unnecessary and will only teach the cat to avoid you next time you try. You might also be injured in your attempt to restrain your cat. Stop grooming before your cat reaches his or her level of intolerance. There is always tomorrow. The idea is to build it into a pleasant experience that your cat eagerly anticipates. The sight of the mitt or comb or brush should make your cat purr! Stop *before* the cat has had enough. Contact with you should be a good thing. After all, that is the basis of your relationship and the key to living happily ever after.

HOW TO DEAL WITH A MATTED COAT

Felicity was a mess. She was a white domestic longhair with silky hair that matted easily. The brush would not undo the knots, and in the winter, static electricity seemed to generate even more tangles. Unable to comb through a particularly large mat, her owner decided to simply cut out the matted hair. Felicity needed sutures to close the inch-long laceration and avoided him for weeks afterward. Needless to say, Felicity's dad felt worse than she did.

Matted coats can be a nightmare. They are not just unattractive and a challenge to groom, the knotted hair is uncomfortable for the poor cat. As the hairs mat together, they pull on the skin. In addition, when the coat is sufficiently matted, the skin cannot "breathe" and this predisposes skin to infection. The cat cannot groom through a heavily matted coat either, and parasites may take advantage of any lack of personal hygiene. Many cats have a few knots here and there, but longhaired cats can develop "body mats." The only way to remove these massive mats is to shave the cat. These frequently come off in one thick solid piece that looks like a rug shaped like the cat! Negligence of this kind is difficult to understand when it is so easy to make grooming, either at home or by a professional, a routine.

If the knots form faster than you or your cat can manage, or when the cat seriously resents your grooming attempts, it is best to have your pet professionally groomed. If there are only a few knots, however, try separating the strands with your fingers. Avoid pulling on the skin, just divide the knot into smaller ones and then work on each small one in turn. Frequently, the small knots can be easily removed by holding the hairs at the base (to keep the skin from moving) and then combing or pulling them out. Remember, the hairs don't have sensation but the skin does! If you can't reduce the knot size in this manner, a pet groomer will be able to do it for you. It is generally unwise to go anywhere near your cat with scissors. However, if you are confident that you will not harm your cat, use scissors with rounded tips and carefully snip just a few strands at a time with the *tips* of the scissors only. Make certain you can see where the knot and your cat's skin meet. If you can't, don't even try.

GROOMING BEHAVIOR IN CATS

Gidget, a shorthaired blue-cream calico, was a bouncy pussycat who was always very very busy. After she was done with her daily chores of chasing flies, climbing the bookcase, watching the birds in the yard, and tripping her owner as she carried carefully folded fresh laundry, Gidget liked to make sure she was looking her best. She would find a stream of sunlight and stretch out. She groomed a bit before her nap and did a more thorough job when she awoke. One day Gidget took a nap on the back of the sofa. When she woke up, she began grooming herself as usual, but much to her surprise, rolled backward off the couch. She looked up casually as if to say she "meant to do that," found a sunny spot on the carpet, and resumed her primping. Her owner laughed until her sides ached. Gidget was not easily embarrassed.

Cats normally groom themselves up to 8 percent of their waking moments or about 4 percent of a twenty-four-hour day. This is almost an hour a day! Under certain conditions, grooming is prolonged. For example, cats with external parasites such as fleas can be expected to spend more time grooming themselves. Grooming behavior is also an important indicator of a cat's health. Sick cats, especially if they have a fever, often stop grooming themselves. Chronically ill cats frequently have a dull and ragged coat. This is partly because of their illness but also because of a decrease in maintaining normal behavior, such as self-grooming.

Grooming behavior is stereotyped in cats. This means that most cats groom the same way because it is primarily under genetic control. Cats use the front paws to clean the head and ears, licking the paw to wet the hair and then wiping the paw in circular patterns over the top of the head. The head is cleaned with the cat in a sitting position. The rest of the body is licked while reclining or half sitting.

The feline tongue is nothing less than a marvel. It is a muscle that is used to feed, to groom, and even to show affection. The surface of the tongue provides the cat with important sensory information. Taste buds are located on the sides, tip, and back of the tongue. The center of the tongue has no taste buds. Instead, it is covered with hooked spines composed of keratin (the same protein in human fingernails). These are what give the cat's tongue its abrasive texture. The spiny tongue is a special adaptation to aid in shedding old hairs as the cat licks herself or a close companion, to clean her kittens, to remove meat off the bone, or to wipe the dinner plates clean! Pussycat kisses can be an irritating experience if the cat licks too hard, but once your cat has learned to check the pressure against your naked skin, there are few things more delightful than a soft pussycat kiss.

HAIRBALL TIPS AND FACTS

Phoebe was coughing. Her owner thought she might have caught a cold, but a trip to the veterinarian soon determined that she was perfectly healthy. It seemed that Phoebe was vomiting hairballs every now and then, too. When Phoebe coughed, she would crouch down with her head and neck extended. She also swallowed a bit when she was done. Her owner's description of the behavior, along with an absence of any other physical problem, allowed her doctor to diagnose hairballs.

Did you know that rabbits and calves can also have problems with hairballs? Hairballs are clumps of hair, removed during grooming, that become compressed in the digestive tract. More often than not, these are eliminated in stools. Occasionally, however, hairballs become large enough to plug up the intestine and stop the normal passage of food and fluids. The hairball cough is not really a cough but a specialized gagging that helps to promote the movement of hairballs that may be lodged in the intestine. It is a dry, wheezing kind of sound that originates not in the chest but in the belly. Irritated by hair in the gut, the abdomen contracts and forces the cat to exhale in short, staccato breaths called a "hairball cough."

Hairballs are vomited up when they cannot pass the other way. Occasionally, hairballs form a serious bowel obstruction, and surgery may be necessary to remove the foreign body and repair the injured bowel. Fortunately, this is rare. Hairballs can cause problems in pet cats, but longhaired cats are at higher risk. They have the same number of hairs as shorthaired cats, but each hair is, well, longer. Hairballs are easily prevented by regular grooming, which helps the cat to remove shed hair that would otherwise be swallowed during self-grooming. Petroleum jelly and remedies that contain petroleum jelly are also effective in helping to lubricate the hairballs to ensure their easier elimination. Adding fiber to the diet may also help because it contributes to intestinal motility. Recently, commercial cat foods have been developed that may prevent the formation of troublesome hairballs. If your cat is prone to hairball problems, any one or a combination of these solutions should eliminate the hairball cough and the frequency of hairball-related regurgitation.

PSYCHOGENIC LICKING (OVERGROOMING)

Virginia was a timid black cat who was adopted from a local animal shelter. A previous owner had left her there, both brokenhearted, when he was forced to move to a nursing home that did not allow pets. Virginia seemed to adjust to her new home. Several months after she was adopted, however, her new owner discovered that Virginia was pulling out the hair on the inside of her thighs. She had licked her tummy raw. Her owner was surprised when her veterinarian pronounced that Virginia was anxious and referred them to me. Was her little cat unhappy?

When I met them, Virginia's owner was upset because she felt she had not provided Virginia with a happy home. I gently explained to her that psychogenic licking is common in cats. Virginia had undergone many months of serious upheaval and had resorted to a form of self-mutilation in an attempt to relieve her anxiety. Much like fingernail biting in people, it is a neurotic symptom, but it did not mean that Virginia was unhappy in her new home. It did, however, reflect a significant degree of prolonged stress that had begun with her separation from her first home and beloved owner, her stay at the shelter, and adjustment to her new home.

By definition, change is stressful, even when it is a change for the better. Cats feel anxiety, just as we do, when forced to cope with major life changes. They can't voice their concerns the way we can, and so their behavior becomes an important reflection of their internal state. Cats express their insecurities with a number of odd or undesirable behaviors. Some cats urinate out of the box, others hide, while some stop eating. A new roommate or spouse, a new home, home renovations, unruly children, unfamiliar street noises, prolonged separation from a favorite person or housemate, and inadequate activity and intellectual stimulation are just some of the things that can cause a cat's little world to feel unsafe or unsatisfactory. Psychogenic licking is an obsessive-compulsive form of grooming behavior that is often a sign of anxiety. Some outdoor cats, for instance, will groom excessively when confined during periods of harsh weather. In my experience the most frequent common denominator among cats who overgroom themselves is *separation anxiety syndrome*. Owners who must travel on business, go on vacation, or work long hours may not realize how much they are missed by the little cat who patiently awaits their return.

It is important to identify the source of anxiety in case it is something that can be modified. For instance, owners who work long shifts should concentrate on the quality rather than the quantity of time spent with their pet cats. Play, groom, pet, cuddle your cat at the end of a long day at work. You'll both feel better for it. In many cases, however, neurotic overgrooming in cats persists long after the initial trigger is forgotten. You may have started biting your fingernails, for example, during college exams, but that was long ago and you are still a fingernail chewer! Virginia had found a wonderful home, but we did need to stop her desire to continue licking.

Troubled cats will lick or pluck the hair on the abdomen, back, and legs. Licking frequently perpetuates more licking. When excessive licking irritates the skin, the cat feels itchy and this promotes more licking. This is called the "itch-lick cycle," and medication is frequently necessary to stop it. Virginia did well on amitriptyline, an antidepressant that also has anti-itch properties. She also benefited from two weeks on an anti-inflammatory medication to help her thickened and inflamed skin to heal. After several months, the psychoactive medication was gradually withdrawn. Her skin had healed, her hair had grown back, she groomed normally, and her mom was all smiles. They both deserved a happy ending, little Virginia most of all.

TRAINING YOUR CAT TO TOLERATE NAIL TRIMS

The feisty brown tabby American Wirehair kitten did not want to have a pedicure. Juanita squirmed, wriggled, and twisted her way out of her owner's hands, scratching her in the process of trying to escape. Her owner did not want to have her declawed but was increasingly frustrated with five-month-old Juanita's destructive scratching. Her hand-hooked rugs and needlepoint chair pads and footstools were being ruined. Juanita was beginning to use the scratching post, but her claws were like little daggers. With a bit of coaching, we soon had little Juanita tolerating her manicures. Here's how we did it.

It may seem obvious, but paws are sensitive! Like small children who weep and wail when being fitted for their first pair of shoes, a cat's paws are even more sensitive to the touch. They are sensitive not only to touch but to vibration. It is very important to get kitties accustomed to having their paws handled in a gentle and gradual way. Even cats who are devoted to their scratching post need to have a nail trim done once in a while, and it is an advantage to teach your cat to tolerate pedicures from the start. A destructive or aggressive cat who cannot be trained to tolerate pedicures may need to be declawed, as a last resort, to minimize the use of those impressive digital weapons. Nail trimming should be an uncomplicated procedure that is painless to both you and your cat if you take the time to introduce it slowly and reward the cat for her tolerance. *Don't cut too short!* The negative experience of an overly enthusiastic pedicure is not easily forgotten.

Ask your veterinarian to show you how to safely trim your cat's claws. The claws are unpigmented so it is easy to distinguish the pink portion of the nail bed, which contains the sensitive nerves and blood vessels. Any cat will instinctively resent having the feet touched at first. Don't just grab the foot and try to force the nail trimmer between the toes! Begin by gently using your fingers to casually stroke the legs, feet, and toes, when your kitty is in a quiet, cozy mood. It would be a mistake to introduce any interaction that requires pets to be calm and motionless when they are in the mood to play and bop around. Cats resent restraint when they are agitated or in the mood to have some fun! Practice gently massaging your cat's limbs for a few minutes every day. If your cat seems uncomfortable, practice this for just a few seconds several times a day and build up tolerance from there. Create a positive association with this new activity by offering a small piece of dry kibble or a tiny pet treat. You might even want to give a pea-sized piece of cheese or meat to make it an extra-special occasion.

With each session, your cat's comfort level should grow, and you should be able to manipulate those toes and feet (mimicking the pedicure without the clippers in hand) more each time. Slip your fingers between the kitty's toes, gently squeezing each toe as you flex the nail forward. Once your cat is indifferent to having the feet and toes played with, try your hand at trimming one or two nails. There is no need to do every nail the first time around. Trim just one or two a day over the course of the week, and you'll be right on track. Be casual about it, reassure your cat with a special treat, and then let him or her go. If you tense up, so will your cat. Nail trimming will soon become routine.

Even a skilled professional can make a mistake and trim the nail too short. This can happen, for example, when a nervous cat withdraws a foot during the pedicure. *It is always better to cut less than you think is necessary.* Trim off small portions at a time. Stop before you hurt your cat. In between pedicures, which may be required monthly, gently massage your cat's toes so that it does not become an unfamiliar and unpleasant sensation. If your cat has already had an unpleasant experience with nail trimming, you may have to reintroduce it by starting from the beginning as if those nails had never been trimmed. Clip one nail a week if you must and offer an extra-special food tidbit that is exclusive to pedicure time (they don't call me Dr. Cookie® for nothing!). If your cat overreacts to nail trimming and retraining seems impossible, the staff of your veterinary clinic can safely trim your cat's nails for you.

EXTRA TOES (POLYDACTYLY)

DeeDee was a lynx point Himalayan with beautiful markings. She would have been a showgirl except for one flaw. She had been born with an extra two toes on all four paws. She was sold as a "pet quality" kitten, and her new owners were thrilled. They found DeeDee's extra digits to be charming; and in their eyes, at least, she was flawless. The problems began when DeeDee was about eight months old. They had decided not to have her declawed at the time of her spay and tried to trim her nails as often as they could. Unfortunately, DeeDee's parents were both overextended, and they remembered to trim her nails less often than they should. DeeDee's extra toes were awkwardly wedged between her normal ones. Consequently, the curved nail grew long and easily pierced the skin. The ingrown nails were painful and required veterinary intervention because of the infection that frequently set in. DeeDee's sunny disposition clouded over each time they tried to trim her hidden toenails. Was their little girl flawed after all?

Polydactyl toes are an inherited trait. Cats with polydactyl toes occur spontaneously in any breed, but they are more common in domestic shorthair and longhair cats of the northeastern United States. This is because a polydactyl cat was among the first settlers that landed on the shores of the New World. *Polydactyly* is common among cats in New England. Cats with extra toes look like they are wearing baseball gloves, or oven mitts, depending on your perspective. The only problem with this genetic fluke is that the extra toes can be hidden and difficult to find during nail trims. The claws can also grow in spurts, and the ingrown extra toenail can become infected and painful. It is important to pay close attention to polydactyl nail trims.

Many veterinarians recommend that the polydactyl toes wedged between the others be removed when the cat is spayed or neutered to prevent problems later on. DeeDee's veterinarian suggested this was a reasonable option. Her owners thought this plastic surgery was a great compromise that resolved their dilemma. They did not want her declawed completely because she was faithful to several scratching posts in their home, and yet they did not want to perpetuate her suffering. DeeDee was perfect after all.

13

Golden-Age Cats

I am the cat of cats. I am
The everlasting cat!
Cunning, and old, and sleek as jam,
The everlasting cat!

—WILLIAM BRIGHTY RANDS (1823–1882)

ON AGING GRACEFULLY

Capri was fourteen years old but didn't look a day over ten. He played a little every day with the same ball he had received as a holiday gift when he was just a fuzzy orange baby boy. It was a little blue ball that had faded to a shade of gray, but Capri didn't care. He still trotted to the door when he heard the key in the lock, and he still raced his owner up the stairs to bed at the end of the day. Sure, he was a little stiff in the morning, but a few good stretches and a leisurely breakfast soon put things right. Winter cold and dampness slowed him down a bit and he stayed in bed later or curled himself into a ball in his basket near the radiator. Capri did not complain, he just took things day by day. Despite little aches and pains that slowed him down, some days more than others, the quality of his life was good. He ate well, slept well, appreciated his owner's company, and groomed himself daily. No doubt about it, Capri understood the pleasures of life.

Being a kitten is, after all, a state of mind. Technically, a kitten is an adult by about one year of age when they are physically, sexually,

and behaviorally mature. We used to compare one cat year to seven people years, but this is no longer a realistic measure. More people are taking better care of their pet cats, and veterinarians have more treatments to offer than we did twenty years ago. So the equation is still one cat year for seven human years for the first couple of years, but thereafter, the scale slowly declines to one cat year for six, five, or even four human years. What this means is that more cats are living longer lives. The average life expectancy used to be less than ten years (this used to be the equivalent of a seventy year old by the older scale) but now it is not unusual to see cats living beyond fifteen years (80+ by the updated scale), and some are still spry over twenty years of age.

There is no doubt that indoor cats can be expected to live longer (the average is at least twelve years) than cats who go outside and are exposed to all kinds of stress. Outdoor cats have to contend with territorial rivals, predators, traffic, contagious disease, parasitic infestation, and weather extremes. The life span of pet cats who roam outside is closer to that of the stray cat population, which is less than five years. I always worry about cats who go outside, but I worry even more about older cats who continue to roam. Cats over the age of ten are unquestionably slower to react and slower to move out of danger's way. Their hearing and vision may not be quite as acute to give them early warning of an approaching menace.

Quality of life is still more important than quantity, but quantity doesn't hurt! Some cats seem to age faster than others. Your eight-year-old kitty might look older than someone else's thirteen year old. This is just one of those mysteries of life, which is certainly partly determined by genes, lifestyle, and a little luck. Most cats will age in exemplary fashion. There is something comforting about an elderly cat who unhurriedly patrols from window to window, catches an occasional fly, and then settles down for a long snooze. The rhythms of life go on, they just go on at a slower pace. Elderly cats take their time getting through the day. They live within their abilities. Their lives still have purpose and pleasure. They still need us, and we still need them, for as long as there is.

THYROID DISEASE IN CATS

Sara was sixteen years old when I noticed that she was losing weight despite a healthy appetite. In fact, she was eating more than her usual share of food. It was unlikely that intestinal parasites were the cause because she had lived all her life indoors. Still, in case she had eaten a fly that had been in contact with infested stools, a stool sample was done. It was negative. Her blood test showed an increased thyroid level, which confirmed hyperactivity of the thyroid gland. I started her on oral medication to control the excessive production of thyroid hormone that would have taken her from me. She was difficult to pill, but this was complicated by the discovery that she did not tolerate either of two medications available to treat hyperthyroidism in cats. They both made her vomit and stop eating. This was unusual because most cats do fine on oral medication. And so she underwent radiation treatment at a veterinary teaching hospital. Two weeks after her admission, I collected my precious pussycat. She had come through with flying colors—no side effects, excellent clinical response, and an ideal patient. I considered myself fortunate to hold her close to me awhile longer.

The thyroid gland sets the level of general metabolism. Tumors of the thyroid gland are relatively common in cats and, fortunately, are usually benign. However, as the thyroid tumor grows, so does the production of thyroid hormone. If thyroid activity is too high *(hyperthyroid),* it is associated with a number of serious consequences. Rapid or irregular heart rate, difficulty breathing, weight loss, ravenous appetite, bulky stools, increased thirst and urination, excessive vocalization, and restlessness may all be noted. Diagnosis is by measuring the level of thyroid hormone in the blood. Additional blood tests are important to make certain that these signs are not confused with other diseases or to exclude coexisting illnesses. Most cats do very well if treatment is begun before the disease irreversibly affects other organs.

In cats, thyroid disease is almost always a case of overactivity *(hyperthyroidism)* as opposed to inadequate production of thyroid hormone *(hypothyroidism).* Cats under the age of ten are rarely diagnosed with hyperthyroid disease, although rare cases are discovered in cats as young as five years old. Diagnosis is by palpation of a nodule on one or both of the paired thyroid glands located on the cat's neck and/or by blood tests that confirm an elevated blood level of thyroid hormone. Thyroid tumors are generally benign; nonetheless, they can be fatal if left untreated.

Treatment options of thyroid disease include surgical excision of the affected gland, oral medication, and radiation therapy. Surgical excision of a thyroid tumor is delicate because it is often difficult to separate the thyroid gland from the adjacent parathyroid gland. The problem often affects both thyroid glands, however, and surgery is usually not the treatment of choice for most patients. Many pet owners prefer to medicate their hyperthyroid cat with one of two drugs currently available. Pills may be required two or even three times daily for the remainder of the cat's lifetime, although some cats are well controlled with one daily pill. Some cats resent being pilled, however, and become increasingly intolerant. In a minority of cases, side effects such as vomiting are noted and preclude further medication. Radiation therapy is an attractive but more costly alternative for pet owners. The cat is admitted to a veterinary facility that is specially equipped to provide this treatment. After a series of intravenous injections (with the radioactive iodine isotope I131) and careful monitoring, the cat is tested for radiation level and released only when he or she may be safely handled without special protective clothing. Most cats do brilliantly well with this treatment, as did Sara, and usually do not require additional treatment.

The cause of thyroid disease is not known. Possible contributing factors include a genetic predisposition as well as environmental contaminants. Until a cause is determined, it is important to have your cat examined annually over the course of a lifetime by your veterinarian. Report any health changes as soon as you discover them so that diagnosis of any ailment is timely and appropriate treatment can be instituted as soon as possible. In a peculiar twist, thyroid disease often affects more than one cat in a multicat household. Your veterinarian is a partner who will work with you to maintain your cat's quality of life regardless of the cat's age. *Don't assume that there is no help for aging cats who show signs of failing health.* So many pet owners seem to go into a sort of denial and delay making an appointment because they dread hearing gloomy news when an older cat does not feel well. Give your veterinarian the opportunity to surprise you with some happy options!

KIDNEY FAILURE

Michelangelo was fourteen years old when his owner noticed that he seemed to be drinking more water. After several months the litter box seemed to be getting wetter than usual, too. Michelangelo was losing weight, and his appetite seemed inconsistent. Every few days he vomited bile, and he was becoming more subdued. His owner brought him to the clinic; blood was drawn and a urine sample was obtained. The results confirmed that Michelangelo was in renal insufficiency. This meant that his kidneys were not functioning normally. His veterinarian suggested a prescription diet formulated for cats in renal failure. Because Mickey was dehydrated, he went to the clinic twice a week to get fluids replaced until he was feeling better. Mickey improved dramatically and gained three pounds in a month! He lived another three years before he died in his sleep of acute heart failure, curled in the rocking chair by the fire.

Healthy kidneys are complex filters that serve to maintain water balance. Renal filtration conserves water, reducing urinary output and avoiding dehydration on a hot summer day, or eliminates the excess with higher urine production when water is not required. The kidney also eliminates various by-products of metabolism. Some of these proteins would be toxic if they accumulated in the body. In renal failure, the kidney does not do its job, and water is lost uncontrollably. This causes the symptoms of excessive urination and excessive thirst, as the cat desperately tries to maintain hydration. In addition, toxic metabolic by-products are not eliminated efficiently, and their levels rise to dangerous levels. This is what causes vomiting or diarrhea and the changes in mental attitude of cats in renal failure.

Prescription diets, formulated with lower protein compared to regular adult cat food, help the failing kidneys by giving them less work to do. It can also be useful to add water to the food, whether it is canned or dry, to help your cat replace the fluids that the failing kidneys may not be strong enough to conserve. Unfortunately, no matter how much kidney patients drink, it is barely enough to replace what is lost in their dilute urine. Electrolytes, potassium in particular, are also lost in advanced kidney failure. Fluids will replace some of these, and electrolyte supplements will also be helpful. In some advanced cases, it may be necessary to administer *subcutaneous* (injected under the skin) fluids on a daily basis. Your veterinarian can teach you how to do this if you would rather avoid frequent clinic visits. Your cat will be more comfortable with treatment at home. Some veterinary teaching hospitals offer organ replacement for cats in kidney failure. This may be something to discuss with your veterinarian.

Kidney failure is almost inevitable in aging pets. Congenital kidney diseases can also affect younger cats but the effect of these diseases is usually more devastating in a short period. Infections of the urinary tract can ascend to the kidneys in cats at any age, and cause temporary or permanent renal damage. Geriatric kidney patients often do quite well for years after they are diagnosed. Sara's kidneys showed signs of weakening when she was sixteen years old or so, and that was six years ago. Your veterinarian can evaluate the degree to which your cat's kidneys are affected and advise you regarding appropriate treatment options.

ARTHRITIS AND GETTING BY

On cold, damp days, Alistair's arthritis acted up. His movements were just a bit rickety, and he was a little cranky, too. He seemed withdrawn on those achy days, seldom climbing the stairs, and paid less attention to the birds outside. Alistair cried when getting into or out of the litter box. A urine analysis was normal, so his discomfort was attributed to the inflammation in his joints. I suggested that his owner purchase a litter box with lower walls that would be easier to step into. I also suggested that a box be placed on each floor of her home so that the aging cat did not have to make long trips. Alistair was a bit overweight for his light Siamese-hybrid frame, and this was contributing to the burden on his sore geriatric joints. He eventually lost three pounds and effortlessly hopped into the new boxes. Alistair was feeling good again and so was his mom.

Getting old has its advantages and disadvantages, too. Like people and dogs, cats can get arthritis from old injuries or from wear and tear over time. Because of their small structures, light frames, and stoic natures, most cats tolerate the discomfort of arthritic joints and compensate by avoiding painful movements or taking shorter steps at a more cautious pace. Arthritic cats who are overweight tend to be further incapacitated, and although this may not be the only weight–related health issue, it is an important one.

There are a number of anti-inflammatory medications that can be prescribed for dogs and people. Unfortunately, the majority of these are extremely toxic to cats. For example, acetaminophen is lethal. When a cat's pain impacts the quality of life, plain aspirin may help to control the discomfort and minimize inflammation. However, even the margin of safety of aspirin is extremely narrow in cats. It must not be given more often than every seventy-two hours and at a minuscule dose. *Please do not medicate your cat without first consulting your veterinarian.*

Because arthritis can be difficult to treat in cats, it is even more important to assess those little things that could make a world of difference to a golden-age cat. Cats that experience discomfort when attempting to scale the high walls of some litter boxes may hold their urine for longer periods and develop urinary tract infections. Or they may avoid the litter box and choose another toilet area that you might not appreciate. Replacing the box with one that is more accessible (i.e., more shallow) is a solution. For example, the lid of front entry covered boxes may be removed and turned upside down to become a litter box, too. This is easily entered from the same doorway, but the cat can easily step into it. The high walls of the overturned lid make the cat feel secure. Place additional boxes in quiet corners on every floor of your home. You might even place more than one on each floor, depending on your cat's preferred territory and, of course, the number of other cats in your household. Some folks place the litter boxes in the basement but this may be impractical for an elderly cat with stiff knees and hips who is also being bullied by a younger housemate!

Arthritic cats are not going to be as agile as they were in their younger years. If you used to feed your cat on the kitchen counter (to keep away the dog or kids), for instance, you might need to lift the old-timer up and down or simply feed the cat in a quiet room with the door closed. Be aware of where that new puppy is or what your toddler is up to. Your old pussycat is just not up to taking too much teasing and may not be able to evade a problem as nimbly as before. Your aging friend is more fragile and, perhaps, less patient. Make a list of things that are more stressful to your cat now that he or she is less flexible physically and emotionally. You can help by minimizing unnecessary stresses and any obstacles to the cat's comfort. It's usually the little things that make life pleasant, or not.

HEARING LOSS (ACQUIRED DEAFNESS)
IN AGING CATS

Enrica was a shaded silver Persian. She had always been a placid kind of cat, never too demanding, never too clinging. But when her owner opened a can with the electric can opener, Enrica proved that she was an Olympic-class sprinter. She zoomed to the kitchen from wherever she was or whatever she was doing in the hopes of being rewarded with a bowl of tuna juice. One day when she was about twelve, Enrica did not appear when the can opener called to her. She did not come when her owner called. Her owner went in search of her and found her watching the goldfish in the fish tank. She seemed startled when her owner entered the room. Her veterinarian noticed that Enrica did not respond to little noises he made just behind her ears. He suspected that she had a hearing defect and referred her to a veterinary teaching hospital where a neurologist examined her with special equipment. Enrica did indeed have reduced acoustic sensitivity in both ears. And so her owner saved the tuna juice for her and added it to her evening meal, which Enrica never missed.

Hearing is very sensitive in cats. The ear *pinnae* move toward a source of sound and function as amplifiers. In fact, hearing is so acute in cats that they can hear into the ultrasonic range. This is an adaptation that allows them to detect motion and the calls of small rodents. Cats have a wider hearing range than all other mammals, with the exception of the horse and porpoise! Feline acoustic ability exceeds that of dogs and people, too.

Acquired deafness in an indoor cat is nothing more than a minor inconvenience. You will be amazed to discover the ways in which your cat will compensate for this disability. Cats are sensory marvels. Your deaf cat will become more sensitive to vibrations, thanks to receptors in the pads of her feet. The feline sense of smell and vision will also alert the cat to important sensory information about the world around her. So when the odor of that tuna juice finally wafts up to your bedroom, your cat will come running, even though she can't hear that can opener! Deafness becomes a real liability when the cat is permitted to roam outdoors. An inability to hear can lead to fatal consequences should the deaf cat fail to detect impending danger. Keep your hearing-impaired cat inside where he or she is safe.

HELPING YOUR CAT COPE WITH ACQUIRED BLINDNESS

Cyrano was a crusty old boy. Adopted as a stray, he had lost one eye as a kitten, presumably to untreated infection or trauma. Cyrano was still king of his castle. When he walked by, his other four housemates made way out of deference to the dominant male. His handicap had not handicapped him at all. When he was about eleven, his owner noticed that his remaining eye seemed to be bulging. Cyrano was unusually subdued and eating less than his customary share. His veterinarian was concerned when an ocular exam revealed that Cyrano's retina was torn, which must have been quite painful. His ocular pressure was elevated, and a radiograph of the skull was ordered. To everyone's surprise, the X ray showed that a round mass was pushing against the back of Cyrano's eye. Surgery was performed, and a benign tumor was removed. Unfortunately, Cyrano also lost his eye, but he was alive and well. Within weeks, he was patrolling the house as if nothing had changed, with one exception. He began to follow one of the other male cats, his favorite companion Cornelius, and they became inseparable. The other cats gave them both a wide berth when they walked by. His buddy was gentle, even protective of Cyrano, as he grew older. I will never forget their unusual alliance because of the level of understanding and tenderness it implied. Cyrano and Cornelius—they were quite a pair.

Feline vision is legendary. Among mammals, their visual acuity is unrivaled. Only the owl matches them. Cats can see in dim light thanks to a specialized reflective layer of cells at the back of the eye. This layer, called the *tapetum*, causes the glowing green flashback in your cat's eyes that is such a nuisance to photographing your pet. Siamese cats, and others with blue eyes, lack pigment in the tapetum, and their eyes reflect a reddish color because of the blood vessels in the retina that lie behind the tapetum.

Cats really can't focus well on objects that are right in front of their noses because their eyes are adapted primarily to detecting movement and patterns at a distance. At distances of less than a foot or so (25 cm), cats rely more on scent, hearing, tactile information relayed by sensitive facial whiskers, and vibrations in the pads of their feet. So if a cat begins to lose visual acuity because of untreatable disease, untreated disease, or age-related changes, they will not be left helpless. My Gracie, for example, was born with congenital retinal atrophy, but she has adapted so well that most visitors are surprised when we tell them she is blind. Most Siamese cats do not have normal stereoscopic vision, which affects depth perception, because of neurological abnormalities of the optic nerve fibers in the brain, cross-eyes *(convergent strabismus)*, and *nystagmus* (uneven side-to-side tremor of the eyeball). Siamese cats are at a distinct visual disadvantage, but most compensate well. Of course, any cat with visual deficits should remain confined indoors.

With regular annual checkups and immediate attention to any obvious eye problems, your cat's vision should last a lifetime. Veterinary ophthalmologists can provide advanced care that rivals the options available in human medicine. However, there are some normal changes that occur as your cat grows older. The lens of the eye is normally transparent, but it becomes increasingly opaque with age. When you look at your golden-ager, you may notice that the pupil has taken on a grayish tint. The lens, located just behind the opening of the pupil, is more visible because light is traveling through clouded tissue. These are often referred to as "senile cataracts," but the correct term is *lenticular sclerosis*. It should be distinguished from true cataracts, however, which can be surgically treated to restore your cat's vision. Cats with senile opacity of the lens generally see well, although details may be lost and the world might look a bit hazy.

Diseases of the heart and kidney, associated with high blood pressure, are also linked with eye troubles. High blood pressure can cause retinal detachment and glaucoma. Diabetic cats do not usually develop diseases of the eye. Visually impaired animals may be more prone to traumatic injury of the eye. Pigment changes of the iris, the colored part of the eye that is so glorious in cats, deserve attention, too. Report any brownish or black discoloration to your veterinarian. It might be just an inflammation that doesn't even need treatment, but it should be monitored in case it is the early stage of *melanoma* of the eye. Melanoma of the eye is slow to metastasize and, following removal of the affected eye, your cat should be fine. Just because your cat is getting older doesn't mean that problems can't be treated. Discuss any concerns with your veterinarian without delay. Your cat can adapt to a world in relative or total darkness as long as you are there to brighten the day.

INCREASED VOCALIZATION IN GERIATRIC CATS

Bubba was a bushy, sweet, marshmallow of a cat with long orange hair and yellow eyes. When he was around seventeen years old, his owner noted that he seemed to have more to say. Bubba began to meow more and more. At first, his mom thought that he might be hungry. Bubba gained three pounds. His blood tests showed that his kidneys were a bit weak but not enough to cause any real problems, and other than that, he was fine (except he was five pounds overweight!). Bubba was gaining weight rather than the weight loss associated with overactivity of the thyroid, and his thyroid test was normal. Bubba was crying at odd times of the day, but especially bothersome were his plaintive "meOOOOws!" at around 4 or 5 A.M. I was called in to help his sleepless owner get some much-needed rest. We decided to try to readjust his sleep patterns. His mom woke him up with petting or a game of feather chasing to disrupt his afternoon nap (she admitted to me that this was her revenge on Bubba). We also decided to confine him overnight to the spare bedroom. He could enjoy his favorite bay window along with his own dinner, water, and litter box. Bubba was thrilled. He slept peacefully, and so did his mom.

In my experience there is a difference between a young and healthy cat who keeps his owner awake and an aging cat with unprecedented sleep disruption and excessive vocalization. In a youngster, bouncing off the walls and knocking items off your dresser at 6 A.M. is normal. Young kitties are simply full of energy and looking for stimulation and attention. In an elderly cat, however, when the possibility of underlying problems such as hyperthyroidism has been ruled out, I think it may be a form of senility.

Many aging animals show signs of confusion and lethargy. It remains important to make certain there are no latent physical problems that need attention; however, mild changes in mental clarity may be part of the normal aging process. A syndrome of extreme senile behavioral changes has been recently recognized in dogs. Called *canine cognitive dysfunction syndrome* (CCDS), it is associated with changes in normal sleep-wake cycles, restlessness, regression in house training, excessive vocalization, and other symptoms. From a scientific perspective, it is interesting to note that brain lesions in these dogs are very similar to the changes seen in human Alzheimer patients. Although there is no cure for Alzheimer's disease in people, we are fortunate to be able to offer medication to CCDS dogs. Sadly, CCDS is progressive, and most dogs diagnosed with this ailment continue to degenerate over time; but at least we can offer a temporary remedy. I have often wondered that a similar disease might not be at work in some of our aging cats with similar clinical signs. Indeed, there is preliminary evidence to support the feline equivalent.

Until we know more about brain pathology in aging cats, the best we can do is to keep both owner and cat as comfortable as possible. Unfortunately, the drug that may be helpful to CCDS dogs is not approved for use in cats. Aging cats, like people, can become a bit confused and are slower to adapt to change. It is important to maintain an older cat's routine because it gives consistency and a comforting kind of rhythm to the day. If their schedule is changed, older cats can be thrown off balance and out of synch with their owners' schedule. We gently readjusted Bubba's sleep-wake cycle. He felt more secure in his favorite room rather than pacing in confusion when it was dark, his owner was asleep (or trying to sleep), and he felt all alone. Be patient with your old friend. With a few minor adjustments, you should be able to regain your harmony and live happily ever after.

VETERINARY CARE FOR A LIFETIME

At fifteen, Madeline had not been to see her veterinarian in three years. Her owner had assumed that all was well and that, since the blue tortie Burmese did not go outdoors, her annual checkup was unnecessary. That summer her owner decided to make the trip to a family reunion. Madeline would have to stay at a boarding kennel where proof of current vaccinations was required. During the course of her vaccine appointment, a thorough examination revealed that Madeline had a serious heart murmur. On a scale of one (mild) to six (severe), Madeline's murmur rated a four. Her veterinarian explained that the stress of boarding in an unfamiliar location might trigger acute heart failure. He pointed out that Madeline's gums were slightly bluish when she was anxious, which supported his concerns. Nighttime coughing is suggestive of cardiac coughs, and her owner confirmed that she did cough a bit at night. Fortunately, her veterinarian performed an electrocardiogram and a cardiac ultrasound (echocardiagram) and was able to prescribe medications that strengthened her heart muscle and helped to eliminate the buildup of fluid in her lungs. Within days, Madeline was more active and alert than she'd been in a long time. She boarded at the clinic, where the veterinary staff could administer her medication and monitor her daily, and her owner was able to enjoy her family reunion. Still, the best reunion came when her sweet Madeline was returned to her safe and sound upon her return home.

Veterinary evaluation throughout your cat's lifetime is invaluable. Consistent contact with your veterinarian will allow you to detect any underlying problems before they become big ones. Your veterinarian will be familiar with you and your pet, and be more effective in caring for you both. It will also allow you to keep informed of any new trends or medical discoveries that might improve the quality of your cat's life.

Even cats who remain indoors, can still get sick. Vaccinations prevent infection with airborne viruses that cause upper respiratory infection even if a cat never leaves the house. The rabies vaccine, in particular, may be required by law in your area whether or not your cat goes outside. Rabid animals can occasionally enter your home (e.g., squirrels through your chimney, bats by way of your balcony, raccoons in your garage . . .) and your cat must be protected in case of contact.

Pet owners sometimes assume that nothing can be done to treat a health problem in an aging cat. Sadly, the "end" is inevitable for all of us, but that does not mean that nothing can be done to delay it for a while! If you detect a small problem, have your cat evaluated before it becomes a big problem! For example, treatment of minor conjunctivitis will be far easier and less expensive than the corneal ulcer that could develop if treatment is delayed.

Some pet owners actually base their decision of whether or not treatment is worthwhile on their pet's age. For instance, an owner whose fifteen-year-old cat was diagnosed with a treatable heart problem told me that she would have pursued treatment had her cat been five or even ten years old. She declined an inexpensive medication because "this cat is not going to live much longer anyway." She was right, her cat soon died without treatment. Your decision to treat your cat's problem is yours to make; however, I always advise pet owners to make the decisions that will cause them the least regret later on.

Your cat is the same cat you loved when you were both younger, the same constant friend who was there for you when you went through hard times, day or night. The packaging may be somewhat frayed, but doesn't your cat still look at you as if *you* were unchanged? Cherish your pet throughout your journey together. Your cat is no less valuable at fifteen years than at five years, and still depends on you to do what is best and what is right. As long as your cat's quality of life can be reasonably maintained and you are financially able to manage control of a medical problem, take care of your pet. Your cat would do no less for you.

14

Surviving Your Cat's Death

Like a purr, you drift and fade
Stay, angel, I cannot follow your hushed velvet paws
Like mist against my cheek, now murmur:
Soon, soon, I will wait.

—STEFANIE SCHWARTZ (2000)

COPING WITH THE LOSS OF A PET

Merysa was a painfully thin but infinitely appealing waif turned in to a local
shelter. She was a three-month-old silver tabby domestic shorthair with glow-
ing, green eyes. With some uneasiness as to how my husband would react to
yet another surprise addition to our family, I took her home, but not before
she tested negative for both types of feline leukemia (FeLV and FIV). It is
my practice to keep any new pet in strict quarantine for at least one week,
followed by supervised and brief encounters over several weeks to integrate
smoothly with the household. This is to keep tempers from flaring but also
as a precaution to prevent any latent medical problems from affecting the
resident cats. Merysa failed to thrive. She was treated for several types of
intestinal parasites but grew weak and pale. My sad suspicion was confirmed
when she tested positive for feline infectious peritonitis (FIP). This viral mu-
tation of the coronavirus, which causes diarrhea in young cats, becomes a killer
of kittens or lies silent for years in the adult cat. Merysa put up a brave fight,
trying so hard to eat, lifting her sweet face to me when I went into her room
to treat her or just to hold her next to my heart. My wish, which I repeated

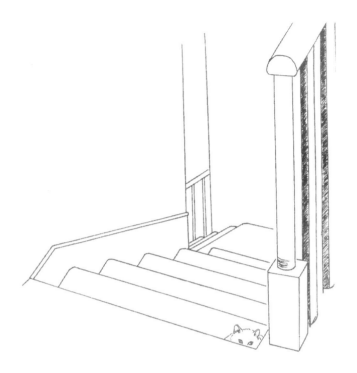

to her over and over again, was to see her grow big and strong. After two weeks I admitted her to the clinic for ongoing care. On the seventeenth day after she came into my life, I lost one of a pair of angel earrings. I later learned that she had died that morning. My husband sweetly suggested that we bury the remaining angel earring with her. I hope that my Jonathan is taking care of her until we can meet again. I pray that she knows, despite so short a time with me, how much she was loved.

She was only a baby. She was born feral and had to fight for her survival. She did not have time to play or sleep on a big soft pillow in the sun. She never saw the leaves change color in the fall or watch the snow softly cover the grass from inside a safe and warm home. She was so young and yet she possessed the wisdom of the ages in her sea green eyes. She was an old soul, but she would not grow old with me. Despite my best efforts and heartfelt pleas, she would never grow big and strong. Merysa drifted in and away when I was halfway through writing this book. I needed to tell you about her because she gave me the impetus to write this chapter. She was my baby, even for a short time; and her brief presence deserved to be recorded. In my grief I was inspired to express what I know and feel about pet loss. It is because of my profound grief for Jonathan, Merysa, and every pet whom I have touched in my veterinary career, that I am driven to reach out to you in your grief. Merysa inspired me with her loveliness and her courage. The memory of her tiny face and illuminous eyes haunt me still. I hope they always will.

The mourning experience is unique for everyone who loses a beloved pet. Indeed, the experience is different for every pet we lose. For some of us grieving is more private, while others seem to recover more quickly. It is comforting for some grieving pet owners to turn immediately toward the search for a new pet. However, you may not be ready to open your heart to another creature. You may feel that loving another pet so soon would somehow be disloyal to the memory of the pet you still miss so much. Be patient and follow your heart. Take the time to work through your grief. It may be necessary to deal with your feelings and resolve them before moving on. Turning toward an immediate replacement could be a form of denial that will prevent you from healing in a healthy way.

A pet becomes a symbol of many things. In fact, your cat probably means something different to every member of your family. A pet may symbolize a child, perhaps a child yet to be conceived or the innocent child in you. Your cat is a playmate and a sibling, or perhaps your idealized mate or parent—patient, faithful, and welcoming, who loves you unconditionally. Your cat is a reflection of you, the embodiment of negative and positive qualities you recognize or lack in yourself. Your pet may embody all of these, alternating between these symbolic roles on any given day. Your cat offers you companionship, entertainment, and intimacy. It is not the length of time spent together that defines the impact of a relationship. Your cat may live with you for a few weeks, a few years, or a few lifetimes. Cherish every moment. Then take a deep breath and release your friend's spirit, knowing this angelic presence has enriched your life forever.

WHEN EUTHANASIA IS APPROPRIATE FOR A PET

Jonathan became ill when he was about five years old. He was a healthy, strong cat. One day, the color of his beautiful green eyes took on a strange brown color, and he developed uncontrollable diarrhea. After many blood tests, radiographs, a barium series, and endoscopy, he was diagnosed with chronic inflammatory bowel disease. His diarrhea was liquid, foul, and explosive. He lost weight, despite a good appetite, and he withered before my eyes over the following five years. I tried everything to control his disease. He seemed to improve temporarily on several medications, but the improvement was short-lived. But he was my boy. As long as he ate well, wanted to be near me, and seemed relatively comfortable, I wanted him with me. When he was almost ten years old, Jonathan took a turn for the worse. An additional blood test revealed that his kidneys were failing. He was increasingly frail and seemed very sad. He suffered from severe intestinal cramps, and his eyes reflected a desolated emptiness. I had kept him with me for as long as he was happy. But my brave little boy, who had fought so hard and so long to keep us together, was tired. So tired. It was time to let him go. It was impossible for me to be present during his final moments; I could not bear to watch him take his last breath and leave me behind. My anguish was unbearable as my colleague carried him away, although I knew it was the kindest thing for my little prince. She later told me that his end was easy. She recalled how he seemed to offer his paw to her for the injection that was to relieve him of so much pain. I tried to take comfort in knowing that he was no longer suffering, but so many years later, not a day goes by that I don't think of him. My Jonathan was magic. His intelligence and sensitivity were extraordinary. He changed my life and made me a better veterinarian and a better human being. If there is an afterlife, I hope he will be among the first to greet me so that I can hold him close to me and, this time, never ever let him go.

Losing a pet may be as painful as the death of a relative or friend. For some people a pet's death may have even more profound impact than the death of a human being. Whether they are aging normally or faced with a terminal illness, dying pets appear to go through a final period of withdrawal. This does not mean that they are conscious of their own mortality. Physical decline alone can resemble the depression that creeps in when confronted with our own impending mortality. It is natural to reach a stage at the end of one's life during which social interaction diminishes. I believe that one of the greatest gifts our cats give us is the demonstration of dying with dignity and grace.

Death can be swift and unexpected, or it may follow a slow decline. You may have little control over how or when your cat dies, but you may be offered some level of involvement. You may passively end your cat's life, for example, by simply deciding not to pursue medical or surgical treatment in an aging or ailing pet. Perhaps the disease has no cure, and the best that can be done is to alleviate any pain so that your pet's remaining days are lived in relative comfort. On the other hand, you may not have any choice or time to prepare if your cat is struck down by a sudden illness or accident. We all hope that our pussycats will be granted a peaceful passing. It would be a blessing to discover your darling cat curled up in his or her bed one sunny morning. If, however, you are called upon to consider euthanasia, the impact of your pet's death may be more severe.

Euthanasia means "good death" and implies the induction of painless death. Veterinarians accomplish this by an intravenous injection of a concentrated dose of barbiturate anesthetic. Your cat will feel no greater discomfort than with any other injection as the needle tip passes through the skin. It takes just seconds to induce a total loss of consciousness; respiratory and cardiac arrest soon follow. Doctors of veterinary medicine are dedicated to the diagnosis and treatment of disease. The option of extending an animal's life and prolonging suffering is not taken lightly by any veterinarian. I have refused to euthanize many healthy or easily treated pets and pleaded with other pet owners for the chance to relieve their pet's agony. Your pet's doctor will help you to decide whether euthanasia is an appropriate option for your cat. You may postpone the decision, hoping that if you wait the decision will not be necessary, one way or the other. You will be flooded with feelings of overwhelming guilt and anger. There is no easy way to let go. The decision to authorize your pet's euthanasia should be guided by one fundamental motive: *Do what is best for your pet.* Do what is best for your cat, in view of short-term and long-term quality of life. Although you may suffer temporarily from the decision to end his or her life, you will have the satisfaction, in retrospect, of knowing that you acted well.

If you must choose whether or not to request the euthanasia of your precious cat, I offer a list of questions to guide your decision. These are intended to facilitate your soul-searching so that you can arrive at the solution that is best for you and your pet. Discuss the options with your veterinarian. Open your heart to family and friends. Seek comfort from psychotherapy or in your faith. Consider what will result in the least cause for remorse after your pet is gone:

- Evaluate the current quality of your pet's life. Is your cat (a) in pain, (b) eating well, (c) playful, (d) affectionate and sociable?
- Does your pet seem tired and withdrawn most of the time?
- Are any treatment options available? (Specialists are available for medical as well as behavioral problems.) Can anything make your cat more comfortable?
- Can you afford any treatment alternatives? Can the clinic offer a payment program?
- Do you resent the restrictions your pet's condition has placed on your lifestyle? Are you angry enough to withdraw from your cat?
- What is the current quality of your life, and how will your pet's death change it?
- Is it reasonable to extend your pet's life?
- Do you want to be present during the euthanasia?
- Do you want to wait in the clinic's waiting room until it is over?
- Do you want to be alone or ask a friend to be present?
- Do you want any special burial arrangements made? (Discuss the options with your veterinarian even if it is only to store the body until you can think more clearly.)
- Do you want to adopt another pet right away or take the time you need to recover from this loss before considering another pet?

SOCIAL SUPPORT FOR GRIEVING CAT OWNERS

Priscilla was a calico Persian, the perfect companion and trusted confidante of a sixty-year-old widow. She was an angelic cat, who lived quietly and sweetly for fifteen years. When Priscilla died suddenly, her owner felt totally alone. She was tearful at work and isolated herself from family. She tried to relay the depth of her loss, but found that many coworkers and family members could not relate to her grief. Several understood grieving for a dog, but did not feel that attachment to a cat was as deeply felt. Those friends who had never loved a pet could not understand her loss at all. This poor lady felt rejected and alone, which accentuated the void left by little Priscilla. We spoke for a long time. She shared her fondest memories of Priscilla, showed me photos of their life together. She grieved for her little friend, and this triggered the dormant grief she still felt for her departed husband. Sometimes all you can do is listen, but that may be enough. Sometimes all you can do is hold a hand and offer a warm hug. And that is everything.

The bond between you and your pet is as valuable as any of your human relationships. Indeed, for some people living far from home, a pet may be the most important and sustaining relationship. The process of grieving a death is the same, whether you have lost a pet or a person. The stages of mourning are identical; the difference lies in the value that society places on pets. When a pet dies, you expect that your pain will be acknowledged. Yet despite the importance of your loss, other people may not understand it. At a time when you most need to rally your support system, it may fail you. If there were a death in your family, you would be expected to take some time away from work. If your cat dies and you need some time to collect yourself, you might lose your job. Yet the grief that you feel when you lose a pet might exceed your grief for a person.

The joy found in the companionship of a pet is a blessing not given to everyone. You do not need anyone else's approval to mourn the loss of your pet. You don't have to justify your feelings to anyone, particularly when they cannot relate to your experience. Share your pain with cat people, who will understand you. Reach out to your veterinarian, veterinary technician, groomer, or another pet owner. Inquire about pet loss support groups or veterinary bereavement counselors in your area. Your pet's passing can revive painful memories that you thought were resolved. Seek professional support to help you through this difficult time. It is, above all, an opportunity for healing.

Priscilla's owner spent a few months of sadness and self-imposed isolation. She needed to work through her grief and heal from the loss of her pet and her husband. She reached out to me and to others and discovered new pet-owning friends who empathized with her loss. She emerged from her bereavement with renewed energy. When she was ready, she went to an animal shelter in search of a new companion. As fate would have it, she met a widower who was also looking for a feline friend. Priscilla's death had become an opening for new possibilities.

Your pet's passing is a chance for emotional growth. Your life was brightened by the time spent with your pet. Your grief is a measure of how fortunate you are to have the capacity to receive and donate a gift of great love. Feel your pain and indulge yourself in the simple pleasures. Let your grief flow through you and out of you, don't hold it in. When it is gone, you will still be there. Take things slowly, be patient with yourself, make sure to get your rest. Then move forward in your journey with an open heart.

EXPLAINING PET LOSS TO YOUR CHILD

Cuddlebug was seventeen years old when he died peacefully in his sleep. It was what his mom had wished for her cuddly cat as she powerlessly watched him decline over the last few weeks of his life. She could barely remember a time when he was not cuddled next to her. He had been with her before she met and married her husband, long before her own children were born. She was grateful for his easy passage, but how was she to explain his loss to her nine-year-old daughter and five-year-old son? How could she keep them from seeing her tear-stained face over the next days and weeks?

It is only natural to try to shield our children from painful experiences. As adults, the concept of death is still ominous, yet it is surprising how well most children adjust to a pet's demise if they are prepared with honest and simple explanations. Children begin to process the concept of death from a young age. Death is first analyzed on an unconscious level in games such as "hide and seek" or fears of the "boogie man" under the bed. Young children pretend to bury their dolls or have funerals for their stuffed toys. By the time they are eight or nine, most children develop a more conscious understanding of death.

It may be more difficult for a child to resolve a pet's death if the child is not told the truth. There are some phrases, for example, that could confuse a child and that are best avoided when discussing a pet's death. A common phrase used to describe the euthanasia of a family pet is "put to sleep." Use of this misleading phrase, which implies an adult's denial of death, has caused sensitive children to develop a terror of bedtime. Another example of an inappropriate explanation is the suggestion to a child that "God has taken" the pet. This often creates conflict in the child, who may become angry with "God" for being mean to him or her as well as cruel toward the departed pet.

Children are capable of understanding that life must end for all living things. Support their grief by acknowledging their pain. Affirmation is empowering. *The death of a pet can be an opportunity for a child to learn that you can be counted on to offer comfort and reassurance.* This is an important chance to encourage a child to express his or her feelings. Sadness and loss are inevitable in life. Grief must be expressed so that healing can follow. Supporting your children through this difficult time and allowing them to see your sadness, will make them stronger and more sensitive adults. And the cycle of life will live on through them and be all the better for it.

GRIEF IN CATS

Mama Kitty became a shadow of herself after her housemate Gino died. She spent long periods hiding under the bed and emerged briefly to use the litter box. She restlessly paced the house, vocalizing in a mournful tone, inspecting one room and then another before returning to her solitude under the bed. She stopped grooming herself, and her appetite declined. Her worried mom was afraid she would lose Mama Kitty, too, and yet her veterinarian could find nothing physically wrong with the little Abyssinian. After three weeks of Mama Kitty's behavioral disruption, I was called in to help.

There are cats who exhibit clear signs of depression and separation reaction when a favorite companion is removed. I have seen some cats become irritable and others withdraw into their own little shell in response to the loss of another pet with whom they were closely affiliated or when an owner dies or suddenly departs. It is unknown, or perhaps unlikely, whether cats have a sense of mortality and death. However, cats are social animals; they are known to develop selectively close alliances with other cats and animals, and demonstrate real sensitivity. Given these facts it is not surprising to discover that they can respond profoundly to separation from an "attachment figure," that is, a favorite human or nonhuman companion.

Grief implies a conscious concept of death or loss. Even if we cannot truly say that cats grieve, it can at least be described as an intense separation reaction (i.e., a form of separation anxiety). Sudden separation from a loved one, and the emotional response it triggers, are inherent elements of grief. Cats may not understand what has happened, why their friend left, or that they are not coming back, but they can respond to their absence and to the void left behind. Cats may show varying depths of depression or anxiety. The hallmarks of depression in cats, like people, include a change in appetite (increase or decrease), a change in sleeping patterns (increase or decrease), social withdrawal and isolation, a decreased interest in grooming, mood swings, and changes in overall activity (increase or decrease).

Mama Kitty was definitely depressed. Because her anxiety level had not subsided after several weeks and was impacting her health, we decided to alleviate her mood and obvious unhappiness by interfering with the brain chemistry that shadowed her perspective. After several days on psychoactive medication, Mama Kitty began to emerge from the isolation of the bedroom. The medication was discontinued a few weeks later, and she remained well. She just needed a little short-term help in coping with a significant shock. A few months later, after she had time to settle in and enjoy the spotlight for a while, she was thrilled to welcome a new companion who had been chosen just for her.

STAGES OF MOURNING

Malcolm's mom was inconsolable. Her beautiful flame point Balinese had lost his battle with cancer at just eight years of age. His mom had trouble sleeping and felt overwhelming guilt that she had been helpless to save Malcolm's life. She was angry with herself for not taking him to seek veterinary help sooner. She was angry with the veterinarian for not curing her cat and for the fee he charged her anyway. She was angry with her husband, who did not seem to be as strongly impacted by Malcolm's death. And she was angry with Malcolm for leaving her. When she was not feeling angry, she wept. She lost weight and did not bother to take care of her appearance. I gently suggested that she was suffering from clinical depression and needed professional guidance to support her through this emotional crisis. When I checked on her several weeks later, she sounded more cheerful or at least optimistic. Her physician had referred her to a psychotherapist, who had prescribed a short course of antidepressant medication. She was able to share with her therapist some more deeply rooted problems that seemed to resurface shortly after Malcolm died. She was also looking forward to the arrival of a breeder's litter of Balinese kittens and had decided to get two kittens this time around.

Mourning, and the more private process of grieving, is an experience that is common to people from all walks of life. Grief is the distress we feel when we are afflicted with great sorrow or loss. It is a dynamic process that takes its time. The duration is different for us all and allows us to reclaim a sense of peace. The stages of grief are universal and occur in response to one's own terminal illness or to the death of a valued being, human or not. Public display of bereavement is influenced by culture and other factors, but it is still driven by a universal expression of underlying grief. When your cat dies, you may be reminded of other losses. Perhaps you will remember other loved ones who have left you or losses of many kinds that your cat helped you to survive. Painful memories associated with your pet's lifetime and beyond may come flooding back to complicate your grieving process. Sometimes we need professional help to untangle the jumble of emotions triggered by a pet's death. Recognizing this and speaking with supportive counselors or perhaps sympathetic clergy will help you recover more quickly and more fully.

There are five stages of normal grief. During the process, you will spend different lengths of time at each one and feel each stage more or less intensely. You will not necessarily experience each stage in the order outlined below. It is common to vacillate between stages before coming to terms with your loss. It is a luxury of sorts to have the time to reach a level of acceptance, which is the final stage of grief. It can take a lifetime to work through grief, and some of us may never find complete resolution. Your pet's death will force you to evaluate your feelings of mortality and the meaning of life. A common thread runs through the stages of grief: Holding on to hope. Hope is life.

DENIAL AND ISOLATION. Your first reaction to learning of your pet's illness or death is to deny it. This rejection of reality is a way to survive overwhelming emotions. Denial is a defense mechanism that buffers an unbearable emotional shock. You will block out the words and hide from the facts. Your denial and isolation will carry you through the first wave of pain.

ANGER. As the masking effects of denial and isolation fade, painful reality will hit you again; but you are still not ready. The intense emotions within you must have an outlet and are directed outward and expressed instead as anger. Your anger may be aimed at inanimate objects, complete strangers, friends, or family. It is natural to feel some anger toward your dying or deceased pet. On a rational level you know your cat is not responsible for your pain; however, on an emotional level you may resent your cat for leaving you in such anguish. You may even feel guilty for being angry, and this will only make you angrier.

You might direct some of your anger toward the veterinarian who diagnosed the illness, was unable to cure the disease, or performed the euthanasia. Health professionals, in veterinary and human medicine, deal with death and dying on a daily basis; but they are not immune to the suffering of their patients or to those who grieve for them. Ask your veterinarian to spend some time with you, even if it is to explain just once more the details of your pet's illness. This might require a special appointment or a simple telephone call at the end of their day. Discuss the cost of treatment options. Discuss burial arrangements. You and your veterinarian will benefit from honest and open communication during your crisis.

BARGAINING. When we feel helpless and vulnerable, the normal reaction is to try to regain control, or at least to give ourselves a sense that somehow we have the power to control the outcome. If only you had sought veterinary attention sooner, gotten a second opinion from another veterinarian, changed your pet's diet, he or she might have recovered. You may make a deal with God or your higher power in an attempt to postpone the inevitable. You are grasping at firmer emotional ground but still being swept away in a current of pain.

DEPRESSION. Grief is associated with two types of depression. First, a sense of sadness stems from practical considerations relating to the loss. You will worry about the cost of treatment and burial. You may regret that your grief has prevented you from spending time with others who depend on you. This aspect of your sadness may be alleviated by a bit of helpful cooperation and a few kind words. The second type of depression is subtler and more private. You must prepare for the final separation from your cat and let him go in peace.

ACCEPTANCE. Not everyone is able to reach this stage of grief. Some of us never emerge from our anger or denial. This final step is characterized by withdrawal and calm. This is not a period of happiness nor is it depression. Accepting the death of someone you love is a sort of release. You are relieved of the pain caused by sudden separation. You must forgive yourself for any responsibility or any sense of failure. You must accept that death is another phase of life. And you must recognize that *you* are still very much alive and have many more things to accomplish in your time. The final phase of grief brings resolution to the past and hope for the future. You had the great good fortune to be touched by one of creation's most exquisite beings. Go forward on your journey and, perhaps, your path will be crossed by another wonderful cat.

MOVING ON

Sara was never really depressed after Jonathan's death. Yes, they had been close companions. They groomed each other, slept together, played together, and ate together. However, the sicker he grew over the years of his illness, the more she withdrew from him. I was so consumed with his welfare that I frequently took hers for granted. She didn't seem to mind. I think she understood how hard it was on all of us. And when he died, I spent a year alone with her. It was our special time together. She was not upset when he left. In fact, she blossomed. She regained a sparkle in her emerald green eyes. We played together, slept together, ate together, and groomed each other. We made peace with his departure and rejoiced in each other's company.

Despite the unique bond between Jonathan and Sara, his chronic illness had long impaired the quality of their relationship. His death brought me great pain but also deep relief. He was no longer suffering, and I was no longer suffering for him. Had Sara suffered for him, too? Perhaps. More objectively, I can say that she must have sensed my anxiety and ongoing tension because of his disease, and this most certainly impacted her. When he was gone, my anxiety was relieved; and Sara had to have sensed the change in me. Our pets are keenly affected by our moods. They learn to read our facial expression, body posture, and tone of voice. It is likely they can even detect our mood by a change in body odor. Your cat is affected by a change in your work schedule, stress from work or family, an upcoming move, financial pressures, school examinations . . . anything that troubles you will necessarily influence the quality of your relationship with your cat.

Our pets are often more resilient than we anticipate, yet they are certainly more sensitive to their environment than we currently understand. Life will distract you from your cat sometimes. Try not to let anything interfere with spending quality time with all the creatures you love and who love you.

EPILOGUE

Delight in me, I am yours to love
Gaze into my serenity as our spirits embrace
And wonder, will you be my cat next time we meet?

—STEFANIE SCHWARTZ (2000)

Closure, when it is possible, is so important in living happily. I felt it would be appropriate to leave you with some parting thoughts. My "Top Ten Tips" summarize the most essential of the practical lessons I have learned about how to make your cat happy and, thereby, how to live happily ever after with your cat. These are followed with observations that are more philosophical in nature and that emanate from my glimpses of the spiritual connection with our cats. Reach for it; it is there. I hope that, in some small way at least, this book has helped you and your cat to live happily ever after.

DR. COOKIE®'S TOP TEN TIPS ON HOW TO LIVE HAPPILY EVER AFTER WITH YOUR CAT

10. Keep at least one litter box for every cat in your household (and consider a minimum of two boxes for a single cat). Maintain the litter box according to your cat's high standards of hygiene and predilection for placement, litter substrate, box size, and box type (covered, uncovered . . .).

9. Think like a cat (or at least consider my recommendations!). Place litter boxes, scratching posts, and cozy baskets in places that are in keeping with your cat's preferences.

8. Two kittens (or two carefully selected and gradually introduced adults) are as easy to keep as one; they provide entertainment and

companionship for each other, and you double the placement of wonderful pets who might otherwise be destroyed.

7. Always introduce new pets gradually over a period of at least ten to fourteen days and not before your veterinarian has examined the new cat thoroughly!

6. Establish and maintain a good relationship with a veterinarian in whom you have confidence to coordinate your cat's health care for a lifetime.

5. Keep your cat indoors; house cats generally live longer and have fewer health problems!

4. If your cat stays indoors (I hope s/he does!), provide alternative daily activities with lots of interactive playtime with you as well as a variety of toys that keep your kitty's interest!

3. If your cat is misbehaving and your veterinarian does not think it is a health-related issue, seek help *immediately* from a veterinary behaviorist to ensure that you and your cat will live happily ever after. Behavior problems are the most common reasons given for the destruction and abandonment of healthy cats. Please don't let your cat be one of them!

2. Good health and a friendly temperament are more important to living happily ever after than how cute a cat looks. Remember, the cat's appearance is just like gift wrap; it may be pretty but what really counts is what's inside the box!

1. Every cat is an individual that is unlike any other cat you have ever known and loved. Nurture the sparkle mirrored in your kitten's eyes; it is a reflection of your love.

WHAT YOUR CAT CAN TEACH YOU . . .

The purpose of this book has been to share my experiences, knowledge, and feelings about my years living with and loving cats. During this project I began to reflect upon a deeper union with cats. The spiritual connection to cats reached its zenith during the days of the pharaohs when cats were revered as deities. Over the centuries, the cat's spiritual symbolism was sometimes negatively labeled, and yet their spirituality *per se* was never denied. For many of us, our cats continue to inspire a glimpse of the divine in all creatures and within ourselves. To live happily with your cat is to have enlightenment within scope and innumerable revelations within view. Here are a few reflections on what my cats, and your cats, have taught me:

Why We Are Here

We live in a fast-paced world surrounded by technology and machinery that were meant to simplify life yet seem to complicate it further. We live in a disposable society where emotions are blunted and relationships are easily disengaged. Disconnected from our families and hometowns, we are alienated from each other and live in emotional isolation and insulation. Your pet helps you to focus on priorities and what is constant and true. *We are here to love each other.* You chose your cat, or s/he chose you, out of a need to connect. The emotional and spiritual bond to your pet, your family, your friends, is what fuels our existence and makes life worthwhile. Regardless of the business at home or at work, your cat is a reminder of your center, your foundation, your connection to the divine. You were born with an infinite capacity to love.

The Power of Touch

The gentleness of your hand gives reassurance and offers connection on many levels. Response to an intimate touch is an act of trust and faith and opens us to the positive forces of the universe. You may have heard that contact with pets can have profound physical effects on animal lovers, particularly those who are recovering from illness or loss. Blood pressure, heart rate, and respiratory rate have been shown to decrease in pet owners when they physically interact with their animal companions. No one has really been able to account for this phenomenon. I'd like to offer an explanation. Physical connection that originates from love is a bridge to a spiritual bond. The caress offered or received in love causes your physical being to focus entirely on the sensation, and the world around you dissolves. In a very real sense, this is a form of meditation. It is a moment of purity that takes you away from your worries, and the world fades away. Similarly, when you pet your cat, your soul is granted a moment of uninterrupted bliss. You have cleared your mind and exist only in the oneness of being with your cat. The power of touching your cat, facilitated by the uncomplicated and unconditional bond between you, draws you in to each other so that you are living completely in that moment. I believe that your mind and your spirit are at peace when you cuddle with your pet, and this results in the physical, emotional, and spiritual benefits of true relaxation. Sensing only the soft fur and the rolling purr brings the profound revelation that your cat can indeed bring you a touch of heaven.

True Friendship

Real friendship means not feeling compelled to converse, feeling content just to be near each other, sitting in meaningful stillness. The most intimate moments are often those spent in silence. Words are not always necessary; in fact, they frequently get in the way. Your cat speaks volumes when s/he finds just the right moment to rub against your cheek and curl up next to you. This tranquil moment is possible only when there is real mutual acceptance and understanding on a very fundamental level. This quality is difficult to achieve in interpersonal relationships because human interaction is often so (unnecessarily) complex. Despite an arduous day, when your cat gazes at you and purrs, it is the gesture of an angel reminding you that, today and every day, you are worthy of being loved.

Instinct and Patience

Watch your cat as s/he stalks a moth at the window pane. If the insect flies away, the cat will track it and wait for it to land. Patient, persistent, and relentless: the cat will concentrate and refuse to be distracted. Jumping and swatting with either or both paws, the moth is knocked to the ground. Peeking under a paw to verify success, the cat is very pleased and rightly so! When you have a goal in mind, plan ahead, work consistently, and be prepared for last-minute adjustments even when your goal is within reach. Trust your instincts. Focus. Be patient. Don't be discouraged with temporary setbacks. Know your abilities as well as your limitations. Pace yourself. And pounce when you feel the timing is right! Listen to your inner voices; they will guide you to make the choices that are right for you.

Bask in the Sunshine

No matter how busy you are, take time to appreciate the world around you. We tend to be overly focused on lofty objectives and forget how important are the simple things that make life worthwhile. What does your cat do at every opportunity, perhaps as a reward after catching that delicious moth? Take a nap and stretch out in the sunshine. There are few things as delicious as feeling the warmth of the sun on your skin. If you do it right (in moderation and with sunscreen, of course), it is an opportunity for another transcendental moment. Feel the sun warm your skin and permeate your being. You are radiant in a celestial bright light and connected only to the sensation of sunshine. You are a part of the sunshine. My suggestion to "bask in the sunshine" is a figurative one. If you get the same boost to your batteries from taking a walk in the woods, watching a crackling fire, holding hands with your best friend, tending to your garden, reading an inspirational poem, do it. The most powerful and empowering moments in life are often the simplest ones: *Reward yourself.*

Learning to Coexist

Hissing and spitting at each other takes a lot of energy. It is hard to keep up all the fussing and fighting; there are so many issues that are more important and demand our attention. And there are so many better ways to resolve our differences, with family, friends, lovers, coworkers, and fellow travelers along the back roads and highways of life. Everyone needs room to breathe, and some of us need a wider berth than others. House cats need time to learn to live together, and there may be spats at first. In most cases they will learn to tolerate each other's presence even if they do not become intimate companions. Observe cats as their relationships evolve and they allocate the space in your home with great subtlety and intricacy. One cat comes along to find another already occupying a favorite chair by the window. He could decide to bully the other and claim priority use of that chair. He could try to share it and risk being rejected or trigger a confrontation, or simply find another perch. In similar situations, we might think something like this: You seem so comfortable there. If it is really so terribly important to sit in that chair, I am happy to let you enjoy it. It means more to you than it does to me at this moment, and I can find another spot. Just let me know when you're ready to cuddle. Walk lightly, like a cat does on silent paws, around the people who are important to you. Wait for an invitation to enter their sphere of being; do not intrude. Keep your claws sheathed. Be kind to yourself and to others. A blunder, an uninvited comment, cannot be retrieved. Tempers may flare, the fur may fly, but try to forgive, forget, and learn how this experience can improve the peace. Tread softly on this Earth because your footsteps echo farther than you know.

Aging Gracefully

So what if you have a few white hairs? Your whiskers still frame the face I love. And if you are not as quick to greet me when I come home? It is enough that you greet me when no one else will. You lost your kitten sleek shape years ago, but your eyes reflect all the memories we share. We are older than we were, but we will never again be as young as we are in this very moment. The past is the past. There is only today. Look at your pussycat. As long as s/he is eating well, grooming daily, sleeping comfortably, and enjoying your company, life is good. It is not about vanity or superficial qualities that fade, just as the stars fade in the morning sky. The stars are still there; it is only the light that has altered the illusion. Enjoy the passage of time. Today is everything.

Dying with Dignity

Every day that we live brings us closer to the day when we will leave our loved ones behind. Growing old is a luxury not afforded to everyone. Tomorrow is a dream that may never be fulfilled. Sometimes death is sudden and leaves us no time to say good-bye. Aging is a reminder that we have a finite period of time to do the jobs we were meant to do in the time allotted to us. Your kitty may live well into the double digits; however, he or she may be gone far too soon. In your cat's final days, when veterinary medicine can do no more, your dying cat will withdraw and retreat. Your pet will become weary and sequester himself. It is almost as if s/he is shutting out the world. There is a sort of calm acceptance of solitude. "I will purr for you, but I will not eat. I will look at you, but I will look away, for I cannot stay with you. Today is tomorrow's yesterday, and I will be gone. Thank you for everything. Let me go; it is my time."

How You Make Me Feel

Have you ever noticed how fleeting is the memory of the spoken word? Can you precisely recall what someone said to you an hour ago, yesterday, or even last year? Verbal communication seems to fade as quickly as the sound waves pass through our ears. Visual memory is not much clearer. If it were, crime witnesses would be infallible, and cameras would be obsolete. Years later, can you visualize with clarity the image of someone's face without referring to a photo? Yet, *you will likely always remember how someone made you feel*. You will never forget how special you felt when your mother sang a lullaby that was meant only for you or when she treated you to a chocolate ice cream soda on a happy spring day. You certainly remember how your dad held you close when the Wicked Witch of the West appeared, cackling in a whirling green cloud of evil smoke, and how you felt when your parents walked you down the aisle on your wedding day. Only you know how much it meant when your cat kept devoted vigil during your recuperation from knee surgery. When you were devastated because of a broken romance, you were not alone; your cat was there. Take a few minutes every day to measure the gifts your cat brings you. Take notice of how this special friend makes you feel. It is true that your cat may not make you feel terrific on the day you come home to a potted plant disaster with soil scattered and leaves tattered. But even this, years later, will make you feel like smiling. And perhaps it is most important to learn not what you feel but that you can feel at all. Your cat has the ability to put you in touch with fundamental emotions and to enrich your life by sharing the life of a divine creature. Your connection to your cat will help connect you to other people who love you. This is your cat's blessing and my prayer for you. Live, happily, ever after, with your cat.

INDEX